S0-AFY-924

THEOLOGY OF WORSHIP
IN 17th-CENTURY LUTHERANISM

FRIEDRICH KALB

THEOLOGY
OF
WORSHIP

IN 17th-CENTURY LUTHERANISM

Translated by
HENRY P. A. HAMANN

CONCORDIA PUBLISHING HOUSE
SAINT LOUIS, MISSOURI

264. 04
K124

158764

Concordia Publishing House, St. Louis, Missouri

Concordia Publishing House Ltd., London, W. C. 1

© 1965 by Concordia Publishing House

Library of Congress Catalog Card No. 65-15934

MANUFACTURED IN THE UNITED STATES OF AMERICA

The German word *Kultus* and the Latin word *cultus,* which occur so frequently in this monograph, present some difficulty to the translator. The word "cultus" has never really become naturalized in English, and "cult" has developed a meaning which is only rarely useful in our context. The work of translating is further complicated by the variety of ways in which the German word *Gottesdienst* is used. Much depends on whether the German genitive in the word is subjective or objective in nature, whether a public or a private act or an external or internal phenomenon is referred to. Fortunately the context usually provides the clue to the correct understanding and therefore the proper translation as well.

All quotations in the text and in the notes, German or Latin, have been translated; only the most familiar Latin theological terms have been permitted to stand untranslated.

H. H.

CONTENTS

INTRODUCTION ... ix

     Part One: The Essence of the Divine Service ... 1

CHAPTER ONE: Fixing the Concept ... 3

CHAPTER TWO: The Divine Service of Christian Faith ... 10

  1. How Worship Is Related to Theology in General ... 11
    a. Worship and Religion ... 11
    b. Worship in Actual Practice ... 13
    c. Worship and the Glory of God ... 14
    d. Worship in the Dogmatical Systems ... 16
  2. Worship and Salvation History ... 18
    a. *Status innocentiae* ... 19
    b. *Status miseriae* ... 21
    c. *Status gratiae* ... 24
    d. *Status gloriae* ... 32

CHAPTER THREE: The Divine Service in the Divine Commandments ... 37

  1. The First Commandment ... 38
    a. The Object of Worship ... 39
    b. The Right Mode of Worship ... 49
  2. The Second and the Third Commandments ... 52
    a. Prayer ... 53
    b. The Sabbath ... 55

     Part Two: The Form of the Divine Service ... 65

CHAPTER FOUR: The Necessity of Form ... 67

  1. The Argument from Creation ... 67
  2. The Pedagogical Argument ... 71
  3. The Theological Argument ... 74

CHAPTER FIVE: The Essentials of Form ... 81

  1. Church and Ministry ... 81
  2. The Proclamation of the Word ... 84

3. The Sacraments   86
    a. Baptism   92
    b. The Lord's Supper   96

CHAPTER SIX: The Adiaphora   104

1. Theological Foundations   104
    a. The Relation of Worship and Ceremonies   105
    b. Ceremonies and 1 Cor. 14   108
    c. The Meaning and Purpose of Ceremonies   110
    d. The Criteria for Ceremonies   112
2. The Most Important Adiaphora in the Judgment of Orthodoxy   116
    a. Exorcism   116
    b. Externals Connected with the Use of the Sacraments   119
    c. Time and Place, Pictures, Fasting, Funerals, Language   123
    d. Sacramental Ceremonies   128

CHAPTER SEVEN: The Theological Evaluation of Music   139

1. Music and the Gospel   139
2. The Danger of Misuse   142
3. The "stile nuovo" (New Style)   149
    Part Three: The Relation of Essence and Form   153

CHAPTER EIGHT: The Tension Between Essence and Form   155

1. How the 17th Century Posed the Problem   155
2. The Worship of the Individual   159
3. The Worship of the Community   166

CHAPTER NINE: Worship and Mysticism   173

1. Mysticism and the Mystic Union   174
2. The Mystic Union and the Presence of Christ at the Divine Service   181

BIBLIOGRAPHY   189

INTRODUCTION

The reorganization of our Evangelical divine service, which has been under way for a number of years, can be achieved only on a well-defined theological basis. For this purpose Luther's view of Evangelical worship must provide our recurring starting point. For it belongs as it were to the very essence of his accomplishments in the Reformation that he reintroduced, in contrast to the Roman cult of the sacrifice of the mass, the true Christian worship, in which man experiences the service which God renders him and is enabled by faith to serve God aright. Again, since Luther could in a sweeping manner equate Christian worship with Christian faith, his teaching on worship cannot be gathered solely from a few liturgical writings but must be understood from the sum total of his theology. There has been no lack of endeavors to find the theological presuppositions for our worship in Luther's rich life-work, the last one being the thorough and comprehensive exposition by Vilmos Vajta.[1]

Unlike the Reformation age, the 17th century, the period of Lutheran Orthodoxy, has hardly been drawn on for undergirding the Evangelical service. In the historical portions of textbooks on liturgics only modest space is sometimes assigned to Orthodoxy. Because of the wealth of purely liturgical subject matter, Graff's history of the

[1] Vilmos Vajta, *Die Theologie des Gottesdienstes bei Luther*, 2d ed. (Göttingen: Vandenhoeck & Ruprecht, 1954). An abridged English translation of this work is Vilmos Vajta, *Luther on Worship*, trans. Ulrich S. Leupold (Philadelphia: Muhlenberg Press, 1958).

dissolution of the traditional forms of worship [2] can only indicate the dogmatical problems; and on the other hand, works on the history of dogma, if they include our period at all, mostly disregard questions concerning public worship or mention them only marginally.

The main reason for the modern disinclination to make reference to the period of Orthodoxy — in contrast to the epoch of Luther — is the popular low estimate of "dead Orthodoxy," which allegedly was satisfied with the dogmatical preservation of Reformation doctrine and lacked originality and contact with real life.[3] Besides, the theology of Lutheran Orthodoxy shows a certain process of reduction, characterized by the growth of the theology of reason and the gradual decay of the theology of revelation. Here the question arises whether the decline of liturgical forms is not a consequence of dogmatic deterioration, in other words, something caused precisely by the representatives of strict Lutheran Orthodoxy.

But even though many a criticism leveled at classic Lutheran Orthodoxy [4] may be perfectly justified, it would be wrong to try to find in classic Lutheran theology the reasons for the decay. And Orthodoxy may doubtless claim some merit for preserving and securing the Lutheran faith laid down in the Confessions. It was always concerned about warding off those foreign influences which in particular caused the disintegration of Evangelical worship. Every appraisal of Orthodoxy will have to bear in mind this double fact: on the one hand, the faithful conservation and the brilliant elaboration of the Lutheran heritage; on the other hand, a dissection of existential truths that gets lost in scholastic systems and a gradual surrender of the religion of revelation for a growing religion of reason.

This consideration also guided the present investigation, which has assumed the task of pointing out the contribution made by Ortho-

[2] Paul Graff, *Geschichte der Auflösung der alten gottesdienstlichen Formen in der evangelischen Kirche Deutschlands* (Göttingen: Vandenhoeck & Ruprecht, I, 2d ed., 1937; II, 1939).

[3] See how modern church history writing speaks of the literature of Orthodoxy in Hans Leube, *Die Reformideen in der deutschen lutherischen Kirche zur Zeit der Orthodoxie* (Leipzig: Dörffling & Franke, 1924), pp. 27 ff.

[4] The translation "classic Lutheran" has been adopted for the German *altlutherisch* in reference to the Lutheranism of the era of Orthodoxy.

doxy to research dealing with the concept and the foundations of public worship. Here the positive aspects of Lutheran Orthodoxy become especially clear. Insofar as it served to fortify the heritage of the Reformation, therefore, we still have reason today to welcome the classic Lutheran theology as it supplements the literature of the Reformation with its systematic precision.

On the other hand, it may be important to learn in what manner a reduction of Luther's theology by Orthodoxy proved to have disastrous consequences for worship. We shall come to the conclusion that, in spite of the descent from the high plane of Luther, the tendencies which really were destructive to liturgy and finally made complete havoc of our divine services never emanated from Orthodoxy itself. Although the transitions from Orthodoxy to Pietism are fluid at times, it must not be supposed that Orthodoxy gradually and consistently turned into Pietism. As regards the theology of worship, we rarely meet a departure from Luther's line within strict Lutheran Orthodoxy. The real impetus for the great process of dissolution proceeded from Pietism; and while the views of this movement were spreading already in the 17th century, they did so against the strong opposition of Orthodoxy.

This book is deliberately not based exclusively on the purely theological works of the 17th century; literature intended for wider Christian circles has also been considered: sermons, devotional books, writings aiming at reform, etc. This was done partly to help counteract the erroneous judgments pronouncing Orthodoxy dead and unrealistic, and partly to accord to our subject no mere detached, theoretical treatment, but to point up its place in real life.[5] In this latter direction the scope of this work could have been greatly extended. One need but adduce the names of the poets Johann Heermann, Paul Gerhardt, and Johann Rist or of the musicians Praetorius, Schütz,

[5] Cf. Paul Althaus, Sr., *Forschungen zur evangelischen Gebetsliteratur* (1927), pp. 5 f.: "We have known a long time that the dominant theology of the day does not constitute a satisfactory or even approximately adequate criterion for understanding and judging the religious life of any period. He who would evaluate the religious life of Evangelical Christendom in the 16th and 17th centuries exclusively by the specifically theological works, especially the dogmatic systems, would get a very wrong or at least one-sided picture. On the contrary, theology itself in its deeper problems ultimately depends chiefly on the prevailing type of piety."

Schein, and Scheidt to indicate that particularly the 17th century gave its best for the worship of God *(cultus Dei)*. However, these areas, lying as they do in the fields of history of literature and history of music, had to be disregarded in the interest of a systematic theological synthesis.

The concept "Lutheran Orthodoxy" is very flexible, and here, too, a delimitation seems necessary. If the raising of the Book of Concord to the status of a Confession (1580) is looked upon as the real consolidation of orthodox Lutheranism, only those who expressly adopted the Formula of Concord can be regarded as representatives of Lutheran Orthodoxy. Nevertheless, Martin Chemnitz, one of the spiritual fathers of the Formula of Concord, although he really belongs to a previous epoch, may be included here, at least insofar as he is not, as in his *Loci,* completely dependent on Melanchthon. The Syncretistic Controversy, precipitated by Calixtus, which disturbed Orthodoxy about the middle of the 17th century, yields nothing for investigations into the nature of worship. If one considers the epoch of Orthodoxy as closing with Hollaz, its last great exponent (d. 1713), the movement coincides pretty well with the 17th century, even though it no longer held undisputed sway since the rise of Pietism (Spener's *Pia desideria,* 1675). To draw the boundary line with Pietism quite plainly, we have occasionally quoted Valentin Ernst Loescher (1673—1749). Though he represented a bygone age, he still continued in a fruitful polemic to set forth the principles of his Orthodox Lutheran conceptions over against Pietism, now already fully developed.

Orthodoxy is here treated as a unit, though strictly speaking it does exhibit an inner development. But since this is in the main immaterial as far as the theological foundation for the worship of God *(cultus Dei)* is concerned, it could be passed by.

In Part I we take up the question how classic Lutheran Orthodoxy understood "the essence of worship." We take "worship" *(Gottesdienst)* first of all in its widest sense, as the fundamental attitude of the Christian who, "worshiping God in spirit and in truth," offers Him his whole life in service. Only from this comprehensive definition of "worship" will "the form of the meeting for divine service" or "of the gathering in the name of Christ" receive its proper character.

The subject of Part II will be the theological principles underlying Orthodoxy's "external divine service," which are to be applied as criteria to the form of the service that has become historical within the Christian church. It will remain for Part III to deal with the relations and the tensions between the theory *(Lehre)* and the concrete form *(Gestalt)* of the historical service with special reference to the ecclesiastico-historical situation of the 17th century.

PART ONE

The Essence
of the Divine Service

CHAPTER ONE

Fixing the Concept

Throughout the 19th century and into the present the concepts "divine service," "ceremonies," "liturgy," "worship," and similar ones have been widely used as interchangeable. Though with some difference of emphasis, these concepts were ultimately to express the same thing: they were to describe "the essence of matters liturgical." In his comprehensive study, "The Theory of the Divine Service of the Congregation Assembled in the Name of Jesus," Peter Brunner has pointed out how complicated and diversified the question of terminology is in this area; in particular, that our "divine service" cannot simply be designated thus in the view of the New Testament.[1] It is agreed nowadays that the concept "cult" *(Kultus)* is not only unsuitable for the Christian divine service but directly opposed to it insofar as it signifies man's attempt at self-redemption by his own efforts. An attempt to define the essence of Christian worship *(Kultus)* with the customary categories of the comparative study of religions would indeed reveal certain parallels as regards outward manifestations; but these are mere externals and really signify nothing. Christian and non-Christian worship *(Kultus)* are so radically different in their essence that one cannot speak of a relationship. One excludes the other. Another conception widely held hitherto, but now overcome, is that of the "liturgy" as a *part* of the divine service — the relatively

[1] Peter Brunner, "Zur Lehre vom Gottesdienst der im Namen Jesu versammelten Gemeinde," *Leiturgia, Handbuch des evangelischen Gottesdienstes,* I (Kassel: Johannes Stauda Verlag, 1952), 99—112.

unchanging portion. Rightly understood, the liturgy is "the entire order of the service including the sermon." [2] Hence in order to grasp properly "the essence and the form of the divine service" as viewed by classic Lutheran Orthodoxy, we shall often have to disregard present-day terminology and appropriate the concepts and terms of that epoch. A genuine agreement with contemporary Lutheran theology will emerge despite terminological differences.

An investigation of the terminology of the Reformation reveals a similar unhesitating interchange of concepts. When Luther states in the *Formula Missae* that it never entered his mind to abolish all *forms of worship (Kultus)*[3] but that he only wished to remove false notions about the *ceremonies (Zeremonien)*,[4] and then explains his thoughts about the various *rites (Riten)* and their proper use,[5] he indicates that for him, too, the concepts that concern us here are interchangeable.

The Augsburg Confession (Art. XV) also speaks, without differentiation, of church usages *(ritus ecclesiastici, Kirchenordnungen)* and human traditions *(traditiones humanae, Satzungen und Traditionen)*. The term "liturgy" was not yet in use at that time nor in the period of Orthodoxy. It had occurred occasionally in the Middle Ages, but was in the main regarded as belonging to Greek ecclesiastical usage. Similarly the Apology [of the Augsburg Confession] discusses the term only in that context.[6]

Of course this synonymity of terms cannot obscure the fact that already at that time the term "worship" *(Kultus)* meant two things. This can be observed when the question of its mandatory character is discussed. On the one hand there is a constant emphasis on the relativity of its importance. It is said that it is not important, that it is not necessary for salvation, and that "ceremonies and other externals instituted by men" had been absolutized by the Roman Church

[2] Paul Althaus, Jr., "Der Sinn der Liturgie," *Luthertum* (1936), p. 236.

[3] Martin Luther, *D. Martin Luthers Werke*, 12 (Weimar: Hermann Boehlaus Nachfolger, 1891), 206, 16. This edition is hereafter cited as WA.

[4] WA 12, 205, 8.

[5] WA 12, 214, 34.

[6] Apology, XXIV, 78 ff. Cf. also *Realencyklopädie für protestantische Theologie und Kirche*, 3d ed. (1896—1913), XI, 545.

in a most unevangelical manner. On the other hand, however, the worship of God *(cultus Dei)* is considered the first and most fundamental commandment, binding under all conditions and without any reservations.

One could therefore divide worship into essential and nonessential elements; yet this leaves open the question where the dividing line is to be drawn. As the Apology explains the matter, the criterion for the binding quality of ceremonies seems to reside in their author: insofar as God ordained them, it would appear, we owe them unconditional obedience; insofar as men invented them, we are reminded of their temporary nature and their insignificance. But this will hardly do. The Old Testament is full of ceremonial directions of which God is the author but which are no longer valid for us, while in the Christian church human ordinances have arisen which have proved both indispensable and theologically defensible.

Appealing to Luther's Large Catechism, one could distinguish essentials and nonessentials in worship by saying that true, God-pleasing worship consists in trust in God,[7] that is, in an *ethical* act, and that ceremonial forms are indifferent and irrelevant. But this distinction is opposed precisely by the fact that God Himself, by instituting the sacraments, made "external signs and ceremonies" absolutely essential.

Finally it is possible to identify essential worship with "inner adoration" and nonessential worship with the "outward service." One meets this conception again and again in church history. The separation into internal and external is found also in modern theology, where at times "worship" and "liturgy" are thus contrasted with each other (for example, by Allwohn). As long as this division is felt to be purely formal, one may accept it. But that which is external, the "liturgy," must never be subordinated to "worship" as quite unessential. It will be shown later that the "liturgy," the physical act of worship, must also retain its place in the Christian service. But despite this unconditional necessity of the "liturgy," which is ultimately occasioned by the proclamation of the Word and the administration of the sacraments, we must be aware of its transitoriness and relativity. The "human rites," without which no service is possible on

7 Large Catechism, I, 16.

5

earth, also form part of the "liturgy"; but they cannot be made binding for the Christian conscience.

Hence a clean line of demarcation between the real essence of worship and its earth-bound concomitants would pass through the *external service*. On the one hand we have the rites which have the command of God, and to which the promise of grace has been added *(ritus qui habent mandatum Dei et quibus addita est promissio gratiae);* on the other, the rites instituted by men *(ritus ab hominibus instituti).*[8]

Classic Lutheran theology met this situation fairly by making a clear terminological distinction between the two spheres of worship, a distinction not yet known in the Reformation age. The term *cultus* became the central concept and was reserved entirely for the "essential" worship. Accordingly, it included only the inner worship and the means of grace to be administered in the external service; it was no longer applied to the external ceremonies instituted by men.[9] This use of the word begins already in the Formula of Concord. While for example in the Augsburg Confession (XV, 2) or the Apology (XV, 17) the "ordinances made by men" are still described by the term *cultus,* a clean-cut distinction is noticeable in Epitome X, 3. True, the word *cultus* is still qualified by the adjective *divinus;* but soon there was no further need of that. In Orthodox theology *cultus* and *ceremoniae* are contrasted as opposites in the sense that *cultus* designates what is necessary, obligatory, and indispensable; whereas *ceremoniae* refers to matters incidental and immaterial.[10] The 17th-century dogmaticians repeatedly urge caution lest rites, ceremonies, traditions, and the like be treated as constituting true worship *(ne cum opinione cultus usurpentur).*[11] The essence of worship *(cultus)*

[8] Apology, XIII, 3.

[9] Here Orthodoxy follows Luther's line. Cf. Vajta, p. 47: "For Luther it was basic that one should be able to distinguish, in the Evangelical mass, what was grounded in the Word of God from external matters lacking God's Word."

[10] Friedrich Balduin, *Tractatus luculentus . . . de . . . casibus . . . conscientiae* (Witebergae, 1628), p. 1135: ". . . That ceremonies are not a part of worship" *(. . . ceremoniae non sint pars cultus).*

[11] E. g., Leonhard Hutter, *Compendium locorum theologicorum* (ed. August Twesten, 1855), pp. 126, 130; Johann Gerhard, *Loci theologici* (ed. Edward Preuss, 1863), IV, 391; V, 248, and often.

and the ceremonies are sometimes brought into the relationship of substance and accidental circumstances.[12] At this point it becomes plain why a state of tension, to be discussed later, clings to the public divine service. For here we enter the borderland where the essence of worship and the ceremonial overlap. This borderland is represented by the sacraments, which are indeed "ceremonies" but nevertheless belong to the essence of worship (cultus).

While Orthodoxy did clearly mark off the substance of worship (cultus) from the accidental circumstances of "ceremonies," yet the content of the concept cultus itself is variously understood. It all depends on what one means by "internal worship." Dannhauer, for example, gives it the widest possible meaning. As all commandments ultimately stem from the First Commandment, which enjoins the worship of God (cultus Dei), so the whole of ethics is finally included in worship (Kultus). The imperative to man that he offer God worship (Kultus) must not be restricted to a solemn ceremonial act; it embraces the totality of human action.[13] In this sense worship (Kultus) and religion are treated as synonyms, or practically so, by Gerhard, Quenstedt, Hollaz (religio = ratio colendi).[14]

Baier narrows the concept somewhat, referring it only to the First Table of the Decalog and including the duties of the regenerate toward God. Thus worship becomes a part of ethics. The duties owed by the Christian to himself and his neighbors Baier assigns to the Second Table of the Decalog and does not include in worship.[15] "Internal worship" is assigned to the First Commandment, "external worship" to the Second and Third.

[12] Gerhard, Loci, I, 157: "Matters pertaining to the real worship (cultus) of God and to the substance of religion and piety are confused with adiaphora, rites, and things permitted."

[13] Cf. the schedule of the cultus Dei in chapter 3.

[14] Gerhard, Loci, VI, 464; Abraham Calov, Systema locorum theologicorum (Witebergae, 1655—77), I, 297; Johannes A. Quenstedt, Theologia didactico-polemica sive systema theologicum (Wittenberg, 1685), I, 19; David Hollaz, Examen theologicum acroamaticum (Rostock and Leipzig, 1741), p. 34; Valentin Ernst Löscher, Vollständiger Timotheus Verinus (1718—21), I, 660, combines Religionssachen, Gottesdienst, and credenda.

[15] J. W. Baier, Theologia moralis (1698), pp. 263 f.

7

With Calov, who pursues a middle course, the commandments of the First Table pertain to the direct worship of God *(immediatus cultus Dei)*, those of the Second Table to the indirect worship *(mediatus cultus)*.[16] In addition to its proper theological meaning, the word *cultus* also occurs occasionally in a secular sense. Balduin speaks of a *cultus animi*, said to consist in the possession of faith and the study of the liberal arts and to lead on at last to the true worship and service of God, who is honored also by the cultivation of the mind.[17] Calov takes advantage of the possibility of using *colere* in the religious sense of "worship" and in the secular sense of "cultivate" in order to illustrate by a play on words the need of progressing from culture to ethics: the doctrine of the singleness and unity of God demands that we actually worship only one God *(unum Deum colamus)*, but with respect to our fellowmen that we cultivate unity *(unitatem colamus)*, that is, strive to be of one mind among ourselves.[18] Calov even places alongside of the worship of God *(cultus Dei)* demanded by the First Table of the Decalog the respectful treatment of our fellowman *(cultus proximi)* demanded by the Second Table.[19] Self-evidently the word *cultus* acquires a totally different content by the change of objects. Still, the profane use of the word is always exceptional.

The only synonyms for *cultus* still found in orthodox theology after this are such words as *veneratio, celebratio, glorificatio*. They serve to emphasize certain characteristic features inherent in worship without effecting a material change.

In summary, the following may be stated. However inappropriate the concept of worship *(Kultus)* may appear to modern theology for the Christian service, it was for Lutheran Orthodoxy the designation for the service of God in its widest as well as in its special sense. *Cultus Dei* comprises *the whole of Christian faith*, as well as, in

16 *Systema*, VI, 440.

17 Balduin, p. 894: "This cultivation *(cultus)* of the spirit is worship *(cultus)* of God Himself; for he who keeps his spirit uncontaminated, reveres God and wins His favor."

18 Calov, *Systema*, II, 288 f.

19 Ibid., V, 390.

8

particular, *all action in the way of liturgy and formal worship,* the latter, however, with the exclusion of all human additions. We can speak of the divine service as liturgy only if "worship" is viewed rightly as the fundamental attitude of believing man. Hence the following chapter will treat of the manifold ties which connect the divine service with Christian faith as a whole.

CHAPTER TWO

The Divine Service of Christian Faith

The "worship of God" *(cultus Dei)* is not a clearly defined division of classic Lutheran dogmatics. It cannot be. It cannot be placed on the same plane, for instance, with the doctrines of the Trinity, of Sin, of Justification. Its content comprises the entire Christian faith and life and therefore the whole subject of dogmatics and ethics. This seems startling at first. But we must not lose sight of the tremendous expansion which the concept has undergone since the Reformation. In the medieval church its content had been restricted more or less to certain liturgical acts; since then it has been expanded to include the entire life of the Christian.[1] Indeed, this was the very starting-point of the Reformation that penitence "became a condition of man instead of a rite, a way of life instead of a liturgical act, a fundamental personal attitude instead of a religious form."[2]

To set forth the doctrine of worship would therefore be tantamount to presenting the whole Christian doctrine of faith. That cannot be our task. Besides, the insight that the entire life of the Christian is to be a service of God remains unimpaired by the conception of ecclesiastical worship as a special act aiming directly at the glori-

[1] WA 1, 233, 11: ". . . that the whole life of believers is repentance . . ."

[2] Heinrich Frick, "Protestantismus und Liturgie," *Theologische Blätter* (1924), p. 145.

10

fication of God.[3] Nevertheless, it will be our purpose to show that the dogmaticians of the 17th century did justice to the broad Reformation view of the idea of worship when they assigned to it a very prominent place in their dogmatic system.

1. How Worship Is Related to Theology in General

This definition of worship *(Kultus)*, which overlaps theology in general, becomes especially plain at three points.

a. First it appears in this, that "worship" *(Kultus)* is identified with "religion" and thus becomes the central subject of theology instead of a subordinate topic. Accordingly, worship usually appears as the organizational factor of religion at the very beginning of the theological system, when the essence of religion is defined. In König we read: "The Christian religion is the way of worshiping the true God *(ratio colendi Deum verum)* by faith in Christ and by love toward God and the neighbor, according to the written Word, so that man, separated from God, may be reunited with God." [4] In German definitions, too, the "service of God" is the characteristic of the Christian religion: "True religion we call the particular duty of *serving God* aright, which is properly learned from Holy Writ and is demanded by God." [5] It is to be observed here that there is never an omission of the reminder that the right way of honoring God can be derived only from the Word of God. Calixtus, it is true, is willing to recognize also the propriety of a worship order according to the principles of reason.[6] But when worship and religion are equated, this implies

[3] See Werner Elert, *Morphologie des Luthertums* (Munich: C. H. Beck'sche Verlagsbuchhandlung, 1931), I, 282 f.; trans. Walter A. Hansen, *The Structure of Lutheranism* (St. Louis: Concordia Publishing House, 1962), pp. 322 f.

[4] Johann Friedrich König, *Theologia positiva acroamatica* (1665), p. 9. Similar definitions in J. A. Quenstedt, *Theologia*, I, 19, and Hollaz, *Examen*, p. 34. For accidental synonymous use of both terms see Gerhard, *Loci*, VI, 353; Balduin, *Tractatus*, p. 143; Quenstedt, *Theologia*, IV, 261, 265.

[5] Johann Adam Scherzer, *Kurtzer Weg und Handgriff . . . die ganze christliche Lehr . . . leicht zu fassen* (1686), p. 3.

[6] Georg Calixtus, *De veritate unicae religionis christianae . . . dissertationes* (1658), pp. 1 f.: "The worship *(cultus)* of God can be instituted either according to the leading of the light of nature, be it from the precept and dictate of reason, be it from what remains of nature without special

11

more than the right to institute certain external orders of worship; it amounts to nothing less than according recognition to a religion of reason.

The indissoluble connection between religion and cultic veneration, by the way, is found not only in the Christian religion. In paganism and Judaism, too, where one can speak of religion only in an improper and perverted sense *(improprie et abusive)*, there is such a thing as religious veneration, even though it is directed toward what is *not* God.[7]

This close coordination of religion and worship rightly characterizes the New Testament designation of "religion." For in the Greek word θρησκεία (Acts 26:5) the concepts *religio* and *cultus* are combined. The abstract expression *religio* by itself has no corresponding concept in the language of the New Testament. Indeed, θρησκεία corresponds to *religio;* but especially "insofar as it shows itself as the service of God, worship."[8] The same is proved by the other New Testament expressions which Quenstedt adduces as synonyms of religion — λογικὴ λατρεία, θεοπρέπεια, εὐσέβεια. These terms might be translated into Latin thus: *cultus, reverentia,* or — *pietas!* Hence *pietas,* too, represents the essence of true religion and service of God. This was so already in the time of Orthodoxy. Balduin simply treats *pietas* and *cultus* as interchangeable concepts. They represent the practical and ethical side of religion in contrast to theology, which embodies the theoretical and intellectual side.[9] Pietism held, however, that to Orthodoxy religion was conceivable without *pietas,* so that it was necessary to insist upon the addition of true piety to religion. Hence in the Pietistic controversies the ambiguous question

divine revelations; or according to revelations of the kind already mentioned, especially disclosed by God and proceeding from Him."

[7] Quenstedt, *Theologia,* I, 20.

[8] Cf. Walter Bauer, "θρησκεία," *Griechisch-Deutsches Woerterbuch zu den Schriften des Neuen Testaments und der übrigen urchristlichen Literatur,* 4th ed. (Berlin: Verlag Alfred Töpelmann, 1952), col. 658.

[9] Balduin, *Tractatus,* p. 143: "[Religion] is otherwise called piety and differs terminologically from theology because the latter is perceived in knowledge, but religion or piety in manifestation and deed. But as regards the matter itself, religion embraces both: the knowledge of God, or wisdom; and demonstration, or the worship of God."

could arise: "Is piety necessary for religion and salvation?" [10] This was possible only because an altogether new and much narrower understanding of the concept "piety" had arisen. Over against this, Löscher points out the "very wide meaning" of the term: "This word includes the service of God, determined by God's revelation and presupposing true faith; also earnestness and continuance in it as well as its fruits; that is, all religion." [11] The attempt to separate piety and religion, he felt, would be self-contradictory.

b. The comprehensive meaning of worship *(Kultus)* becomes evident also at another point. Some dogmaticians added a so-called directions-for-use section *(usus practicus)* to every doctrine treated. This method is found already in Gerhard; it is most consistent and marked in Calov. This appendix contains the practical application of what has before been expounded theoretically. It frequently has two parts: one to comfort *(usus consolatorius)* and one to admonish *(usus paraeneticus, or exhortatorius).* True, the latter *usus* in particular may tend to turn the depths of divine wisdom into the shallows of trivial moralizing admonitions. Gass writes: "The intention was good, but owing to the manner of the time, the execution was very pedantic and even arouses apprehension. . . . It sounds trivial when, after the vision of Christ has been discussed with regard to its dogmatical content, its *utility* finally receives commendation — a meager category, to be sure, when dealing with the Savior as a great religious and moral spiritual potency!" [12] This criticism is justified as long as the "application" aims only at morality. Yet here again there is proof that Orthodoxy did not rest satisfied with a mere intellectual grasp of a doctrine but urged that the saving truths should become effective in the life of the Christian. Besides, with these *usus practici* Orthodoxy emphatically placed the worship elements in the foreground. It was understood that man can respond to the divine mysteries only with wondering and grateful adoration.[13] Calov's "practical application"

[10] Löscher, *Timotheus Verinus,* I, 755.

[11] Ibid.

[12] Wilhelm Gass, *Geschichte der christlichen Ethik,* II (Berlin, 1886), p. 155.

[13] Gerhard, *Meditationes sacrae,* Med. 19: "In the Holy Supper of the Lord there is placed before us a tremendous and in every way adorable mystery."

13

of the doctrine of God, for instance, reads: "That we should think about the divine attributes aright and rightly estimate, venerate, and adore God's nature and majesty."[14] God's holiness wakes its proper echo if we glorify the Holy One and emulate His holiness.[15] It stimulates us to praise God with the heavenly host.[16]

Even when the dogmaticians do not add a "practical application," the exhortation to praise and glorify God for His majesty and mercy runs like a colored thread through their whole fabric. Thus Hollaz concludes each main section of his dogmatics with a prayer and thereby not only issues a call to adoration, but lets his own doctrinal presentation pass over into laud and praise of God.

c. There is a third place where worship plainly appears as the basic theme of all theology. If the entire theological system is pervaded by veneration and reverence toward God as the fundamental attitude of believing man, there must be a corresponding concept on the side of God which also acts as a fundamental principle unifying the individual doctrines. In classic Lutheran dogmatics this principle is the *gloria Dei*. *Gloria* is the term used by the 17th-century dogmaticians to describe the content of the New Testament concept δόξα; that is, the majesty of God, or "the product of might and honor."[17]

Speaking of blessedness, Calov once or twice distinguishes objective and formal blessedness: blessedness is both God Himself and what His blessedness causes in man.[18] This distinction may be transferred to the term "glory," and so the objective glory is God Himself, while, formally considered, it is the glorification of God in the sense of Luke 2:14. Quenstedt follows a similar scheme in his discussion

14 Calov, *Systema,* II, 231.

15 Calov, *Systema,* II, 342: "The application of this doctrine is that we love and glorify God as supremely good and holy, strive for sanctification, avoid and flee evil, and be sustained in all adversity by the goodness of God."

16 Calov, *Systema,* II, 353: "The holiness of God invites us to glorify Him with the holy choir of the angels: Holy, holy, holy is the Lord God of Sabaoth." (Is. 6:3)

17 See Elert, *Der christliche Glaube* (1940), p. 228.

18 Calov, *Systema,* XII, 352: "Here a distinction must be made between objective and formal blessedness. The former is the Triune God; the latter, the fruition of the Triune God."

14

of the final aim of theology. The objective goal of theology is God, the formal goal is the enjoyment and glorification of God.[19]

But this objective goal, God and His glory, together with the formal goal, the glorification or the worship of God, dominates all of theology. Since the glory of God appears as the ultimate aim (*finis*) of every doctrine, it becomes the comprehensive total concept of the Christian faith in general.[20] Following its scholastic method, 17th-century Lutheran dogmatics employs a scheme of distinctions also when dealing with aim or purpose. There is an ultimate, or highest, purpose and an intermediate one, a purpose in respect to God and one in respect to ourselves, an external purpose and an internal one, etc.[21] But no matter how varied the many subordinate aims, the constantly recurring *gloria Dei* crowns the whole as the final purpose of all aims. Nor does this fundamental conception govern only the theology of the pilgrims on earth. To give praise and glory to God is also the noblest function of that creation which never fell into sin.[22]

This emphatic accent on the glory of God could almost be evaluated as a Calvinistic trait. It is strictly maintained. Even when treating of everlasting reprobation, Quenstedt mentions as its final aim the glory of God.[23] However, this *gloria Dei* does not clash with the evangelical proclamation of salvation, as the Reformed teaching does particularly in the doctrine of Predestination. For it is the glory of

[19] Quenstedt, *Theologia,* I, 550: "So far we have dealt with the objective aim of theology, which is God. There follows the formal aim, which is the enjoyment and glorification of God."

[20] Calov, *Systema,* I, 8: "The absolute aim [of theology] is the glory of God."

[21] Gerhard, *Loci,* I, 7: "Theology has a chief or highest and an intermediate aim. The chief and highest is the glory of God; for God revealed Himself in His Word and gives theological wisdom to men to this end, that He might be rightly known by others and be glorified, worshiped, and called upon in this life and the future life. . . . The intermediate and nearest aim is either internal, making men wise to eternal salvation; or external, the very attainment of beatitude or eternal life."

[22] Quenstedt, *Theologia,* I, 450: "The functions and works of the good angels are to adore and praise God and to carry out His commands."

[23] Quenstedt, *Theologia,* III, 23: "The aim of reprobation must be considered rather with respect to God who condemns than with respect to those who are condemned. But no other aim of Him who condemns can be given than His own glory, which results from the exercise of His divine justice."

the Father of Jesus Christ in the sense of John 1:14. The side of the glory that is turned toward man is eternal salvation. Hence, side by side with the glory which is the aim of salvation history so far as God is concerned, there always appears the eternal salvation which is the goal so far as men are concerned.[24] The glory of God and the salvation of men: these are always placed together as two sides of the same thing. It is in His good and gracious will that God's glory becomes rightly known to us.

This should suffice to make clear the fundamental significance of worship as a concept correlative with the basic principle of all theology — glory and glorification.

d. But also worship in the narrower sense of a particular congregation assembled for the specific purpose of worship is looked upon by the 17th-century dogmaticians as the very center of ecclesiastical action. They did not separate liturgics from dogmatics, as is the case today. On the contrary, the problems of form in worship arising in connection with some specific doctrine were discussed by them in that very section, though without systematic completeness. In consequence, such liturgical subjects emerge at many points in the course of their dogmatical system, often unexpectedly.

[24] Quenstedt, *Theologia*, I, 56: "The purpose of Holy Writ is one with respect to God, another with respect to ourselves. With respect to God it is saving knowledge and worthy praise of Himself. For God revealed Himself in His Word so that He might be rightly known by men and glorified in this and the future life. With respect to men the aim is either intermediate, that is, their instruction, conversion, coming to faith, sanctification, and guidance to eternal life . . . or ultimate, that is, eternal salvation."

Hollaz, *Examen*, p. 1292: "The immediate purpose of the church is the edification both of the whole body and the individual members. The ultimate object on the part of the church is eternal salvation, on the part of God praise of the glorious divine grace." P. 1347: "The ultimate aim of the church ministry is on the part of God the glory of the divine name; on the part of man, eternal salvation. Intermediate aims are illumination and conversion, regeneration, reconciliation with God."

This dual concept extends even to sin: "The aim of sin is properly none; yet incidentally, as regards sin itself, it happens that it is directed to good, to the illustration of the divine glory and the salvation of man" (Calov, *Systema*, V, 55). This also applies of course to the practical work of the pastor: "Let him seek only the glory of God and the salvation of his hearers. Let the evangelical preacher direct all his actions to increase the glory of the one God and to promote the conversion and salvation of the souls committed to his care." (Quenstedt, *Ethica pastoralis*, [1678], p. 351)

16

Naturally, the doctrine of the Sacraments most frequently suggests the treatment of liturgical questions. Besides the purely dogmatical treatises we find sections like "Concerning Organization," "Concerning Materials," "Concerning Circumstances of Time and Place," "Concerning Administration," "Concerning Ceremonies." In Gerhard, these "liturgical" chapters take up more than one half of the locus "About the Holy Supper" *(de sacra coena),* though to be sure much dogmatical material is introduced as well.

The doctrine of the Word of God, more particularly the doctrine of the Law, offers much material for questions of worship. The moral elements of the Mosaic legislation are distinguished from the ceremonial and judicial elements; the former retain validity for the Christian, the latter are abolished. A more or less extensive treatment is given to the Ten Commandments. The first three, which pertain to the "direct worship of God" *(cultus immediatus Dei),* are particularly rich in matters affecting worship. Questions about Sunday observance, the public services, church music, the veneration of images and saints, festivals, vestments, colors, lights, etc. are examined. Occasionally, however, liturgical matters are discussed in connection with the Second Table of the Decalog. Thus Calov treats ceremonies at Holy Communion, festivals, rites at marriages and funerals, and the laying on of hands under the Fourth Commandment.[25] For such ceremonies were then determined by the civil authorities, to whom the Christian owes obedience under the Fourth Commandment. The detailed treatment of the Decalog, by the way, was taken over in the 17th century by theological ethics, which at first confined itself to casuistry, but gradually became an independent discipline.

The doctrine of the Angels furnished occasion for extensive discussions of angel worship.

A very important problem was presented by the so-called adiaphora. Chemnitz treats them in the very beginning of his *Examen* in the section "On Traditions."[26] He does not, like Calov,[27] simply equate traditions and adiaphora but undertakes an exact classification,

[25] Calov, *Systema,* XI, 158 ff.

[26] Chemnitz, *Examen concilii Tridentini,* ed. Edward Preuss (Berlin: Gustav Schlawitz, 1861), pp. 69 ff. So also Hollaz, *Examen,* p. 189.

[27] Calov, *Systema,* I, 306.

which assigns the proper place to ecclesiastical ceremonies on the total spectrum of binding and nonobligatory traditions. Gerhard on the other hand takes up this subject in the doctrine of Good Works, giving it the last place; [28] while Hafenreffer expatiates on it under Church Government.[29] Finally, Eschatology also suggests important viewpoints for the whole realm of worship, inasmuch as the perfect worship of the redeemed in eternity serves as an ideal for our worship on earth.

By not removing worship from the sphere of dogmatics but rather viewing it as included in all affirmations of Christian revealed faith, Orthodoxy merely illustrated an attitude already found in Luther and recently pointed out clearly by Vilmos Vajta: "As soon as Luther speaks of God, he speaks also of the worship of God, which is inseparable from the God revealed in Christ. Worship of God is not so much the human reaction, the human reply to a relation established by God, . . . rather, where God deals with us (that is, as the revealed God), the worship of God is also present. Revelation and worship are actually one and the same reality: the communion of God and man in earth-bound conditions." [30] So Lutheran Orthodoxy brings home to us that one cannot speak comprehensively of the Christian faith without drawing a picture of Christian worship, just as vice versa Christian worship in all its aspects must have reference to the total contents of the Gospel.

2. Worship and Salvation History

God's revelation and the faith of man are not static entities. As the self-witness of God proceeded and proceeds dynamically as the history of salvation, so faith, or worship, respectively, is not a completed and quiescent event but has part in that tension which results from God's revelation in Law and Gospel. Classic Lutheran dogmatics doubtless weakened this tension as was understood by Luther. Following Roman Catholic Scholasticism, it substituted a scheme of four successive epochs, viz., the four states of man *(status hominis)*, in which worship likewise takes on a correspondingly different character.

[28] Gerhard, *Loci,* IV, 4.

[29] Matthias Hafenreffer, *Loci theologici,* rev. ed. (Tübingen, 1603), p. 516.

[30] *Theologie,* p. 24; trans. Ulrich S. Leupold, *Luther on Worship,* p. 15.

18

These four states may be briefly sketched here. The first, the paradisaical state of man *(status innocentiae)*, was marked by the perfect agreement of the human with the divine will. It was superseded by the state of wretchedness *(status miseriae)*, which man brought upon himself by his sin and which holds him fast in guilt and wretchedness. From this state man may be set free by being translated, through faith in Christ, into the *status gratiae,* in which he knows himself to be released from guilt and misery by the atoning death of Christ. Now he still awaits the entrance into the *status gloriae,* which will bring the final release from all earthly limitations and provide enduring blessedness; but he also faces the possibility that he may be plunged instead, through impenitence, into the *status damnationis,* which means everlasting despair.[31] The Christian divine service is celebrated in the *status gratiae.* It can be rightly understood only by looking backward and forward.

a. What, in the opinion of the classic Lutheran Orthodoxy, were the content and the form of the divine service in the primal state of man? Calov developed a *theologia paradisiaca,* which attempts to picture the relation of God and man as it existed before the fall of man and would still continue if the Fall had not happened. Worship and prayer make up *Locus VIII* of this paradisaical theology.[32] Worship is consequently grounded in the creation; it did not enter in only after the Fall. Yet it differed totally from worship after the Fall. Elements that later belong to the essence of the service, such as sacrifices and sacraments, are still lacking.[33] Worship is reduced to its original form, which in spite of all later modifications was bound to remain the common and constant element; that is, prayer. Thus prayer *(invocatio)* and worship *(cultus)* are used synonymously.[34] Balduin calls prayer the chief element of religion *(praecipua religionis pars).*[35]

[31] Thus Quenstedt, *Theologia,* I, 513. This partition appears in every dogmatician, sometimes with different terms.

[32] Calov, *Systema,* I, 23 f.

[33] Gerhard, *Loci,* III, 118; IV, 137.

[34] Ludwig Dunte, *Decisiones mille et sex casuum conscientiae* (1628) p. 892: "So that, by a more general term, prayer stands for the whole worship of God in Scripture."

[35] Balduin, *Tractatus,* p. 215.

19

The relation, Creator — creature, which involves a relationship of dependence, itself gives rise to prayer which thankfully, obediently, and worshipfully acknowledges this dependence, and which is the answer to the creative Word of God that called man into being.[36]

In the estimation of these dogmaticians, worship is thinkable only within the protective setting of the Law. Hence worship becomes a function of the Law already in the primal state: it exists because and insofar as it is grounded in the Law. Even for Adam there was, according to Calov, a natural law *(lex naturalis)* and a formal law *(lex positiva):*[37] the latter referred to the injunction not to eat of the Tree of Knowledge;[38] the former was written in the hearts of the first human beings and comprised all commandments of the later Decalog.[39] It possesses eternal validity; it existed before creation in the mind of God.[40] The Sabbath was doubtless observed already in the primal state (Gen. 2:3). All this forms *Locus IX* in Calov's theology of Paradise.

This yoking together of worship and law even in the original state of man is significant. As early as in Melanchthon's *Loci* worship is one of the three natural laws.[41] Only in the form of law has wor-

[36] Elert, *Das christliche Ethos* (Hamburg: Furche-Verlag, 1949), p. 47; Peter Brunner, *Leiturgia*, p. 120.

[37] Calov, *Systema*, IV, 695.

[38] The Tree of Knowledge was for the first man "an altar and a temple, from which he was to recognize the benign will of God the Creator toward himself and the blessing of his concreated integrity." (Gerhard, *Loci*, II, 131)

[39] Calov, *Systema*, IV, 697: "It must be noted that that law of nature embraced all moral precepts which are comprehended in the Decalog and were solemnly repeated on Mount Sinai."

The reflexions of the orthodox fathers about the worship of the first-created man grew out of Luther's Lectures on Genesis, 1535 ff., chiefly from his exposition of Gen. 1:26 ff. (WA 42, 41—87). These thoughts were disregarded by the theology of the 18th and the 19th century; but they have been taken up again recently and given new consideration. See Peter Brunner, *Leiturgia*, I, 119—125.

[40] Gerhard, *Loci*, III, 5: ". . . before the foundations of the world were laid, that norm and rule of righteousness existed in the mind of God."

[41] Philipp Melanchthon, *Loci communes*, eds. Gustav Leopold Plitt and Theodor Kolde (Leipzig, 1900), p. 112; *Corpus Reformatorum*, XXI, 1024.

ship really been given to men.[42] If our first parents in the state of innocence could not get along without the Law as their rule and mirror, then of course the regenerate need the Law as the rule for their service of God. Here is the preparation for the third use of the Law.

b. The situation brought about by the Fall, the state of wretchedness (status miseriae), effected certain changes also with respect to worship. Worship and the Law were united still more closely and all but indissolubly. In the solemn legislation on Mount Sinai God's will regarding veneration of Himself was expressed clearly and exhaustively.[43] All self-invented forms of worship were excluded.[44] The scrupulous fulfillment of all directions, whether moral or ceremonial or political, was made the condition for the fulfillment of the promises given.[45] Increasingly the observance of the Ceremonial Law was regarded as the worship of God. Ceremonies occupied the center of formal worship. While the etymological origin of the word "ceremony" is dubious,[46] there is no debate about its meaning as religious

[42] Gerhard, Loci, III, 5: "Even before that solemn promulgation the Moral Law was given and revealed to men at the very beginning of the world. Indeed, it was inscribed in their hearts at creation, if indeed they were created in the image of God, Gen. 1:27. This consists in righteousness and true holiness, Eph. 4:24, the norm and mirror of which are found in the Law."

Luther saw Gospel and Law included in the Word of God Gen. 2:16 f. (WA 42, 80, 4). Brunner rightly asks whether the word "Gospel" was put first by accident (Leiturgia, I, 123, Note 55). Orthodoxy certainly saw no trace of the Gospel in this context.

[43] Calov (Systema, XI, 6) affirms that the Law of God exhibits the worship of God in such a way that no addition is required, but that addition and subtraction are excluded.

[44] Calov, Systema, XI, 5: "The application of this doctrine (of the Decalog in general) is that we do not invent for ourselves forms of divine worship, but honor God according to the laws and the testimonies."

[45] The Old Testament consists of two parts, command and promise. The object of the command is religion and divine worship; by it the Israelites were ordered to keep exactly and completely all divine laws, moral, ceremonial, and political. The object of the promise are blessings of every kind sent by God and bestowed on the Jews. . . . (Quenstedt, Theologia, IV, 261)

[46] Brochmand offers various explanations. Livy and Valerius Maximus derive the word from the Tuscan city Caere, where the Romans took their sacred vessels when Rome was captured by the Gauls. Augustine, Gellius, and Macrobius point to the verb carere (caremoniae=caeremoniae) since ceremonies have to do with the lack of something. They think of the Jews'

21

rite.[47] Sacrifices now became the principal rite.[48] This cult had been — in the opinion of the dogmaticians — a human obligation already in the primal state; now man was bound to it not only as a creature, but as a sinful creature: he was to expiate his guilt by means of ritual. Worship no longer existed for its own sake, that is, for the glory of God; it had become a means for the end of setting right the disturbed relation between God and man. Here we have come very close to the meaning of worship and ritual as a common phenomenon in the history of religion, which Bertholet defines thus: "Worship *(Kultus)* is the activity of religiously motivated man, manifesting itself by certain sounds and words, gestures and actions which have the purpose of entering into communication with the supersensory powers (or supersensory Power), so as to make sure of their aid or to deflect the dangers emanating from them." [49] The question is whether these cultic exertions achieve their intended object, that of being justified before God.

At this stage the Gospel enters with its totally different viewpoint. Judaism expected to be able to make satisfaction through its ritual; but Christian faith knows that such attempts only reveal our helplessness and lost condition. The Law, which was to serve as a means of justification particularly also through worship, merely brought the impossibility of this to light. And, viewed from the Gospel, all notions of merit through worship as a legal requirement are fallacious and illusory.

This antithetical evaluation of the Old Testament worship ritual, demanded by the New Testament, is not found so sharply delineated

abstinence from unclean foods, of the Nazirites' abstaining from wine. The third and most common derivation, and the one adopted by Brochmand, is from the Etruscan word *cerus*=*sanctus*. (Jesper Rasmussen Brochmand, *Universae theologiae systema* [1633], II, 73)

[47] Quenstedt, *Theologia*, IV, 11: "Ecclesiastical ceremonies are nothing else than external rites and motions about sacred things."

[48] Hollaz, *Examen*, p. 1017: "A sacrifice is an external sacred act, in which some visible object is offered to God by the priest through a ritual commanded in the Law, the purpose being to make known the gravity of sin and the future sacrifice which the Messiah would offer for sin on the altar of the cross."

[49] Alfred Bertholet, "Kultus," *Religion in Geschichte und Gegenwart,* 2d ed. (Tübingen, 1927—32), III, cols. 1365 f.

in the 17th-century dogmaticians. To be sure, the nature of worship that flows from the Gospel is admirably delineated, as we shall see. But the Old Testament worship is not set off against it in clear contradistinction; on the contrary, it is drawn into the Christian area by a reconciling and attenuating interpretation.[50] These Lutheran dogmaticians are well aware that all human actions, including specifically the actions of worship, have no value in God's sight, but disclose our sins all the more.[51] In such contexts, however, they speak of the worship of the people of Israel only implicitly. It is quite different when the worship of the regenerate is described. Then the Old Testament rites, which are understood as types, play a large part. It is not strange, then, that the "Law" has its place in the section "Concerning the Means of Salvation" *(De mediis salutis)*. Thus the meaning of all Jewish legal institutions is positively referred to the Gospel. There is significance in the transformation of the triple use of the Law into a quadruple use, which made its way into 17th-century theology almost without exception. The *usus elenchticus* was divided. One of its functions was to reveal sin and to accuse man; the other, to act as "our schoolmaster to bring us unto Christ" (Gal. 3:24). It now has a negative and a positive side: in contrast to the one negative function *(usus elenchticus)* there are three positive functions *(usus politicus, paedagogicus, didacticus)*.[52] It was therefore not difficult to invest the Law, in most cases, with a kindly intent.[53]

[50] Cf. the definitions of the Old Testament rituals. They are represented only as connected with the New Testament, as preliminary to it, but not as standing in contrast to it.

See Hafenreffer, *Loci*, p. 457: "The ceremonial laws are external ordinances about sacrifices and the entire Levitical worship, by which the Hebrew people was not only separated from other nations, but also Christ with His benefits was foreshadowed and through faith applied to the true worshipers." See also Note 48.

[51] Gerhard, *Loci*, I, 276: "Although the works of the pagans may appear splendid, yet because they are not 'done in God' (John 3:21), they are sin in God's judgment. Nothing in us pleases God except what He Himself works in us."

[52] König, *Theologia*, p. 222; Brochmand, *Systema*, II, 13.

[53] Balthasar Mentzer, Jr., *Evangelisches Handbüchlein* (1698), p. 50 f.: "Among the Jews there were laws of various kinds. Of what use were they? The Ten Commandments bind Jews and Gentiles alike and cannot be changed (Matt. 22:36). Besides these the Jews had church laws about sacrifices and

23

Here we touch the problem caused by the treatment of the Law in classic Lutheran theology. Luther's line has been relinquished. A marked kinship with Reformed teaching appears in the coordination of Law and Gospel. The "third use of the Law" *(tertius usus legis)* becomes, though not in name, yet in fact because of its frequent application, the "principal use of the Law" *(praecipuus usus legis)* particularly with reference to worship. The service of God *(Kultus)* anchored in the Old Testament Moral Law is now given a place alongside of good works in the "state of grace" *(status gratiae)*, whereas according to Luther it belongs absolutely to the "state of wretchedness" *(status miseriae)*.[54]

c. The *status gratiae* is a complete reversal of man's relation to God. Instead of struggling to render to God satisfaction for sin by his own power, he receives as a free gift the abundant grace of God in the forgiveness of sins. Simultaneously the "service of God" undergoes a complete change. Under the Gospel, "service of God" no longer primarily means that man serves God, but that God in Christ serves man. Divine service is a work of God, a gift of God *(beneficium)*. As such it cancels the old service, the work of man and the offering of man *(sacrificium)*. It is the merit of Vilmos Vajta to have pointed out how the contrast between true and false service of God constantly recurs in Luther.[55] When elaborating this contrast, Luther directed himself not only against the Old Testament ritual, long since abolished, but also against the sacrifice of the mass, in which a relapse into the Old Testament-legalistic religion of achievement is manifested.

One could ask whether the concept of "service" is still appropriate for the nature of worship in the *status gratiae*. In the German word *Gottesdienst (Gottes-Dienst)* the genitive *Gottes* may be read

the worship of God (Lev. 1 ff.). These were types of Christ and are ended and abolished by His coming (Col. 2:17; Heb. 10:1). Again, there were other laws that had been given to the Jews in the land of Canaan for the preservation of the government, the law courts, and justice. These have likewise come to an end, since the Jewish state has passed away completely."

54 WA 40, I, 514, 27: "Whatever is outside of Christ and the promise, whether it be the Ceremonial Law, whether the Moral Law or the Decalog, whether divine or human, is without exception concluded under sin."

55 See especially Vajta, *Theologie*, pp. 43 ff.; *Worship*, pp. 27 ff.

24

as a subjective genitive as well as an objective genitive. The Latin term presents greater difficulty. But when our Confessions teach: "The chief worship of God is the preaching of the Gospel" *(Praecipuus cultus Dei est docere evangelium)*,[56] it is clear that the concept *cultus* was retained by Lutheran Orthodoxy but must be filled with a new content. For it cannot be the meaning of the Apology that the human activity of teaching or preaching was to take the place of the human service expressed in sacrifices. Man is only indirectly the subject of *docere evangelium*. In reality the preaching of the Gospel proceeds from God; it is He who acts and works. Men are involved in this service inasmuch as they let God deal with them. Viewed from man's position, therefore, worship *(Kultus)* is no longer an activity *(actio)*, but an experience *(passio)*.

Already Melanchthon places the main emphasis on the receiving aspect of worship,[57] and this same interpretation of Christian worship runs through the 17th century. The element of passivity predominates in all definitions of worship. Dannhauer and Balduin regard devotion and submission as the two chief component parts of worship; that is, two qualities in man which describe his total dependence on God and his receptiveness over against Him.[58] The devotion manifests itself in faith, love, and hope; the submission in fear,[59] patience, prayer and thanksgiving.[60] Thus faith appears as

[56] Apology, XV, 42.

[57] Melanchthon, *Loci,* p. 119: "The Third Commandment enjoins that the Sabbath be sanctified and that we rest from our work; that is, that we suffer and accept the work of God, the mortification of ourselves. The First Commandment demands faith; the Second, the praise of God's name; the Third, submission to the works of God in us."

[58] Johann Konrad Dannhauer, *Collegium decalogicum* (1669), p. 51: "Worship *(cultus)* has two aspects: religious devotion and religious submission. Devotion clings to God with all its strength and powers. . . . Submission, born from a comparison of our worthlessness and the divine majesty, subjects the whole man to God." See also Balduin, *Tractatus,* pp. 148 f.

[59] Fear does not mean blind terror, but it must be taken as childlike reverence. "Fear means childlike reverence, distinct from the fear of evil, whether servile or mundane" (Calov, *Systema,* V, 392). It is the fear that recognizes the seriousness of the commandments: "Fear is reverence for the will of God, which is always before the eyes of the pious man; he will therefore do nothing against the commands of God or against uprightness, even if it could be hidden before the world." (Balduin, *Tractatus,* pp. 148 f.)

[60] Cf. the schedule in Chapter 3.

25

the primary, determining element of worship, even though it is incorporated in a Scholastic system. Here again Orthodoxy walks in the steps of Luther, who unceasingly inculcates that worship does not consist merely in such things as "singing, reading, playing the organ, celebrating mass; praying Matins, Vespers, and other hours; endowing and adorning churches, altars, monasteries; collecting bells, gems, vestments, metalwork, treasures; and in addition to this, going on pilgrimages to Rome and to the shrines of saints," [61] but that "faith, faithfulness, confidence of the heart" constitute the true service of God.[62] It may be that in Orthodoxy that concept of faith — divided into knowledge *(notitia)*, approbation *(assensus)*, trust *(fiducia)*[63] — no longer possess the existential power of Luther's concept. Nevertheless, what Vajta asserts in the case of Luther still holds true for the 17th-century dogmaticians: "The character of faith as communion with God . . . is not restricted to some region within man, but consists quite concretely in the divine service *(Gottesdienst)*, which is an expression of Christian faith or of unbelief." [64] The nature of worship is determined by faith. Where the service of God is of faith, the works of man are at an end.[65]

Of course the dogmaticians admit that man still can and must do something of his own toward worship. But this concerns some few externals which man can perform by virtue of the powers of volition remaining to him after the Fall; for example, going into the church, or listening to the sermon,[66] though even these possibilities are beset by hindrances. But everything else — the spiritual processes which

[61] WA VI, 211, 14 ff.

[62] WA VI, 209, 33.

[63] Gerhard, *Loci,* III, 350.

[64] Vajta, *Theologie,* p. 17; *Worship,* p. 12.

[65] The Gospel requires faith, not in the manner in which the Law requires works, by way of coercion; but it is the efficacious means by which the Holy Spirit kindles faith in the hearts of men. The Law requires works but gives no power to do them; the Gospel requires faith and gives the power to believe. (Gerhard, *Loci,* III, 155)

[66] Quenstedt, *Theologia,* II, 177: "To the lower hemisphere belong external sacred things and preparatory acts, which are from nature and outwardly subserve spiritual acts, whence they are called pedagogical acts or acts of guidance toward conversion; for instance, the physical going into the church and the physical lending of the ears to hear the Word of God."

men experience in divine worship, the faithful hearing and receiving of the Word of God, and therefore also the passive attitude of him who lets God enrich him with gifts — all this is not *man's* work, but the work of God's Spirit.[67] God is the principal cause in everything. His activity in worship is more far-reaching than appears at the first glance, for it includes the passive attitude of man. All this has nothing in common with non-Christian worship as a work of man.

In principle, there can no longer be a performance of ceremonies as part of the divine service in the sense of the Old Testament, which would be an act of man. For man in the state of grace these ceremonies lie on quite another plane. They are symbolical devices for illustrating the Atonement, in the manner in which the Epistle to the Hebrews uses the Levitical ritual as typical of the Christian service.[68] The priesthood has been taken over by Christ once for all;[69] He is at the same time the sacrifice that rendered satisfaction to God.[70]

The upshot is that Christian worship transcends the usual pattern of worship at two points. First, it no longer knows of a concrete ritual: if it is mentioned at all, it is in a figurative, spiritualized sense.

[67] Quenstedt, *Theologia,* II, 178: "To the upper hemisphere are referred also: going to church to receive instruction from the Word of God with a mind to profit thereby, to be held by the desire of enlightenment from the Word. These are all works of prevenient and incipient grace. Here belongs also the outward and historical understanding of the true sense of the Biblical propositions that hand down the mysteries of faith."

[68] Heinrich Müller, *Ausgewählte Predigten,* ed. Leonhardi (1891), p. 20: "There was (that is, according to the Jewish law) hardly a single ordinance and ceremony in their worship that did not adumbrate and prefigure something particular in the kingdom of Christ."

[69] Brochmand, *Systema,* I, 388: "He is properly called a priest who intervenes between God and man to give and communicate to men things sacred and divine as a minister of God, and who in turn offers to God for men gifts, prayers, and sacrifices." But there are four points of difference between Christ and the Levitical priesthood: (1) Christ was not a sinner like the Levites; (2) the Levites offered other people's sacrifices, Christ offered Himself; (3) the Levitical sacrifices were ineffectual, Christ wrought eternal redemption; (4) in contrast to the Levitical sacrifices that of Christ has no temporal limits, but continues in heaven. (I, 389)

[70] Gerhard, *Loci,* I, 603: "Christ's priestly office consists in this that He, placing Himself between God and sinful men, reconciled the whole human race to God by perfectly satisfying the divine law, by taking the punishment of the sinners upon Himself, and by interceding with God."

Second, the concept worship with its expansion into the ethical field no longer describes an "activity" (Bertholet), but a receiving, an experience.

However, there still are ceremonies also in the state of grace. What is their significance? It is clear from what has been stated that no more than a purely external consonance exists between Christian worship and the ceremonies of Judaism and paganism. The observer may note certain similarities, but the basic ideas are totally different. At this point it must become manifest that the doctrine of Justification, called by Quenstedt the chain that binds together all parts of the Christian teaching,[71] has the power to assert its influence throughout the whole dogmatical system. For every ceremonial act, no matter of what kind, seems to be an achievement on the part of man after all. But the few liturgical acts from which all the ceremonial in the Christian service originates are *receptive acts*. They are the use of the external Word and the sacraments *(usus externi verbi et sacramentorum)*.[72] The passive role played in this by the believer is emphasized again and again by expressions like "hearing the Word of God," "listening to the Word," "receiving the sacraments." In the sacramental act, divided into δόσις *(administratio, dispensatio, exhibitio)* and λῆψις *(acceptio, sumptio)*, man is in reality a participant only with regard to the λῆψις.[73] He is the object of the transaction; something is happening to him; something is being given to him.

The acting subject in these "ceremonies" is God Himself, who offers us His salvation through the Word and the sacraments.[74] The

[71] Quenstedt, *Theologia*, III, 514: "Most divine is this doctrine of the free justification of sinful man before the tribunal of God through Christ accepted in true faith. It is the Acropolis of the whole Christian religion, the connecting principle by which all members of the body of Christian doctrine are held together; if it is broken, all the other articles are weakened and undone."

[72] Baier, *Theologia moralis*, p. 264.

[73] Cf. Gerhard, *Loci*, IV, 160.

[74] Gerhard, *Loci*, IV, 148: "God not only instituted the sacraments, but He also dispenses them; not indeed directly (if we except the first Supper, which was administered by Christ Himself), but by ministers of the church. For since the minister dispensing the sacraments does not act in his own name, but in the name of God, and does not dispense some gift of his own, but that of another; therefore God Himself is rightly declared to be the principal dispenser of the sacraments."

28

incumbents of the sacred office, to whom preaching and the administration of the sacraments have been committed, stand in the stead of God.[75] They are only the earthly agents, who give nothing of their own but merely pass on what has been entrusted to them.[76] Every baptized Christian could really take over this intermediary service and will not hesitate to do so in an emergency. Yet it is the will of Christ that specifically designated men should execute this office of stewards as their life's calling.[77] Classic Lutheran theology understood the special position of the spiritual office as a divine right.[78] As in the case of Luther, this conception of the ecclesiastical office served to "emphasize that the divine service is the service rendered us by God through the Word and the sacraments." [79]

Since according to the clear teaching of the Scriptures the passive position of man toward God is not the only or the final fact to be noted in the relation of God and man, Christian worship must likewise not give exclusive expression to this one feature. But only after full recognition has been given to this paradox that letting oneself be enriched with gifts by God constitutes the true Christian divine

[75] Theodore (Dietrich) von Reinkingk, *Biblische Polizey* (1701), p. 1: "The principal and immediate object of those who hold the spiritual office is the provision and performance of the divine service, whereby the way is shown to truth, salvation, and the one supreme, eternal, immortal Good. Hence they are called servants of God or Christ and stewards of the mysteries of God (1 Cor. 4:1; Heb. 13:17; 2 Cor. 5:20)."

[76] Quenstedt, *Ethica pastoralis* (1678), p. 106: "The ability to preach rightly, in agreement with the divine will and to the profit of souls, is not a work of human industry, nor does it depend upon the rules of some art; it is the gift of God."

[77] Gerhard, *Loci,* VI, 32: "The Son of God Himself in His assumed human nature performed this office; He chose apostles, equipped them with enough necessary gifts, and commissioned them to preach the Gospel to all the world. Seated at the right hand of the Father, He still gives to His church pastors and teachers for the perfecting of the saints, for the work of the ministry, for the building-up of His mystic body (Eph. 4:11, 12)."

[78] Hollaz, *Examen,* p. 1326: "The ecclesiastical ministry is a sacred and public office, divinely instituted and entrusted to certain suitable men through a legitimate call, so that, equipped with a peculiar power, they may teach the Word of God, administer the sacraments, and preserve church discipline to the glory of God and to promote the salvation of men."

[79] Vajta, p. 206. Gerhard, pointing to John 15:1 and 1 Cor. 3:9, calls God the husbandman *(agricola)* who has His fellow workers (συνεργούς) in the spiritual husbandry *(Loci,* VI, 32).

29

service in the Evangelical sense, can and must the sacrifical element also claim its due. It follows the sacramental element as Sanctification follows Justification. Man in turn becomes the acting subject; freely as in the primal state he proffers his adoration, yes himself, for the service of God. Good works are wrought by the Spirit of God and are in turn offered to Him;[80] yet they also have to do with the neighbor.[81] At this stage the concept of a sacrifice of praise and thanks enters; but in a figurative sense, as the words show. All that the redeemed man does is "sacrifice," since his actions flow forth from faith. In gratitude he presents himself and his life as an offering (Rom. 12:1; Heb. 13:15, 16).[82] This offering of the Christian is conceivable only as a thank offering (sacrificium eucharisticum).[83] The non-Christian notion of an expiatory sacrifice has no place in Christian worship.[84] At this point the inherent inadmissibility of the sacrifice of the Roman mass becomes apparent.

Man can give only what he has received. By looking only for "fruits" and remaining indifferent towards the means of grace, Pietism blocked up the spring whence new life could gush forth.[85] All action of regenerate man is reaction, because he previously allowed God to act on himself; he is capable of glorifying God only because he experienced the glory of God. For this reason all definitions of religio and cultus [86] refer to the passive element in faith and the active element in love. This division into sacramental and sacrificial action must of course not be applied to specific external portions of the divine service, as though, for instance, the proclamation of the Word

[80] Brochmand, Systema, II, 228: "Good works are called fruits of the Spirit (Gal. 5:22) from their first Cause; works of faith (James 2:22) from their formal cause; worship of God (Rom. 12:1) and service of God (Luke 1:74) from their final cause."

[81] "Because of their twofold object, the Creator and the creature, good works are placed in a twofold order; some look to God, others to men." (Gerhard, Loci, IV, 4)

[82] Müller, Predigten, p. 62: "In the New Testament rational man is himself the sacrifice, and his worship is a reasonable, inward, spiritual service of the heart, guided by reason not left to itself but enlightened by God."

[83] Apology, IV, 19 ff.; Gerhard, Loci, IV, 3.

[84] Cf. Hollaz, Examen, p. 1134.

[85] Löscher, Timotheus Verinus, I, 756 f.

[86] See note 4.

30

and the administration of the sacraments made up the sacramental part, the other features (prayer, confession, hymns) the sacrificial part. We are here dealing with the service as a whole. The determinative factor is our position in salvation history. The Christian is saint and sinner at one and the same time (*simul iustus, simul peccator*). As a sinner he can only receive; as a justified person he can also give, or give back.[87]

In connection with this "giving back" another task is assumed by the one who holds the office of the ministry. He acts not only "in the stead of Christ" (2 Cor. 5:20), but at the same time on behalf of men. He becomes the mouthpiece of the congregation of Christ assembled before its Lord. Insofar as it can be viewed as sacrificial, the part of the officiating minister is but one individual note in the service which all Christians, together as one liturgical unit,[88] desire to offer to God.[89] Classic Lutheran theology does indeed stress both the passiveness of the Christian, who receives everything as a gift, and also his activity manifesting itself in the performance of good works. In contrast to Luther, however, it does not rightly view these two as existing in each other. When these theologians speak of the service of God in connection with the doctrine of Good Works, which opens the way to man for actions of his own, there is often nothing more than a faint echo of that grateful receiving which is the characteristic of the Evangelical service. All is done by command.

[87] Theodosius Harnack, *Praktische Theologie* (Erlangen, 1877), I, 276: "Hence every act of worship can and should be considered on the one hand sacramental, on the other sacrificial."

[88] Elert, *Das christliche Ethos,* pp. 467 ff.

[89] Reinkingk, *Biblische Polizey,* p. 10: "Religion is an obligation and a duty which every man owes to God as the Creator and Preserver of all things . . . and therefore a "bonum" common to all men of all estates, for it has to do with their eternal welfare. Hence our axiom is that the clergy is to a greater extent engaged in serving God than is otherwise imcumbent upon all men and every man."

This assertion of Reinkingk could be understood as a repudiation of Orthodox teaching on the ministerial office, as though this office originated with men for reasons of expediency. The direction of the service of God must be kept in mind. Reinkingk is speaking only of the service rendered by men to God, not of God's service to men. Hence his statement is not wrong, though incomplete. Also in the present discussion about the proper understanding of the office of the ministry, it is necessary first of all to inquire about one's understanding of the service of God.

The Law has again found a lodging place here in the seemingly harmless form of the "third (or fourth) use of the Law." Good works are prescribed and commanded by God through the Law.[90] No wonder, then, that Baier, enumerating the motives for acts of divine service, whether inward or external, always assigns first place to God's Law (mandatum Dei). When discussing the motives for calling upon God in the spirit,[91] he indeed notes the passage Ps. 50:15, where the evangelical response is clearly pictured. One hopes that here at least the receiving (deliverance) will appear as the motive for the giving (praise). However, Baier is not interested in the third clause of the verse, the praise of God; but only in the first, the cry for aid, which he also traces back to the command of God. Similarly with Meisner; the motives for good works do not really seem to have their roots in faith, though the concept Law (mandatum) is missing. He would have good works performed (1) to honor God, (2) to please the angels, (3) in loving service of the neighbor, (4) for our own sake (to receive the reward of grace), (5) to spite the devil.[92] Of the power of faith and of gratitude there is no mention. Point 4 even suggests the idea of merit.

If and when the Orthodox theologians base the service of God rendered by Christian faith on the correlation of God's Law and man's obedience, they have thereby departed from the line of the Reformation. Faith is essentially trust (fiducia), even though the element of obedience is contained in it. But of course the obedience of faith is never related to a commandment, but to the imperative form of the offer of grace.[93] The obedient carrying-out of the sacramental acts are to be understood in the same way: we are not coerced into doing something but encouraged to receive something. It follows "that Christ commands the use of the sacraments only in order to offer Himself, and that compliance with His ordinances represents not moral achievement but simply readiness to receive." [94]

d. In the status gloriae, too, the reciprocal relation of receiving

90 Brochmand, Systema, II, 218.
91 Baier, Theologia moralis, p. 395.
92 See Dunte, Decisiones, p. 896.
93 Elert, Das christliche Ethos, pp. 295, 321—324.
94 Elert, Morphologie, I, 283; Structure, p. 323.

32

and giving will not cease. The difference from the present aeon will pertain only to the degree of perfection.[95] Our receiving will consist not merely in believing but in seeing, and our giving will no longer be limited by human lassitude.[96] Early institutions which now are of service to us in the transmission of God's salvation — the preaching of the Word, the use of the sacraments, and offices — will then be superfluous, just as there will be no need of food and drink.[97] Every limitation in the praise of God caused by our boundaries of time and place will be removed.[98]

Man's act of receiving will also in eternal life properly express the relation between Creator and creature.[99] It is treated ahead of human giving, and it is comprehended by the Lutheran dogmaticians in the terms "seeing" *(intuitio),* "beholding" *(visio),* and "enjoying" *(fruitio).*[100] The vision of God represents the promised fulfillment of faith. It takes place "face to face" (1 Cor. 13:12; Rev. 22:4).[101] Man no longer needs to hide before the face of God. (Gen. 3:8)

[95] Gerhard, *Loci,* I, 341: "As we in this life do not yet know God perfectly, so we do not love Him perfectly; as we do not love Him perfectly, we do not praise Him perfectly. But in eternal life there will be perfect knowledge, perfect love, perfect praise of the Supreme Good."

[96] Gerhard, *Loci,* IX, 343: "Yonder we shall see God without faith, love Him without revulsion, praise Him without weariness."

[97] Calov, *Systema,* XII, 180: "There God will not operate through magistrates, ministries, the Word and the sacraments, the neighbor, or angels; but He Himself will directly work all things by Himself. There we shall not need the light of the sun, nor the refreshment of food and drink, nor a church, nor the office of the Word, nor any other thing; because God will be all in all to us. Whatever we shall desire, we shall have completely, desiring nothing more."

[98] Gerhard, *Loci,* XII, 354: "In this life we agree to praise God, though we are not assiduous in that praise; but in eternal life we shall be kept from the praise of God by no distractions of business. The subject matter for praise will be the eternal and infinite blessings bestowed by God on the blessed, and in the same way the praise will also be eternal and infinite."

[99] König, *Theologia,* p. 63: "Generally speaking, the essence (of eternal life) consists in the ineffable, most ample, and never-ending receiving of incomprehensible blessings."

[100] Calov, *Systema,* XII, 352: "The essence of eternal life is the enjoyment of God, consisting in the vision of the Holy Trinity, together with perfect, continuous love and praise of Him and exultation therein."

[101] Brochmand, *Systema,* II, 632: "We shall see God face to face and eternally enjoy ineffable bliss."

It is, nevertheless, unmistakable that in classic Lutheran eschatology the concept of the beatific vision contains thoughts not exclusively drawn from Scripture but influenced by mysticism. The vision is understood as mystico-contemplative. This becomes still plainer from the concept of *fruitio*, which quite evidently is used only in connection with mysticism. On the problem of the relationship of mysticism and 17th-century Lutheran worship more will have to be said later. For the present it is enough to state that the *fruitio Dei*, a term introduced mainly by Augustine,[102] is simply equated with the *salus aeterna*.[103] It appears as the comprehensive concept for the mode and manner of eternal life generally, or at least for its *passive* aspect, for the receiving aspect. From this springs the *active* element, the eternal glorification.[104] The spontaneous bursting forth into the praise of God, no longer requiring legal directions, is here described even more powerfully than when the doctrine of Good Works was treated. All who are permitted to see God are quite automatically led to love and glorify Him.[105]

Another important feature of the heavenly glorification of God is its corporate character "in the heavenly community, together with all the elect and the choir of all the holy angels." [106] The congregation, the church, has not reached its end with the ceasing of its earthly marks; on the contrary, it finds its real consummation and goal in heaven. Its unity achieves ultimate reality only in the united chorus

102 Cf. Heinrich Scholz, *Fruitio Dei, ein Beitrag zur Geschichte der Theologie und der Mystik.* An excursus to "Glaube und Unglaube in der Weltgeschichte" (Commentary on Augustine's *De civitate Dei*), 1911.

103 Calov, *Systema,* III, 1216: "Man's ultimate goal, to which not only the guidance of man but also the government of the entire universe looks, is eternal salvation or the eternal fruition of God."

104 Gerhard, *Loci,* IX, 353: "From the vision of God and the inner exultation of the heart which it causes, there will arise everlasting glorification of God and jubilation."

105 Gerhard, *Loci,* IX, 354: "That Supreme Good cannot be seen without being loved at once. From love, praise and glorification are generated spontaneously. Because the blessed are before the throne of God, they also glorify Him who sits on the throne."

106 Calov, *Systema,* XII, 278.

of praise in heaven [107] and in the loving fellowship of all the blessed.[108]

This heavenly service of praise receives very strong emphasis in Eschatology, so that the didactic and ethical portions recede somewhat. Calov exhibits these three elements as forming a climax, the progression running from knowledge via love to the laudation of God.[109] The strong accent on the doxology could not but influence the liturgy of the earthly divine service. The praise of God is the final, real purpose of all of salvation history.[110]

This sketch of the four stages of God's saving acts with respect to men has shown that Lutheran Orthodoxy, like Luther himself, rightly presented the nature of the Christian service of God against the background of worship in the primal state and in the Old Covenant, and also its significance as foreshadowing the worship of eternity. Divine worship is always both "work of God" and "the work of faith" (Vajta). Only "work of faith" was no longer seen to be so deeply involved in "work of God" as in the case of Luther. To be sure, God enables believing man to perform the new work. But according to the 17th-century dogmaticians man is dependent on further commands and directions. The epoch of Orthodoxy felt the need of authority and in the final instance desired security for its faith; it was therefore grateful for receiving from the Holy Scriptures clear directions and commands of God for its liturgical thinking and acting.

[107] Gerhard, *Loci*, V, 260: ". . . thus after this life the whole multitude of the elect will be assembled in heaven to praise God with eternal acclaim and to enjoy Him in perpetual bliss. In this life the whole number of the faithful is 'one church by the bond of faith and love; after this life it will be one united and eternal fellowship,' as Augustine says in his *Enchiridion ad Laurentium.*"

[108] Brochmand, *Systema*, II, 632: "Eternal life has its setting in the most pleasing association with the blessed angels and the saints."

[109] Calov, *Systema*, XII, 278: "Eternal life . . . consists in the beatific vision of God, in which we shall know God perfectly, love Him whom we know with the same perfection, and praise Him whom we love with the same perfection without end."

[110] Calov, *Systema*, XII, 359: "The application of this doctrine is that we should here regard God with eagerness in the Word, be refreshed together by the love of God, piously be filled with love of the neighbor, and, glorifying God with the utmost desire, advance more and more to the praises of the Lord."

The starting point was legal and hence not in the spirit of the Reformation. As to its content, however, the divine service (as the work of faith) was nonetheless set forth according to the will of God, who expects not only the offering of man's bodily life in the works of his calling but also the thankoffering of prayer and praise.

CHAPTER THREE

The Divine Service
in the Divine Commandments

After the position occupied by worship and divine service in the Orthodox doctrinal system has been sketched, there are still some matters of principle to be clarified in order to complete the picture. Only questions of internal worship come into consideration here, since the formal divine service is to be treated in Part II. In view of what has been said about the legal setting given to the teaching on worship, the Orthodox interpretation of the Decalog, or at least of the first three commandments, provides an important source.

Since we are to turn first to the internal service of God, we seem to be limited to the First Commandment. The ancient Scholastic tripartition, found also in Luther [1] and still more in Orthodoxy, would have the First Commandment kept *corde,* the Second *ore,* the Third *opere.* [2] In that case the Second and the Third Commandments, which would then cover the external side of the divine service, do not enter into consideration here. But the partition has not been carried out

[1] E. g., WA 1, 436, 19 f.

[2] Thus the First Commandment concerns the heart with respect to trust, love, hope, worshiping God in mind or spirit, joy in the Lord, resting in the one true God. The Second concerns the mouth with respect to praise of the divine name and avoidance of misuse. The Third concerns the outward deed with respect to observing the Sabbath, which had to be done by rest from ordinary works and by undertaking sacred works, both internal and external, on that day consecrated to the Lord (Calov, *Systema,* VI, 444). See also Calov, *Systema,* XI, 3; Hollaz, *Examen,* p. 1004.

consistently in practice; besides, it would endanger the evangelical principle that thought and deed must harmonize. This remains true even though, as in Orthodox dogmatics, it is pointed out again and again how closely all the commandments are connected and interwoven. Mentzer quite rightly asserts the principle: "All commandments of God require the complete obedience of the entire man, both inwardly and outwardly." [3] This principle was practiced by all when expounding the commandments, the schematic partition nothwithstanding. [4] Hence the first *three* commandments, after all, come into focus when the *internal* service of God is presented.

1. The First Commandment

Dannhauer offers the following overview of virtues and vices, as far as they concern the worship of God demanded in the First Commandment: [5]

The Worship of God is	Vices
A. *Devotion*	
1. In the intellect and the will, Faith	As to knowledge: simple ignorance, error. As to assent: doubt. As to confidence: in excess, bold presumption not supported by the Word of God, or tempting God, to which belongs also superstition or confiding in means that ought not be trusted; in defect, skepticism, to which also the inquisitive speculation on matters divine may be assigned
2. In the will, Hope Love	Despair Hatred of God, aversion from God, and love of the world
3. In the affections, Zeal	Religious lukewarmness, syncretism, hypocrisy
4. In action, External ceremonies	Complete rejection of all ceremonies Insistence upon adiaphora
B. *Submission*	
1. Fear (awe)	False security and atheism, pusillanimity, including superstitious fear of what should not be feared
2. Humility	Pride and fighting against God

[3] Mentzer, *Handbüchlein*, p. 241.

[4] Thus in Calov (see note 2) the *internum opus* recurs in connection with the Third Commandment.

[5] Dannhauer, *Collegium decalogicum*, p. 52.

3. Adoration   Worship of false gods

4. Obedience according   Self-chosen worship ("will-worship")
   to the Word of God

5. Patience   Impatience

6. Gratitude   Ingratitude

This extensive tabulation, it will be observed, which incidentally is typical of the Scholastic teaching method of Orthodoxy, attempts to say all that can possibly be said on the subject of "internal worship." The specifically liturgical element takes up very little space. This is significant, for it proves that for Orthodoxy, too, "worship" embraced the totality of the Christian life and did not mean only the liturgical area. As the author himself notes, the external ceremonies (A, 4) do not really belong here at all.[6] Only the adoration and the obedience according to the Word of God (B, 3, 4) with their corresponding vices come under the category "service of God" in the narrower sense. This distinction touches two series of problems to which we shall turn in the following.

Altogether one can distinguish four sets of problems relative to worship in classic Lutheran theology: questions regarding the object, the mode and manner, and the aim of the worship of God.[7] The question concerning the *aim* has already been answered: it is the glory of God. This aim is perverted when man in worship seeks his own justification and hence his own honor. The question regarding the *subject* must be taken up later at various points — in connection with a position over against *opus operatum,* the relation of worship and church, and the problem of mysticism.

a. The topic of adoration and its counterpart, the worship of false Gods *(alienorum deorum cultus),* can lead us to the question concerning the object of worship. The reply seems to be universal and simple: the object of the worship of God is of course God. But other questions arise at once. Who is God? How do we know of Him? What is His essence and which are His properties? The ques-

[6] Ibid., p. 109: "To action belongs the outward worship of God by prayer, the hearing of the Word of God, the use of the sacraments, outward adoration, confession, oaths, vows, fasting. The place to discuss them individually and concisely will be under the Second Commandment.

[7] Worship is to be understood here from the viewpoint of a man already justified, who can offer God his devotion as a fruit produced by Him.

39

tion has not met with a uniform reply even within a theology based on the self-witness of God as revealed in the Holy Scriptures of the Old and the New Testament. From the *worship of God* we must revert to another question: that of the right *knowledge of God*.[8] It is unavoidable. Wherever worship is mentioned, the need of the right knowledge of God somehow also crops up. Either "cognition" is defined together with worship as one of its essential characteristics,[9] or it appears in close context with worship as a necessary hypothesis. "The worship of the true God presupposes the knowledge of the true God." [10] Thus Chemnitz, when dealing with worship *(adoratio)*, puts the necessity of *knowing* the right object and the right mode of adoration ahead of the act of prayer in petition and thanksgiving.[11] In general, knowledge *(agnitio,* or *cognitio)* and worship *(cultus)* very often occur in close coordination.[12] The dogmaticians observed that the name of God is frequently closely associated with the glory of God, especially in the Old Testament. "Name of God" means "knowledge of God." A stranger becomes known through his name. Knowing the name of God is a presupposition as well as an incentive for honoring Him aright.[13] The oft-repeated formula "glory due to God's name" (e. g., 1 Chron. 16:29; Ps. 29:2; 66:2) involves the duty both of the right knowledge and the right worship of God.

For Orthodoxy, right knowledge or purity of doctrine necessarily formed part and parcel of "beholding the beauty of the Lord and in-

[8] Vajta also proceeds in Luther's case from the principle "that the concept of God determines the conception of worship." (P. 3)

[9] Inward worship embraces: (1) knowledge of God, (2) reverence or awe before God, (3) faith in Christ . . . (Baier, *Theologia moralis,* p. 263)

[10] Calov, *Systema,* I, 190.

[11] Chemnitz, *Examen,* p. 322: "Worship *(adoratio)* embraces these three things: First, that we rightly know the God upon whom we call, think of Him aright, and thus address Him as He has revealed His nature and His will in the Word. Second, that we ask of Him what He has promised to give. Third, that we give thanks for benefits granted."

[12] Dunte, *Decisiones,* p. 45: "Theology is the teaching about knowing and worshiping God." Similarly Hafenreffer, *Loci,* p. 71; Gerhard, *Loci,* I, 7: König, *Theologia,* p. 9; Quenstedt, *Theologia,* III, 19 and passim.

[13] Calov, *Systema,* II, 138: "The name and the glory of God are joined together everywhere, because knowledge of the name of God ought to be conjoined with the glory and the praise of God."

quiring in His temple" (Ps. 27:4). When Johann Saubert, bidding farewell to St. Lawrence's Church at Nuremberg, recalled the "beautiful divine services," he thought first of the fact that the *pure doctrine* was always held in high esteem, and only in second place mentioned the godly zeal and brotherly unity of his colleagues and the fruitful reception of the Word by the congregation.[14]

In 17th-century Lutheran dogmatics, therefore, fundamental questions affecting the worship of God are discussed precisely where there seems to be room only for theoretical doctrines, that is, in the teaching of God and in Christology. This follows Gerhard's rule: "To worship God is nothing else than to recognize the divine nature in Him, just as divine honor does not pertain to him to whom the divine nature does not pertain." [15]

The First Commandment requires knowledge and worship of the *one* Creator-God. What is on the level of the creature dare not be invested with divine honor; for that would make of the creature an idol and make the act of worship idolatry.[16] Such an act need not be directed to an object of sense-perception; it is to be condemned even if it is purely mental.[17]

From what has been said it might appear doubtful whether the worship of Jews and Mohammedans must be called idolatry. Calov, at any rate, cites theses of his theological opponent Calixtus,[18] who held the opinion that Jews and Mohammedans adoring the Creator-God mean the true God even though they do not recognize the Trinity.

[14] Johann Saubert, *Predigten* (appendix to *Die neue Kreatur;* no pagination): "I should like to remain in this house of the Lord all my life; not on account of the beautiful building, equaled by no other main church here, but rather to see the beautiful services of the Lord and to visit His temple. But most beautiful seemed to me (I will say nothing to anyone's prejudice) for some years the orthodoxy and purity of the doctrine which was, praise God, publicly confessed and preached by the entire reverend ministry of this place."

[15] Gerhard, *Loci,* I, 478.

[16] Idolatry always takes place "when that is reverenced religiously which is not the true Godhead, but another god; when beings are worshiped which are by nature not Gods." (Calov, *Systema,* I, 195)

[17] Calov, *Systema,* I, 194: "Idolatry is thus described in the Scriptures, that it includes not only that crass form in which creatures and images are invoked, but also the worship of any idol conceived in the mind."

[18] See Calov, *Systema,* I, 189 ff.

41

Calixtus also maintained that insufficient knowledge of an object cannot effect a change in that object. God does not cease to be the true God because He is incompletely known. Sun and moon are conceived of quite differently by a mathematician and by a peasant without ceasing to be what they are; and just so, Calixtus thought, matters stood in the case of the Creator.

The reply to this view indicates an interesting divergence of fundamental philosophical positions which is reminiscent of the Scholastic dispute between Realism and Nominalism. Calov states that it is less important to agree in the *matter* than in the *perception*. He advocates a theory of cognition that is subjectively orientated: "It is not enough to agree in the matter if people disagree in their understanding; for estimating the truth of worship arises from the latter." [19] Otherwise the heathen, too, could be absolved from the charge of idolatry, if they say that in worshiping Jupiter they adore the Creator of heaven and earth. Of course, Calov admits, our false perception does not change the reality of the object; but the idea of the idol arises just from our wrong perception.[20] What is decisive is not who the adored God is in Himself, but who He is in the mind of the worshiper.[21]

What is stated here is, with the use of different concepts, just what Vajta has noted as a fundamental insight in Luther: "A God is by definition One to whom one should look for all that is good and for refuge in all needs. To have a God means nothing else than to trust and believe in Him from the heart; as I have often said, only the trust and faith of the heart makes both God and idol. If your faith and confidence are right, your God is the right one; and again, if your confidence is false and wrong, the true God is not present either. For these two belong together — faith and God. Whatever

[19] Ibid.

[20] Calov, *Systema*, I, 191: "Although nothing changes in the object through our false perception, nevertheless, our false concept provides opportunity for the idol to arise."

[21] Calov, *Systema*, I, 193: "Let Calixtus learn to distinguish between an objective and a formal concept. In the former nothing is changed by a false apprehension, the latter is vitiated; and in place of the true God an idol of the mind is substituted; or, as Luther says, a vain dream and a lie, not God but rather the devil."

42

you rest your heart and your trust on (I say it again), that is really your God." [22] God is apprehended only where there is faith. But the prevalence of ignorance and unbelief necessarily turns worship into idolatry.[23]

Idolatry is always present in the case of polytheism. It occurs also in that form of monotheism which does not include the confession of the Triune God. On the other hand, the Trinitarian doctrine entails that worship is to be rendered to each Person of the Trinity.[24]

Other points of controversy arose in the field of Christology. The Roman Church and the Reformed Church agree in denying that full divine honor is due to Christ with respect to His human nature. Calvinists dissociate the human nature from all adoration, even condemning it as a sin of dreadful idolatry (horrendae idololatriae crimen).[25] These Christological questions are properly dogmatical in kind; yet the nature of the reverence received by the earthly Jesus from His disciples is not the last criterion for gauging the real nature of the God-man. Here theology for once reverses its course: instead of deriving worship from dogma, it derives dogma from worship. One of the Scripture proofs for the full deity of Christ is the fact that He on earth claimed divine honor for Himself (John 5:23).[26] This worship consisting of religious adoration was applied also to His human nature by virtue of the communication of attributes (communicatio idiomatum).[27] The Scriptures offer enough instances of

[22] WA 30, I, 133; Vajta, Theologie, pp. 5 ff., Worship, pp. 4 ff.

[23] Here again it becomes plain that by faith Luther means "to attach one's heart to," "to rely on," "to trust." He means something far deeper than Orthodoxy, which sees in faith a function of the intellect and the will (see p. 38) and defines it chiefly in terms of "right knowledge or perception."

[24] Balduin, Tractatus, p. 162 f.: "In spite of the essential oneness of the Persons of the Trinity I can nevertheless think, speak, and discourse about one separately without the other. So I can also adore one without the other. The Father is God, the Son is God, the Holy Spirit is God. He who worships the Father separately, at the same time worships the Son and the Spirit, since the Father's essence does not exist outside of the Son and the Spirit. All are one divine essence to be worshiped and adored."

[25] See Quenstedt, Theologia, III, 201.

[26] Gerhard, Loci, I, 478.

[27] Ibid., p. 567. Hollaz, Examen, p. 726: "To Christ's human nature, subsisting in the person of the Son of God, there was communicated by the

43

divine honors paid to the incarnate Logos.[28] If this veneration was rightfully given to Christ, He *is* God.[29]

As is well known, the Roman Church has since Augustine complicated the question of the rightful worship by distinguishing certain grades of veneration. The list is headed by the *latria*, the veneration consisting in adoration and the offering of sacrifices, which belongs only to God. Then follows the *hyperdulia*, which is rendered to Christ according to His humanity and to the Virgin Mary. To the angels and the saints pertains only the *dulia*. *Hyperdulia* and *dulia* are practiced by veneration and invocation.

Thus the clear line of demarcation between the Creator and the creatures disappears. There is no dogmatical justification for this gradation. For if there is only *one* God, there can be only *one* worship.[30] Besides, a distinction between various grades of worship is without any Biblical foundation. In the New Testament, according to Scherzer, *latria* is offered to God the Lord 30 times only, but *dulia* 49 times.[31] Hence there is no difference between the two expressions.[32] On the other hand, there are cases in Scripture where "worship" *(adoratio)* is offered in the sense of civil courtesy *(cultus civilis)*.[33]

personal union religious worship and adoration, so that the flesh of the Mediator Christ is to be revered and worshiped with the same adoration as the divine nature, the Logos."

[28] See Gerhard, *Loci,* I, 569.

[29] Quenstedt, *Theologia,* III, 199: "Is the human nature of Christ in the personal union to be worshiped and adored in the same manner as the divine nature of the Son of God itself? Christ's human nature, in the personal union or subsisting in the person of the Son of God and made a partaker of the divine majesty and glory by the hypostatic union, is to be worshiped and adored with the same adoration as the divine nature of the Logos."

[30] Quenstedt, *Theologia,* III, 200: "Religious worship is so univocal that it admits of no species. For divine and religious worship are identical, whether called λατρεία, or δουλεία, or προσκύνησις."

[31] Scherzer, *Kurtzer Weg und Handgriff,* p. 30.

[32] See Quenstedt (*Theologia,* I, 487), who speaks only of the Papalist distinction, calling it made up and invented, both as to matter and terms, outside of and beyond and against Scripture.

[33] Quenstedt, *Theologia,* I, 486. Cf. Gen. 18:2; 19:1; 23:7,12; 33:3; Num. 22:31; 1 Kings 1:23; 2:19.

44

The differentiation of worship into various stages has therefore no support in the linguistic usage of the Scriptures, as the Roman Catholic Church itself admits.[34] It is futile to operate in this fashion with Biblical terms of manifold significations; the underlying matter itself must decide. We are then constrained to recognize but *two* different forms of veneration — religious and nonreligious,[35] and these two are as far apart as God and man. The former is applicable only to God, the latter to whatever is created;[36] and with respect to the second kind one may distinguish degrees as required. All these are purely secular and relative in the sight of God.[37] The criterion for the proper distinction between the two is furnished by the teaching about God. Where the Triune God is, there we owe divine service — but to no one else. All creatures, be they who they may, must together with us earthbound, sinful men worship God.

The Evangelical nonreligious, or civil, veneration must not be mistaken for the Roman Catholic *dulia,* which is expressly described as "halfway between divine and human." [38] Again, the Roman Catholic distinction between *latria* and *dulia* is not identical with the distinction between worship *(cultus)* in the wide sense *(late dictus)* and in

[34] Wetzer and Welte, *Kirchenlexikon,* 2d ed. (1882—99) III, col. 1233: "This difference was established by self-chosen words."

[35] Calov (*Systema,* IV, 108) calls them *dulia religiosa, pietatis;* and *dulia officiosa, civilis et dilectionis.*

[36] Quenstedt, *Theologia,* I, 486: "One must distinguish between religious veneration, which is owed solely on account of excellence that is not merely supernatural, but infinite and uncreated, and hence only to God; and nonreligious or civil veneration, which is due on account of created excellence of whatever kind, whether natural or supernatural, whether of grace or of glory, as long as it is created. This latter we show to lords, magistrates, parents, and other outstanding persons, both absent and present, including also the angels, in view of their virtue, standing, or dignity."

[37] Ibid. "The general civil respect *(cultus)* shown to creatures must be distinguished from certain degrees of that respect. For as there are various degrees of excellence and dignity among the creatures, so also certain degrees of respect. Yet these degrees do not change the kind *(speciem)* of respect; they differ only as to the more or less and belong to the same kind of civil or official honor. It is not therefore one kind of respect which we accord to angels and the blessed, and another which we show to men living with us; these are various degrees of honor according to the greater or smaller dignity and excellency of the person to be honored."

[38] Brochmand, *Systema,* I, 321.

the narrow sense *(proprie dictus),* which occasionally turns up in Lutheran theology. The *cultus late dictus* coincides with the Roman Catholic *dulia* insofar as it is shown not to God but to men and objects. When in the Evangelical Communion service the Christian receives the body and blood of his Lord kneeling, he kneels not before the elements but before the Lord, who comes to him in the bread and the wine. The contrast to the Roman Church lies in this that such reverence on bended knees is not shown to "sacred objects," whether they be the elements of the Sacrament or symbolical presentations of the Deity, but goes past them to an altogether different goal; that such "sacred objects" merely point to Him toward whom the devotion is in truth directed — God, who is Spirit.[39]

Here are the firm foundations of the Evangelical principles which are of importance for the entire controversy affecting the veneration of angels and saints, of images and relics, etc. With respect to these matters the Roman Church is in the habit of leveling two charges against Evangelical theology. The one is that the denial of the *cultus duliae* and *hyperduliae* entails a deliberate undervaluation of those who are to be honored thereby;[40] the other, that Evangelical theology consciously understands *dulia* and *hyperdulia* exactly in the sense in which the Roman Church does *not* mean them to be understood, viz., as divine adoration.

The first rebuke is easily invalidated. The Confessions (especially the Apology, XXI, 4—7) declare emphatically that the proper honoring of the saints [41] and the emulation of their virtues were regarded as self-evident even after the abolition of the wrong cult of saints. No dogmatician omits pointing out that it becomes Christians to dis-

---

[39] Johann Konrad Dannhauer, *Theologia casualis* (1706), p. 322: "In the distribution of the Eucharist, the cultus used by the communicants presents an analogy, at least as regards the manner in which the sacred elements are customarily received. But reverence is not directed to them as its end, nor as to instruments properly so called, but as to signs useful for reminding them of that which is really present. Thus in Exodus 3 the place where Moses stood is called holy, not in an ultimate sense, but because in those signs God Himself appeared."

[40] Chemnitz, *Examen,* 655: "Andradius imagines that we teach, with the Cainites and Eunomians, an impious, sacrilegious contempt of the saints . . ."

[41] In this connection "saints" is of course always to be understood in the Roman Catholic sense.

46

play a reverential and respectful attitude over against angels, saints, images, and sacred objects and actions in general, corresponding to their degree of importance and within the framework of earthly honors.[42] In this question especially the Lutheran Church has always maintained the right means between two extremes, between Roman Catholic overemphasis and Reformed depreciation and even repudiation.[43]

The second accusation is likewise ill-founded. To be sure, the Roman Catholic Church is quick to assert that the *cultus duliae* by no means includes divine honor; and that, if nevertheless in connection with this *cultus duliae* the word *adoratio* should be used (for instance, *adoratio crucis*), "it must be understood in its etymological sense, not in the transferred sense of 'adore.'"[44] But when Roman theology demands, for example, that they who venerate the saints of the Bible *call upon* them, it has in the Evangelical understanding already entered the sphere of religious worship, which is the preroga-

[42] Gerhard, *Loci*, VIII, 280: "That the saints are to be honored we concede, but we deny that they are to be invoked." — P. 66: "We by no means teach that the bodies and bones of the saints are to be held in contempt, or treated irreverently, or cast upon the dungheap; nor do we approve the intemperance of certain Calvinists . . . But we deny that the bodies and bones of the saints should be venerated in the papistical manner with that religious observance which is flourishing in the papacy."

[43] Chemnitz, *Examen*, p. 762: "There have been and still are those who hotly contend that no images at all are to be tolerated, even though not used for religious acts or offered for adoration. . . . On the other hand, the papists . . . teach that honor and even religious veneration is to be shown to images, and that they should be venerated with the same rite as the thing signified by the image." — Quenstedt, *Theologia*, IV, 372: "There is a double controversy about images, and both are very old. The one concerns the making and possessing of images, the other their veneration. The former we have with the Calvinists, the latter with the Papists. Without abuse but rightfully according to the example of the ancient church, we call the former iconoclasts and image-haters, the latter image-worshipers."

What the Evangelical veneration of angels is like we are told by Gerhard (*Meditationes sacrae*, Med. 26): "Reflect, devout soul, that these angels are holy; therefore strive for holiness if you desire their company. Likeness of morals most strongly wins friendship; accustom yourself to holy actions if you wish for the protection of the angels. In every place and corner show respect for your angel, and do not do in his presence what you would blush to do in the presence of man."

[44] Wetzer and Welte, III, 1233.

47

tive of God alone. No word of Scripture is warrant for the invocation of the saints; on the contrary, the worship of angels (Rev. 19:10; 22:8,9) and of the apostles (Acts 10:25; 14:25) is expressly declared to be sin. Transferring the act of invocation to creatures constitutes a very serious diminution of the honor of God and Christ.[45] All Roman arguments in favor of it disregard the fact that the believer, in the liberty of the sons of God, always has free access to his Father.[46] The invocation, to be described more fully in connection with the Second Commandment, is for Evangelical understanding a concept associated with religious worship *(cultus religiosus)*.

In spite of this clarification of principles regarding the variance in worship, the dogmaticians still entered upon detailed and often farfetched disquisitions in order to show the theological untenability of veneration based on the *cultus duliae*. A most careful investigation of the Scriptural position, consultation of the ancient Fathers, and an examination of contemporary practice are the most important means of argumentation employed.[47] The effect of the polemic is, however, greatly weakened because the dogmaticians proceeded from *their* presuppositions and not from those of their opponents. Gerhard begins his polemic against the Roman veneration of images with a statement of the following principle: "All who pay divine honor to a thing that is not God commit idolatry"[48] — a principle which the Roman Catholic Church will also affirm unhesitatingly. When Gerhard continues: "The Papists pay divine honor to images, which are not God," this will be energetically opposed by Roman Catholics. For they introduced the *cultus duliae* for the very purpose of setting

[45] See Calov, *Systema,* IV, 142 ff.

[46] See Chemnitz, *Examen,* p. 703 ff. The Roman Catholic Church argues: At earthly courts, too, there is no immediate access to princes. Or: True humility forbids our turning directly to God, etc.

[47] Thus Gerhard (*Loci,* VIII, 66) has 13 reasons for rejecting the cult of relics: (1) the lack of a divine command, (2) the contrary command, (3) the absence of a divine promise, (4) the lack of an approved example, (5) opposing examples, (6) God's own way, (7) the lack of a certain and strong reason, (8) the origin of that cult, (9) the voice of the primitive church, (10) the fraud and impositions connected with relics, (11) the superstition in that cult, (12) the absurdities and dangers attending the cult of relics, (13) the admission of older Papists.

[48] Gerhard, *Loci,* III, 41.

the veneration of images apart from divine honors! Hence Gerhard's rebuke, which proceeds from the Evangelical distinction, does not really hit the mark. The veneration of pictures is in the Roman Catholic conception no *cultus divinus*. The question must be decided by asking whether the distinction between *latria* and *dulia* is legitimate. The veneration of angels, saints, and relics presents parallel cases.

b. Having examined worship with regard to its object, we must also study it with respect to its mode and manner. Here Dannhauer speaks of "obedience bound to the Word of God"[49] and sees in ἐθελοθρησκεία (superstition) the real offence against it. That the right manner of worship has been strictly regulated by God and that consequently human alterations and additions are sin, is a thought which in the opinion of the 17th-century dogmaticians pervades all Scripture.[50] Jesus warns against self-chosen service of God (Matt. 15:9) by quoting the words of Is. 29:13. Paul uses the term ἐθελο-θρησκεία in Col. 2:23 (its only occurrence); the matter itself he touches Rom. 1:23, 25. The Apology, too, treats this subject at length.[51]

Self-evidently such rejection of the "commandments of men" is not meant to rule out all regulating and ordering which proceeds from men within the church. The "doctrines of men" come into consideration in relation to the teaching of the Gospel. All divine worship, even in so far as it is given shape by men, must be appropriate to the nature of the Gospel; its point of orientation is not some product of the human mind, but the revelation of God. When human ordinances run counter to the Gospel, either because they are bound up with the thought of achieving merit or because they are represented as indispensably necessary for the worship of God, they are not of God's Spirit and must be abolished.

This was also the judgment of Orthodoxy. The right way of honoring God does not lie in the scrupulously exact execution of

[49] See the schedule at the beginning of this chapter, pp. 38 f.

[50] See Calov, *Systema*, VI, 445—449, and also the Scripture passages cited there: Num. 15:39 f.; Deut. 12:8; 13:1; Is. 1:12; Jer. 7:31; Micah. 6: 7, 8; Gal. 6:16; 2 Tim. 3:16 f.

[51] Apology XV: Of Human Traditions in the Church.

some forms of worship prescribed by Him. But all service of God must clearly and unmistakably correspond to the saving counsel of God extended to us in Jesus Christ.[52] Where this is not the case, we have ἐθελοθρησκεία.[53] Failure to honor God "after a godly manner," that is, in the name of Jesus Christ, is not confined to paganism and Judaism. Within Christendom, too, where the mediatorship of Christ may seem to be presupposed and preserved, worship may take on a form that can no longer be harmonized with that inspired by the Gospel.[54] This happens when Christian ceremonies are defended under the authority of prescribed worship, necessity, and merit *(opinione cultus necessitatis et meriti);* that is, when they are looked upon as if they belonged to the substance of worship instituted by God Himself, as if they were absolutely binding, or as if they possessed justifying virtue.

However, Orthodoxy went beyond this thought that the service of God must be determined by the general will of God as revealed in His Word; it insisted that also the details in the content of worship are determined by God's will. This is connected with the legalistic conception of the Gospel already noted. God is the lawgiver; He prescribes not only the standard by which worship is to be measured but also a certain manner of worship.[55] The Old Testament admonitions not to disregard anything connected with the service of God or to change it[56] retain all their weight. The doctrine of Verbal Inspiration had a fateful effect on the doctrine of Worship. The Word of God was no longer heard as a living voice to be grasped as a whole, but as legal command. The breakthrough from Law to

[52] Quenstedt, *Theologia,* I, 20: "The essence of religion consists in the agreement of worship with the will of God revealed in His Word."

[53] There is ἐθελοθρησκεία when God is not worshiped in a godly manner or according to His will . . . Jews and Mohammedans are idolaters because they do not worship God in a godly way, through the Mediator Christ and in the name of Jesus Christ; for no one comes to the Father except through Christ Jesus. (Calov, *Systema,* I, 195)

[54] Gerhard, *Loci,* VIII, 309: "The invocation of the saints does not agree with the essence of invocation laid down in Scripture."

[55] Every ἐθελοθρησκεία violates the majesty of God the Legislator (James 4:12), to whom alone it is appropriate to institute religious worship. (Calov, *Systema,* VI, 447)

[56] See Note 50.

50

Gospel was not carried out with the necessary consistency when establishing the basis for the service of God.

All transgressions of the First Commandment are gathered together in the term idolatry. This may be divided into *idololatria crassa* and *subtilis*. The first means the primitive, material form; the second, the inward, spiritualized form.[57] It must not be supposed that the use of the former term was restricted to heathen peoples barely touched by the progress of civilization. Schröder complains that it was found everywhere in the 17th century. Like a missionary to the heathen, he felt he had to direct himself against "crying to Woden after the rye harvest, idolatry in casting horoscopes and in palmistry, pernicious misuse of the name of God, and the reverential mention of the names of heathen deities."[58] Dunte, for instance, lists melancholy as a subtle form of transgression against the First Commandment.[59]

Still adhering to the partition given above, one may also divide "idolatry" with respect to its object and its mode and manner.[60] There will of course be duplications. The moment I serve "other gods," the mode and manner of my worship is no longer in accordance with the divine will; and if I serve God according to human devices, hoping thereby to achieve merit before Him, it is questionable whether I am still adoring God, the Father of Jesus Christ.

A multiple partition of idolatry is offered by Calov, who charges the Greek Church with ἀρτολατρεία, οἰνολατρεία, σταυρολατρεία, ἁγιολατρεία, ἀγγελολατρεία, λειψανολατρεία, Μαριολατρεία (bread-, wine-, cross-, saint-, angel-, relic-, Mary-worship).[61] It was a serious

---

[57] Gerhard, *Loci*, III, 27: "The former occurs when stones, wood, and metals are held to have some divine quality; the latter, when divine honor is paid to some idol erected within the heart."

[58] Joachim Schröder, *Hellklingende Zuchtposaune* (1671) pp. 136 f.

[59] Dunte, *Decisiones*, p. 104: "Melancholy conflicts with the First Commandment; it removes from our eyes God's power and His paternal mind towards us; it takes away trust and fear . . ."

[60] Gerhard, *Loci*, III, 28: "The first species of idolatry occurs when divine honor is paid to what is not the true God, whether it be a natural object like the sun or the moon, or one made by the hand of man, like sculpture. The other kind occurs when the true God is not worshiped in godly fashion; that is, otherwise than He has directed in His Word."

[61] Calov, *Systema*, VIII, 232.

51

concern of his to expose the confessional difference at its most important point, the First Commandment, because the partisans of Calixtus had asserted that a consensus with the Greek Church existed.[62] All Christological opinions deviating from the pure doctrine are likewise considered a variety of "idolatry." Thus the Socinians must be accused of ἀνθρωπολατρεία (worshiping a man) because they do not recognize the deity of Christ and nevertheless demand more than human respect for Him.[63] Confessional differences cannot be relegated to some corner of dogmatics; they can all be reduced somehow to their original form — idolatry.

Mention must be made, finally, of the direct opposite of all true worship of God. The reverse of the glorification of God is blasphemy. A component part of this word is the Greek word βλάξ, which according to Brochmand means futile, empty, inane, or contumelious.[64] If the glorification of God is the all-embracing duty of man, then its conscious negation and express antithesis is the all-embracing fundamental sin of man. As blasphemy of the Spirit it is unpardonable (Matt. 12:31).[65] As the eternal glory of God is represented as the sole aim and purpose of the state of glory, so unceasing blasphemy is mentioned as the most important characteristic of the state of damnation.[66]

2. The Second and the Third Commandments

In the eyes of Lutheran Orthodoxy the Second and the Third Commandments belong to the "external worship." [67] Hence this section could properly be assigned to the chapter on "The Form of the

[62] Ibid. p. 199.

[63] Dannhauer, Collegium decalogicum, p. 78: "To the worship of men belongs also the adoration of Christ on the supposition that He is not the true eternal God. This error the Socinians commit, who would have Christ adored yet deny that He is God. Hence they do not worship God and fall into bi-deism."

[64] Cf. Brochmand, Systema, II, 36: "To blaspheme is to malign some superior with insulting and stinging words, and in this way to detract from his honor and dignity."

[65] Dannhauer, Collegium, pp. 351 f.: "Blasphemy is this kind of sin — without doubt on the list of the gravest sins."

[66] Calov, Systema, XII, 265.

[67] Cf. Baier, Theologia moralis, p. 263; Hollaz, Examen, p. 1004.

Divine Service"; and the exposition of these two commandments will indeed receive special consideration in Part II. Still, the commandments dealing with outward observances cannot be thought of as separated from internal worship. "Prayer" and "The Sabbath," to mention the chief themes of Commandments Two and Three, are first of all matters of the heart. This inner service is of course not something different from what is demanded in the First Commandment; but for methodological reasons the peculiarities pertaining to these two commandments will be treated separately here.

a. Prayer. The relation between worship and prayer is seen by the dogmaticians in a twofold manner. Praying and the prayerful attitude of man may be that which generates ethics and worship, or the habitual outlook which is the presupposition for right conduct. Or again, it may be understood as a portion of man's inner and outward devotional life with its manifold manifestations. In the first case, prayer amounts to the equation: worship is religion $(cultus = religio)$. In the second case, prayer is not only marked quite generally by gratitude, humility, confidence, readiness to receive — all qualities which we have already met as constituting "service of God," but in particular by the urgent desire for God's help and by resignation to His will.[68] Thus prayer is distinguished primarily by *petition*. This is expressed in the four kinds of prayer enumerated by classic Lutheran dogmatics in connection with 1 Tim. 2:1: (1) *deprecatio* (δέησις), petition for the averting of evil; (2) *precatio* (προσευχή), the petition for the granting of positive good;[69] (3) *interpellatio* (ἔντευξις), intercession; (4) *gratiarum actio* (εὐχαριστία), thanksgiving.[70] Petition builds the bridge, as it were, by means of which

[68] Brochmand, *Systema*, II, 492 f.: "To make inward prayer, there is required first faith . . . true and sincere conversion of the one praying . . . true humility of heart . . . a sincere intention of the heart to present its plea, a strong and ardent desire for divine help, the readiness to submit to the divine will . . . assiduity, constancy, and perseverance in prayers."

[69] Petitions for temporal benefits must be made conditionally, prayers for spiritual blessings may be brought before God without limitation. Brochmand, *Systema*, II, 495: "In the name of Jesus we ask for bodily benefits conditionally, but we ask for spiritual gifts for ourselves and others without condition."

[70] Brochmand, *Systema*, II, 491; Dannhauer, *Collegium*, p. 363; Hollaz, *Examen*, p. 1209.

God's gracious gifts come to us.[71] Quenstedt calls trust (*fiducia*) the soul of prayer.[72] But one cannot speak of *fiducia* as of an act limited in time. As it is to be in the Christian unceasingly, and because God's compassion is pouring down on us continuously, so our prayers of thanks may return to Him without ceasing.[73] Limitations of time and place do not exist for him who prays aright. When Jesus calls the quiet chamber the God-pleasing place for prayer,[74] this *cubiculum* is to be understood to be the human heart.[75] Prayer in spirit and in truth is the kind that is not modified by external criteria because it is entirely rooted in the believing heart.[76] Hence if the one who prays meets the three main requirements, that is, if he prays in the name of Christ, with an upright heart, and well prepared;[77] then the prayer will be of such a nature as to please God, that is, it will contain nothing useless and improper.[78] True, in agreement with the nomistic trend of Orthodoxy the first motive assigned for prayer is the clear

[71] See the picture of Augustine, which Gerhard repeats in his "Meditations" (No. 25): "The prayer of the righteous man is the key to heaven; the petition ascends, God's deliverance descends."

[72] Quenstedt, *Theologia*, IV, 351.

[73] Gerhard, *Loci*, I, 345 f.: "As there is no moment when man does not enjoy God's mercy, so there should be none in which he does not remember Him and render due thanks for His kindness."

[74] Gerhard, *Loci*, VIII, 88: "Our Savior teaches, that effective prayers pleasing to God can be made in the bedroom (Matt. 6:6)."

[75] Ibid.: "When you enter into your heart, you enter into your bedroom" (after Augustine).

[76] Gerhard, *Loci*, I, 303: "To worship God in spirit and in truth means: (1) to call upon God, who is present everywhere, without discrimination as to place, to lift up holy hands in every place (1 Tim. 2:8); (2) to call upon God with a true and earnest intent of the heart, not with a hypocritical observance of outward ceremonies and circumstances; (3) to call upon Him in true faith kindled by the Holy Spirit."

[77] Balduin, *Tractatus*, pp. 216 f.

[78] Ibid., pp. 215 f.: "There are three conditions for prayer: (1) that it be godly, that is, directed to the one God from whom every good and perfect gift descends; (2) that it be necessary, for things whimsical, headstrong, useless, or even unlawful are not to be asked of God; (3) that it be becoming, asking of God what becomes Him to grant, such matters as concern the glory of His name and the growth of His kingdom."

54

divine command; then follow our need and the example of Christ and the apostles.[79]

b. The Sabbath. The Third Commandment in particular furnishes proof of the pronounced legalistic involvements into which Orthodoxy entered by adopting the "third use of the Law." For if there is a law that is no longer valid, it is that concerning the Sabbath, which Jesus Himself made an object of His criticism. Men thought that they needed the Sabbath commandment to give theological support to the observance of the Sunday, although the latter developed along altogether different lines. They stripped the Sabbath of its Jewish peculiarities and read from what remained a will of God obligating all men equally. Hence the definitions of "sanctifying the Sabbath" were quite general, and, except for the naming of the day, the complicated Jewish ceremonial was not mentioned, in order that the Evangelical observance of Sunday could be included.[80] The keeping of the *seventh* day, the last of the week, was supposed to be a ceremonial portion of the Sabbath commandment meant only for the Jews, the general moral law consisting in the setting aside of a certain day every week for rest and the celebration of the service.[81] The weekly recurring day of rest was held to belong to the moral law already written in the hearts of the first men. The remnants of the divine image in us as well as general consent *(consensus gentium)* would testify to the truth of this contention. According to Clement of Alexandria, the Greeks also knew of a weekly recurring sacred day.[82] Thus the Sabbath law given by God to the Jews is partly formal

[79] König, *Theologia,* p. 268: "The impelling causes are: (1) God's will, declared by the divine command, promises, and threats; (2) our lack and necessity; (3) the examples of Christ and the apostles."

[80] Calov, *Systema,* XI, 133; "The sanctification of the Sabbath is a religious act whereby we consecrate the seventh day of each recurrent week to God in such a way that we do not attend to any of the ordinary tasks and are free and ready to worship the one God."

[81] Hollaz, *Examen,* p. 1005: "The moral part is, that one day of the week is to be set aside for sacred worship; the ceremonial, that precisely the seventh day of the week must be fixed for the exercise of divine worship."

[82] Calov, *Systema,* XI, 450; Hollaz, Examen, p. 1005: "For it is affirmed by nature that some time should be given to divine worship. The divine institution in paradise designated the seventh day."

law and partly natural law.[83] It was not kept naturally with the full details that appear in the law given on Sinai, but it was kept with respect to its general divine content. To dedicate some day to the service of God is therefore said to have been in vogue even before the Sinaitic legislation.[84]

Brochmand does not draw the distinction between the moral and the ceremonial aspect of this commandment, but opposes the general to the specific features and points out that the Jewish Sabbath differs from the observance of Sunday not only in the diversity of the days but also in the use of different rituals.[85] Baier undertakes a still more precise partition, finding the demands of four different legal spheres met in the Third Commandment: (1) The Natural Law demands in general that a time be set for the worship of God; (2) the Moral Law demands that one day be set aside for the worship of God every seven days, or once a week, without specifying a particular day; (3) the Ceremonial Law demands the observance of the last day in every week; (4) the Political Law stipulates a day of rest for man and beast.[86]

[83] Calov, *Systema,* V, 390: "The sanctification of the Sabbath is in part formal, so far as it concerns the seventh day of the week; and in part natural, or in harmony with the eternal moral law, because it is just that in the seven-day cycle one day should be hallowed for God and designated for His worship."

[84] Calov, *Systema,* VI, 437: "For this commandment could not be derived from the law of nature, and hence there was need of the direct expression of the divine will concerning the regular time for the worship of God. Meanwhile we do not deny that, even before the promulgation of the Sabbath law, it was a matter of natural knowledge that a certain day should be consecrated to the worship of God; and that therefore that day was regularly observed from the beginning of the divinely proclaimed first Gospel in the church of the sons of God, as they are called Gen. 6:2. Hence we judge that there is no need of odious contentions about the lawfulnes of the seventh day of the week, or the Sabbath."

[85] *Systema,* II, 41: "The general [aspect] is, that although the whole life-time should be devoted to piety, a certain day be chosen as directed by God, which is to be employed religiously for the public worship of the divine name, ordinary labor both public and private being laid aside. The specific [aspect] is, that this public worship of the divine name is confined to the seventh day of the creation, to be kept from evening to evening, with the prohibition of lighting fire, cooking food, etc., and not without earnest and holy meditation on the liberation from Egyptian servitude."

[86] Baier, *Theologia moralis,* Suppl. p. 101.

There could be no objection to these Scholastic distinctions if they were not made the basis for the assertion that the Law in a certain sense has eternal validity. To retain the Jewish Sabbath, which has been abolished once for all by the Gospel, as a moral law, although with various modifications and changes, is not in keeping with the mind of Luther, who would concede no exceptional position to the Moral Law.[87]

Like all other Old Testament worship arrangements, the keeping of the Sabbath is raised to a spiritual plane in the New Covenant. Classic Lutheran dogmatics speaks of a *temporal*, a *spiritual,* and a *heavenly Sabbath*.[88] But the meaning is not, as one might expect from the analogy with the spiritualizing of the ritual of sacrifices, that the Jews were bound to keep the temporal as the Christians the spiritual Sabbath, so that the three kinds of Sabbath observance would correspond to the three states — of corruption, grace, and glory *(corruptionis, gratiae, gloriae)*. That is what the Sabbath commandment meant for Luther, as is well known.[89] Orthodoxy, however, thought that the duty of keeping the temporal Sabbath applied to Christians as well as Jews and that for both the temporal Sabbath was the real content of the Third Commandment,[90] though the mode of observing it might differ in details.

The heavenly Sabbath will be celebrated only in the eternal kingdom of God, where we shall be free from all sins and the imperfections of this world and rest entirely in God (Is. 66:23; Heb.

[87] WA 40, I, 672, 12 ff.: "When Paul says that we have been set free by Christ from the curse of the Law, he certainly speaks of the whole Law, and principally of the Moral Law, which alone accuses, curses, and condemns consciences, which the other two kinds do not."

[88] Calov, *Systema,* XI, 134; similarly Brochmand, *Systema,* II, 40; Dannhauer, *Collegium,* p. 545; Quenstedt, *Theologia,* IV, 30. Gerhard (*Loci,* III, 64 f.) knows six stages: (1) The Sabbath of creation (Gen. 2:2); (2) the Mosaic Sabbath (Ex. 20:20); (3) the Sabbath of redemption (Luke 23:54-56); (4) the Christian; (5) the spiritual; (6) the eternal Sabbath.

[89] Large Catechism, I, 82: "This commandment, therefore, according to its gross sense does not pertain to us Christians." See also Vajta, pp. 235 ff.

[90] The exposition of the Third Commandment really busies itself only with the temporal Sabbath: "Properly, the temporal Sabbath is being treated here." (Calov, *Systema,* XI, 134)

57

4:6). The earthly Sabbath is a type pointing to the heavenly one.[91] The spiritual Sabbath, finally, forms the content of the Christian life.[92] It is not bound to any particular time.[93] To cease, to "rest" from all evil deeds, from the works of the flesh, is our lifelong task; it is also the inner presupposition for the right external observance of the Sabbath.[94]

This modified and spiritualized conception of the Sabbath calls for two observations: (1) The mystic ideas that became prominent again in the 17th century fit in very well with this train of thought. In fact, they receive excellent theological support from the imagery of the Sabbath rest.[95] (2) On the other hand, these thoughts on the Sabbath are very appropriate for illustrating the receptive attitude toward God which is characteristic of the Evangelical Christian. According to Luther, the fulfillment of the Third Commandment does not consist in doing something but rather in not doing anything.[96]

[91] Gerhard, Loci, IX, 310: "That Sabbath was a type of the eternal Sabbath in heaven, where the elect, both soul and body, will rest from the sins, calamities, and miseries of this life; God will be in them and they will rest in God."

[92] Cf. Large Catechism, I, 87. Johann Michael Dilherr, Heilige Sonntagsfeier, (1649), pp. 55 f.; "Hence I always say that all our life and work must move in the Word of God if they are to be pleasing to Him and holy. If that is the case, this commandment is in force and being fulfilled."

[93] Calov, Systema, XI, 134: "The spiritual [Sabbath] is bound to no day, but pertains to all days, all hours, all minutes, as long as we are here in the kingdom of grace."

[94] Johann Michael Dilherr (Heilige Sonntagsfeier [1649], pp. 26 f.) says of the spiritual and inner Sabbath: "On it we cease and rest from all carnal desires and sinful works and allow God to work in us. This Sabbath we are to keep always; and without this spiritual and inner Sabbath God never took pleasure in the Mosaic or the apostolic or the Christian Sabbath."

[95] Cf. Note 91. Dannhauer (Collegium, p. 545) calls the inward spiritual Sabbath "the Sabbath of the soul, a ceasing from the works of the flesh, resting in the Highest Good." Dilherr, Sonntagsfeier, pp. 81 f.: "Hence, because God rested on the Sabbath, you too are to rest in God and say: Come to me, O Holy Trinity, and keep Sabbath in my heart. Thou hast helped me to labor these six days. Thou who art the strength of my life hast worked in me; therefore rest now in me on the seventh day and let me rest in Thee."

[96] WA 1, 436, 16: "Therefore in this Third Commandment the important thing is not work, but rather quiet, so that God is not offended by works."

This characteristic thought, produced solely by the doctrine of Justification, was somewhat shifted by Orthodoxy. The "not doing anything" was now referred only to evil works *(cessatio ab operibus malis)*, while there was a strong emphasis on doing, viz., the doing of "holy works." The celebration of the Sabbath dare not be merely theoretical (contemplative; a meditation on the works of God); it must also be practical, bound up with faith and the practical employment of Godliness.[97]

That inward sanctification and spiritual worship were represented by Orthodoxy as commanded by God is not strange.[98] It is similar in the case of prayer. But whereas in the case of prayer only the right attitude of the heart appears as commanded, while the external form was left to human choice, it is otherwise in the case of the Sabbath. Here we must note a very pronounced relapse into legalistic thinking in so far as also the *external manner* of "sanctifying the holy day" was closely prescribed for the Christian, as it had been in Judaism. Alongside of the proclamation of the Word and the administration of the sacraments there enters a third form of divine service ordained by God. It is the "apostolic or Christian Sabbath," transferred to the first day of the week and continuing the Mosaic Sabbath in a changed form, but retaining all its moral and obligating validity.[99] Insofar as it bears only the marks of the Moral Law, it is impossible to demand its abolition.[100] The fixture of the Christian

[97] See Calov, *Systema*, XI, 135. P. 136: "Hence the aim of the Sabbath is both rest and activity: rest from ordinary labor; activity, in that we are engaged in divine work . . . namely, the work of faith, which God wants to be active in us, if only we are quiet and do not put anything in His way." — It is noteworthy that Calov despite his "divine work" returns to the fundamental Lutheran thought of "letting God work in us."

[98] Gerhard, *Loci*, III, 60.

[99] Dilherr, *Sonntagsfeier*, p. 25.

[100] Calov, *Systema*, XI, 140: "The first day of the week, commonly called the Lord's Day, does not come under the abrogation of the divine law, because six days are assigned for work, which number would not be constant unless terminated by the rest of a seventh day; because, unless one day out of the cycle of seven is consecrated for divine worship, there is no reason why the 20th or 30th or the 200th could not be chosen, which would clearly militate against the divine institution; and because the apostles always observed the seventh day."

Sabbath on the first day of the week was not accidental but due to an act of God especially distinguishing this day.[101]

In connection with the transfer of the Sabbath to Sunday the *duration* of the "holy day" is sometimes considered. When Schröder castigates "the profanation of the Sunday and of festive days" and refers to such matters as sitting in taverns on the evening before and working during the night preceding Sunday,[102] he is thinking of the Sabbath as beginning, in the Jewish fashion, on the previous evening. Whether he held Sunday evening to be exempt from the duty of observance does not appear. Brochmand considered the reckoning from evening to evening, just like the keeping of the last day in the week, as belonging to the peculiarities of the Jewish Sabbath.[103] Dannhauer thought that the "day" to be kept holy did not mean the day in contrast to the night but included the latter [104] and consequently lasted from midnight to midnight.[105] In Dunte we read, on the other hand, that the Sabbath lasted from sunrise of the "holy day" till sunrise of the following day [106] because Christ hallowed the Sabbath by His resurrection; this had occurred very early as morning dawned. Besides, Paul had protracted his Sabbath address until midnight and finished completely only at dawn. (Acts 20:11)

To this elevation of the Sunday as a divinely-given part of worship objections have been raised from various quarters, as by the Roman

---

101 Dilherr, *Sonntagsfeier*, pp. 47 ff.: "Let no one think that the Sabbath law concerned the Jews only. No! The sanctifying of a certain day of the week is part of the Ten Commandments, which concern and bind to obedience all men. That it had to be the Saturday pertained to the Jews alone. This the apostles abolished in Christian liberty and instituted that day of the week which we call Sunday, or according to Rev. 1:10, the Lord's Day, because on that day God began the work of creation and separated the light from darkness (Gen. 1), and because on that day Christ rose from the dead." In this connection Dilherr later mentions the "institution of the ministry" (John 20) and the outpouring of the Holy Spirit (Acts 2), so that all three Persons of the Trinity had part in the institution of Sunday.

102 Schröder, *Zuchtposaune*, p. 145.

103 Brochmand, *Systema*, II, 41.

104 Dannhauer, *Theologia*, p. 370.

105 Dannhauer, *Collegium*, p. 552.

106 Dunte, *Decisiones*, p. 250: "One must begin with dawn and go to the next dawn, not from one evening to the next."

60

Catholic Church, which derives the authority of the Sunday from canon law. Yet it is expressly emphasized: We are certain that this day was instituted not by human, but by divine authority.[107] In proof it is urged that the Lord of the Sabbath (Mark 2:28) can institute and change the Sabbath; that the apostles, who designated the Lord's Day for public gatherings, only handed on what they had received from Christ; that Christ repeatedly appeared to the disciples on Sunday and poured out His Spirit on that day: "Whence it is probable that the keeping of this day was instituted directly after the resurrection of Christ." [108]

It is remarkable that a man like Stryk, who demanded the abolition of many ceremonies and thereby contributed not a little to the deterioration of the Lutheran service, had a more Lutheran conception of the keeping of Sunday than the representatives of Lutheran Orthodoxy. His criticism of the Sabbath commandment begins with Old Testament facts: The real founder was undoubtedly Moses. Before the Fall the Sabbath would certainly have been absurd, for then man was of course distinguished by the right worship of God, which he offered always and everywhere! Besides, at that time man was not in need of rest, since work was not a heavy burden to him.[109] Stryk also regards as wrong the division of the Third Commandment into a moral and a ceremonial part; he held it to be an exclusively ceremonial law given only to the Jews.[110] The natural law did indeed demand the worship of God, but not for one day of the week in particular.[111] Much weight is given by Stryk to the examples of

[107] Ibid., p. 245.

[108] Ibid., p. 246.

[109] Johann Samuel Stryk, De iure Sabbathi (1733), p. 35.

[110] Ibid., p. 43. The dogmaticians, on the other hand, expressly contended that the Sabbath commandment must be a continuing law, if only for the sake of the completeness of the Decalog: "It is not to be doubted that the commandment about the Sabbath belonged to the Decalog and its integrity, since otherwise the Decalog would not have been entire but would have consisted of only nine commandments. But the law about sanctifying the Sabbath did not belong to the temporary laws." (Calov, Systema, VI, 440)

[111] Stryk, p. 45: "All considerations of natural law that urge the worship of God have this intent that God be worshiped, and worshiped even daily. But that one day weekly must be especially designed for divine worship, and not one day in two weeks or two days in every week or a certain time every day, cannot be proved by any natural consideration."

61

Christ, the apostles, and the church (Rom. 14:5, 6; Gal. 4:9-11). He sees quite correctly that the reasons underlying the development of the Christian celebration of Sunday were altogether different from those generally alleged. It took place for the sake of the weak [112] and for reasons of utility, [113] and it still remains within the sphere of Christian liberty. [114] To be sure, Christian Sunday observance also imposes certain obligations (Heb. 10:25); it also demands abstention from labor. But these obligations grew out of the nature of the matter itself and are of purely human coinage. [115] Löscher was unfortunately too closely enmeshed in the Orthodox tradition to recognize the elements of truth which (apart from many pietistic abridgments of ceremonies) were doubtless present in Stryk's pronouncements on the Sabbath. Hence his judgment on Stryk is altogether negative. [116] It is nevertheless true that the same Stryk

[112] Cf. Luther's words, WA 1, 436, 33 ff.: "Hence (Gal. 4:10) that commandment has properly ceased; yes, all as far as perfect Christians are concerned, since the law is not made for the righteous. The ancient church retained holy days from the necessity of ministering the Word of God to the weak; for the truly righteous is so godly that, as God is indifferent to all days, places, persons, so every day is a holy day to him too. But the weak, who are not yet mortified as to the old man, have need of being engaged with certain duties, days, customs, vigils . . ."

[113] Stryk, p. 52: "Since there were among them unlearned and weak persons, and so that these could be publicly instructed about the true faith and admonished to lead a pious life, it seemed to meet the case to fix a certain day, so that they might know when to come together."

[114] Ibid., p. 53: "Sunday was designed for divine worship not because of an absolute necessity and to be kept forever in the manner of a law, but only on account of good order, yet so that Christian liberty is not abridged thereby."

[115] Ibid., p. 56: "The obligation of bodily rest is not the same as it once was on the Sabbath day. . . . But I think one should still abstain from ordinary labors on that day; yet not from obligation under the Mosaic Law, from which we have been set free, but from another principle, namely, from the nature of the worship requisite in the New Testament."

[116] Löscher, I, 73: "Much offence was also given by the action of Dr. J. S. Stryk of Halle, who in 1702 published his great dissertation De iure Sabbathi, in which he not only mocked and maligned our entire divine service, but declared the Sunday or Sabbath to be a purely Jewish affair not binding on Christians, . . . surrendered it to the decisions of secular governments . . . also taught that really perfect Christians were not in duty bound to take part in external services, etc. This was printed and approved in Francke's Orphanage at Halle. This same Dr. Stryk, in his defense published in 1707,

who had first spoken of the Sunday quite correctly as an institution subject to Christian liberty ended up with the idea of a legally obligatory keeping of Sunday. This was due to his fundamental Pietistic convictions. The difference was that pressure was no longer exerted by an appeal to divine authority but proceeded from the government, while it nevertheless touched things divine and adiaphora which really have nothing to do with regulation by legislation. Visiting taverns, dancing, and theatrical performances on Sundays were strictly forbidden.[117] Even attendance at public divine service could be enforced.[118]

To sum up. The theological basis given for the observance of Sunday by classic Lutheran theology is un-Lutheran throughout. With the aid of the Third Commandment the celebration of Sunday is turned into an ever-valid moral law and vindicated as "divine law." In place of the freedom from the Sabbath proclaimed by Christ and the apostles, a new obligation is formed on another hypothesis. The traditional pericope for the 17th Sunday after Trinity is always interpreted to suit this view. Although it stresses Jesus' right of disposal over the Sabbath, the practical application is always that the Sabbath must be kept and observed rightly, even though the precedence of works of charity over liturgical activities is conceded.[119]

This concludes Part I, in which we endeavored to grasp the nature of divine worship as it appeared to Lutheran Orthodoxy. In doing this, we were concerned with the basic presuppositions, which are indeed also fundamental for man's ethical conduct but which operate somewhat differently in the sphere of worship. The conclu-

insisted that in our present-day divine services everything was corrupted from head to foot . . . All external customs were useless, and there was nothing in any part of the church ceremonies that would stand the test; indeed, God was not worshiped by any external matter, but only in the spirit, that is, in the heart."

[117] Stryk, p. 86.

[118] Stryk, p. 92: "The weak and much more the ignorant or those who as yet have no faith are bound not to neglect the public service of the Lord's Day; not because of the Old Testament law about keeping the Sabbath but because of their own need, to help their weakness, to make good their defects, to reduce their ignorance, to break through from darkness to light . . ."

[119] Dilherr, *Sonntagsfeier*, p. 19: "The Lord proves to them that not all work on the Sabbath is forbidden, but that works demanded by love of the forsaken neighbor and by absolute necessity are permitted."

sion is that classic Lutheran theology maintained the fundamental evangelical concept of trusting faith *(fiducia)* also with respect to the worship of God, but that with regard to the liturgical activities of the regenerate it cannot be acquitted of a legalistic conception of worship, which appears especially in its teaching regarding the Sabbath.

In the following chapters the form of the divine service is to be treated. The reference is of course to the external manifestation, limited as to time and place, of the inward service of God in spirit and truth. Here the following questions arise:

1) Is this form admissible at all? Is it necessary? Is it indissolubly connected with the nature of divine worship?

2) Is this form left to the Christian liberty of individuals, or is it subject to definite norms?

3) Did the liturgical practice of Orthodox times remain true to its theological foundations?

The procedure will be to point out first the right and the meaning of the public service and the position of Orthodoxy over against the most important liturgical problems (Part II). Then the question of the relation between the essence and the form of the service will be examined, with special attention to the conditions actually prevailing in the 17th century. (Part III)

PART TWO

The Form
of the Divine Service

CHAPTER FOUR

The Necessity of Form

L utheran Orthodoxy found the form of the service a well-established reality. At the time of the Reformation men had debated heatedly whether it was justifiable and necessary; but ever since Luther's views on the indispensability of some kind of liturgical embodiment for the Evangelical service had prevailed everywhere, and church constitutions as well as the habituation of decades were exerting a steadying influence, the problem was no longer so acute as when Luther had met it, for example, in 1522. Still, Orthodoxy made its contribution to the discussions with spiritualistic tendencies. The ideas of the Enthusiasts survived in small sectarian movements, and soon the inquiry into the meaning of the external conduct of the service was to be initiated again by the Pietistic movement.

But in the era on which our interest centers the polemics about the outward form of the service had almost ceased. It had been taken up unquestioningly as part of the doctrinal system; its necessity was demonstrated with reasons already used by Luther. Orthodoxy proved the need of public services with three arguments.

1. The Argument from Creation

The first thought that meets us here is this: God, who created man *body and soul,* demands the action of our entire person, that is, of body and spirit.[1] The corporeal is not simply a more or less im-

---

[1] Luther also opposed the tearing apart of body and soul, which made possible the "enthusiastic" conception of the Lord's Supper. Cf. Vajta, *Theologie,* pp. 248 f.; *Worship,* pp. 135 f.

portant concomitant of the spiritual, but it brings the spiritual part of man to its full realization.[2] Just as we operate in other spheres of life with the totality of our being, with body and soul, so the emotion of the heart directed toward God as praise and thanksgiving may have its visible outward expression.[3] Judged by the nature of prayer, what is offered only within the soul may certainly be adequate. But if we think of the one who prays, whose whole personality is to enter into his prayer, it is not adequate.[4] The outward form or expression (the "out-pressing") is not the last remnant of being shackled to corporeality — something still to be sloughed off. It is a part of creation and needs no apology. Its total absence must be regarded as an exceptional case.[5] All our activity takes the shape of "thoughts,

[2] Althaus, "Sinn der Liturgie," p. 242. Wilhelm Stählin, *Vom Sinn des Leibes* (1930), pp. 110 ff.

[3] Dunte, *Decisiones*, p. 143: "It behooves us to render honor to our Savior with soul and body, thoughts and gestures, words and deeds, and thus to give evidence of our reverence and gratitude toward Him. For if we show this honor to kings and those in high places, why not to the King of kings and Lord of lords? We do not doubt that it is a sign of a profane spirit if someone stubbornly refuses to uncover his head or to bend his knees in honor of Christ. It is certain that, as living faith shows itself by good works, so true piety manifests itself by outward gestures. While such baring of the head or genuflexion is not in and by itself worship of God, it is a ceremony pertaining to worship whereby we attest our humility and reverence."

[4] Ibid., p. 893: "Is it enough to pray with the heart and the mind? (1) It is enough as regards the essence of prayer, because the power of faith *(religio)*, which is practiced in prayer, can be exercised by an inward act without the addition of any outward act (1 Sam. 1:13; Neh. 2:4). God well knows the internal act even if expressed by no external sign (Ps. 139:4). (2) It does not always suffice to complete the duty of the one who prays: 1. because God is to be glorified and worshiped by us not only with the soul but also with the body and hence with the voice (1 Cor. 6:20), 2. because the voice, proceeding from the heart, is heard again and received back into it, so that it becomes a means of stimulating, continuing, and increasing the pious impulse from which it emanates, 3. because we must often pray together with others, who are edified by our voice as they endeavor to take part in the same petition." Here Orthodoxy goes even beyond Luther, for whom ecclesiastical ceremonies had "an essential duty in relation to the neighbor" (Vajta, p. 324). As for Dunte, the external form possessed significance even for the individual worshiper. Whether the Christian thereby exercises himself in the faith and at the same time helps the faith of his neighbor, is a question by itself.

[5] Brochmand, *Systema*, II, 493: "The external mode of prayer consists partly in speech, partly in bodily motions. Although this is not absolutely

words, and deeds," [6] and the "deeds," the operations of the body, must be allowed full scope.[7] The humble attitude of faith before God extends to the outward position of the body. Orthodoxy carries the demand for externalization so far as to include, for instance, a visible expression of the respect due to the angels. This naturally leads to a real danger of involvement in the Roman Catholic cult of angels. Therefore, so the argument runs, showing respect to angels by means of bodily gestures is to be reserved for the actual appearance of angels — a very remote contingency. Otherwise the betokening of reverence before angels is merely acknowledged as an ethical requirement.[8]

When speaking of good works, the Evangelical ethics rightly places the accent first of all on what goes on within man. This does not at all mean that less importance attaches to outward works; for good works are almost invariably described as internal and external necessary for the essence of prayer, but the inward thought of the mind and sighs heaved from the depth of the breast and the secret talk of the heart with God suffice, as is shown by the example of Moses (Ex. 14:15), Hannah (1 Sam. 1:13) and others, and especially because God perceives the inner act of the heart without any outward sign; nevertheless, prayer only of the heart and mind does not always suffice to complete the office of prayer, (1) because God is to be glorified not only with our heart but also with the body and hence with our tongue and lips (1 Cor. 6:20; Phil. 2:11); (2) because God tells us directly to praise Him with spiritual hymns (Eph. 5:19; Col. 3:16), Christ Himself setting the example (Matt. 26:30); (3) because such is the weakness of the heart that unless it is aided by the support of the voice in praying, it easily wanders and goes astray. Therefore, in order both to show and to aid the inward emotion, pious men have always been careful to add outward speech and cries, especially in great distress (Heb. 5:7)."

[6] See Ch. 3, n. 2.

[7] Balduin, *Tractatus,* p. 174: "God requires the outward form of worship as well as the inward, since we are to love Him with all our strength; hence all our words, gestures, and deeds are to testify to our faith and love toward Him. And as Christ is the Redeemer of our soul and our body, both must be directed toward God."

[8] Quenstedt, *Theologia,* I, 487: "We honor angels (1) with the intellect, by recognizing them as the noblest creatures; (2) with our emotions, by beholding them with love and reverence; (3) with outward actions, by showing them also marks of respect if they should appear in visible form or shape, obeying the mandates which they bring us by God's command, and imitating their virtues."

acts *(actiones internae et externae)*.[9] But the sequence is decisive: the way leads only from within to without.[10] When Gerhard marshals good works in due order,[11] the first place is occupied by the inner obedience of the heart to God, and more particularly by the fear and love of Him. Second place is given to the fulfillment of the moral precepts contained in the First Table of the Decalog: calling upon God, thanksgiving, hearing the divine Word. Here we are already within the area of the external service of God. There follow the Christian's duty toward his neighbor and toward himself and, as the fifth stage of good works, the fulfillment of the ceremonial of the First Table.[12] Here we come once more upon the necessity of liturgical acts, where the fundamental distinction between moral and ceremonial precepts must not be overlooked. Of this more later.

That which is within tends toward outward expression (as in prayer) not only in the individual Christian, but also in the Christian community. The congregation as the body of Christ is a unit which manifests itself as such by coming together. This implies the duty of the individual to associate himself with the congregation also externally.[13] The church must be visible. Its true marks, the right preaching of the Word and the administration of the sacraments, are perceptible to the eyes of man. Therefore the means of grace must not be alienated from the purpose of making known the presence

[9] Hafenreffer, *Loci,* p. 483; Hutter, *Compendium,* p. 101; Gerhard, *Loci,* IV, 3; Brochmand, *Systema,* II, 228; Hollaz, *Examen,* p. 1185.

[10] Not also vice versa, as the Roman Church teaches, which attributes educative values even to purely external prayer, believing that superficial attention will pass over into attention to the words and eventually rise to spiritual attention (Cf. Wetzer and Welte, *Kirchenlexikon,* 2d ed., V, 141).

[11] *Loci,* IV, 4.

[12] See Ch. 6, n. 38.

[13] Heinrich Müller, *Predigten,* p. 121: "He who neglects the gatherings, disregards the Holy Spirit. As the father of a family does not feed its members individually, the one in this corner and the other in that; as the soul does not give life and motion to separated members, to one here and to the other there, but to all joined together in one body: so we are to receive the Holy Spirit not in dispersal, but as a gathering. . . . Hence do not say: I can read God's Word at home and need no congregation. He who thinks thus despises the office of the Spirit and reads what he reads without the Holy Ghost. . . . Reading the Scriptures is not to do away with the public service, but rather to establish it."

of the church by being restricted to purely private celebrations.[14]
When speaking of the gathering of the congregation, which is effected
by the means of grace together with the calling into being, the nour-
ishing, and the preservation of the church,[15] we must not think exclusively of the *spiritual* gathering, but also of the bodily gathering
in the name of Christ, the assembly for divine service, which has the
promise of Christ's presence.[16]

2. The Pedagogical Argument

The second reason for the necessity of the outward observance
(res externa) is closely related to the first. It is the *pedagogical* factor,
much stressed already by Luther. As long as we are in the flesh, the
spiritual must become more impressive for us through external signs.[17]
That which is external acts as a sort of reenforcement for that which
is within, though this is necessary only so long as we are living in
the present aeon.[18] The Third Commandment in particular is designed to assist us in the difficult duty of keeping the Word of God
in our heart at all times; for it sets certain times when we can devote
ourselves to the Word with full concentration.[19] The pedagogical

[14] Andreas Kesler, *Theologia casuum conscientiae . . . d. i. Schriftmässige
und ausführliche Erörterung unterschiedener . . . Gewissensfragen* (1683),
pp. 137 f.: "The theological rule is known that the holy sacraments are to be
administered publicly in the congregation, except in case of necessity, as they
are also the nerves of the public gatherings. Similarly it is proper that sermons be delivered ordinarily publicly in church."

[15] Gerhard, *Loci*, V, 375.

[16] Ibid., p. 375: "Matt. 18:20: Where two or three are gathered together
in My name, there am I in the midst of them. That assembly is a true church
because it gathers in the name of Christ."

[17] WA 6, 338, 35; 359, 6.

[18] Gerhard, *Loci*, III, 60: "Inner sanctification and spiritual worship are
required in the first two commandments. But because in this life that spiritual
inner worship needs the outward exercise of the public ministry, through
which God produces, preserves, and increases in us that inward holiness, and
in which the principles of that inner sanctification are set forth, therefore this
Third Commandment is to be understood as referring to the public ministry
of the Word and the sacred rites."

[19] Dilherr, *Sonntagsfeier*, pp. 52 f.: "We Christians should always keep
the holy day and be busy with sacred things, that is, daily use the Word of
God and have it in our heart and mouth. But since (as stated) not all have
time and leisure, we must use some hours weekly for the young, or at least one

71

implication of externals will be felt not only by him who makes use of this external aid. If the inner feeling of my heart is given concrete form, it at the same time takes on significance for others, whether as an act of confession or as an encouragement to do likewise.[20]

There is no need to be ashamed of the aids supplied to us by means of outward institutions. They are gifts of God to be received with thanksgiving. Where perfectionism holds sway, indeed, men think that they can do without the aid of external worship. According to Gottfried Arnold it is possible to attain to such a state of perfection in this life as no longer to require the sacraments.[21] Thus Pietism taught: "All external means are to be used only as scaffolding for a wall or as the star was used by the Wise Men from the East, so that the external cease in time and be swallowed up by the spiritual." [22] The consequence of this is a conflict between inward and outward worship, in which the outward form naturally suffers curtailment.[23] If even the sacraments fell a prey to this perfectionism, it is not surprising that the aids of faith (subsidia religionis) were to be

day for all, in order to deal exclusively with these matters and teach the Ten Commandments, the Creed, and the Lord's Prayer, and thus direct our whole life and being by God's Word."

[20] Joachim Lütkemann, Harfe von zehn Saiten (ed. Heinrich Lütkemann, 1909), Ps. 34, p. 15: "The soul desirous of praising God does not keep silent but speaks of His glory among men. With the heart man believes unto righteousness, with the mouth confession is made unto salvation. If I praise God in my heart, I praise Him for myself; if I praise Him with the mouth, I praise Him before the neighbor."

[21] Gottfried Arnold, Unparteyische Kirchen- und Ketzerhistorie (1729), I, p. 53: "On this foundation those who were perfect, Phil. 3:5, required no external aids, such as had been ordained for the weak in whom Christ was not yet rooted and grounded. Hence they did not bind one another strictly to the Lord's Supper, neither for the strengthening of faith nor in remembrance of Christ nor for fellowship among themselves, but left it to each one's liberty. . . . With those to whom the Lord Himself had come and revealed Himself according to His promise, this practice probably ceased after the steady indwelling of the Lord, and there began in them the marriage of the Lamb, an earnest of the future public home-bringing."

[22] Cf. Löscher, Timotheus Verinus, I, p. 270.

[23] Ibid., p. 277: "The inner processes in worship have been placed in opposition to external ones, especially those that belong to the public service, in such a way that the latter necessarily had to suffer."

abolished.[24] The divine service was affected thereby, since "church gatherings and church buildings" were to be done away with gradually.[25] The same demand was raised with respect to church orders (*Kirchenordnungen*), among which Löscher enumerates Confession and Absolution as "profitable and most valuable portions." "Baby walkers" was the term contemptuously applied by Pietists to the aid given by set prayers; and Lange taught "that an adult Christian would do well to throw them away." [26]

These perfectionist sentiments, voiced already in the 17th century, are in the strongest opposition to the conceptions of Lutheran Orthodoxy. The latter was still aware that even the "adult Christian" remains a sinner requiring those external aids; for he daily needs the forgiveness of sins available for him in the congregation through the Word and the sacraments only.[27] Fendt rightly points out that Luther, who at one time proposed a special order of service for those "who seriously desire to be Christians," never thought of abolishing outward order; what he had in mind was a special kind of gathering, but a gathering nevertheless. "A gathering, a congregation there must be, especially for the believers." [28] The sermon and the sacraments have not accomplished their appointed purpose with

[24] Löscher reckons under *subsidia religionis* those things "which indeed do not possess the high dignity and virtue of the means of grace, but still have been ordained or approved by God for man's spiritual benefit, and which are very profitable for the general condition of Christians and for the preservation of true religion; such as the external visible church, apologetics and polemics, the Symbolical Books, dogmatical books, similar teaching materials, the art of theological teaching, earnestness against errorists, church buildings and meetings, also church orders, etc. Because these matters are less than the means of grace and the fence is lowest here, people surmount it more boldly. Now where this is done under the pretext of piety, or with the object of increasing piety, there Pietism stands revealed." (*Timotheus*, I, 555).

[25] Cf. Löscher, *Timotheus*, I, 616 ff.

[26] Löscher, I, 627.

[27] Gerhard, *Loci*, V, 279: "The proper benefits of the church are regeneration, renovation, illumination, sanctification, the gift of the Holy Ghost, the promise of the eternal inheritance, etc. Since these have no place outside of the church, or outside of the assembly of those called by the Word and the sacraments, there can be no salvation outside of the church."

[28] Leonhard Fendt, "Der reformatorische Gottesdienstgedanke," *Grundfragen des evangelischen Kultus*, ed. Curt Horn (1927), p. 30.

having once awakened faith. Those who have become believers stand in need of continued strengthening and preservation.[29]

3. The Theological Argument

It is not really our business at all to decide whether or not man needs these auxiliary means. God has determined that we are to use these external aids by instituting them for us. In the sacraments, where external visible things become the bearers of things spiritual and invisible,[30] it becomes particularly clear that what is inward should take some outward shape. *God's institution* is the third and most important reason for all external divine service.[31] Liturgy is inherent in the commission to proclaim the Word of God and to dispense the sacraments. Both acts are without doubt perceptible processes belonging to earthly reality. Thus the external part of our services, still further accentuated by the ordinance of the sacraments, has been directly authorized by God Himself. True, for Orthodoxy this authority was not "God in Christ," but God the Legislator. The acts of worship under the New Covenant were included in the larger context of the Third Commandment. This was held to have as its contents all outward features of the divine service and hence to demand the institution of public, regulated gatherings of the congregation, with features already known to the Jewish ceremonial in its own way. These traits common to the Jewish and the Christian outward service[32] are first the *assembly* (*convocatio sancta,* Lev. 23:2, 3, 7, 8, 21, 27). There follows *the preaching and hearing of the Word*

[29] Brochmand, *Systema,* II, 265: "By the true preaching of the Word and the right use of the sacraments the church is brought together, and then preserved, nourished, sustained." Vajta, p. 232: "Luther cannot conceive of a Christian faith which at any time attains to a maturity, so to say, through which its passivity (the receiving of God's work) would cease and give way to an activity of faith that would be free from the necessity of continued receiving."

[30] Quenstedt, *Theologia,* IV, 75: "The matter of which a sacrament consists is twofold: earthly and heavenly. The earthly or external matter is corporeal, visible, and tractable, divinely ordained to be the vehicle and exhibiting means of the heavenly matter. The heavenly, or internal, matter is invisible, exhibited by the earthly visible matter or by the divinely ordained means."

[31] Cf. Vajta, *Theologie,* p. 230; *Worship,* p. 128.

[32] After Gerhard, *Loci,* III, 63. Cf. Calov, *Systema,* XI, 136; Dunte, *Decisiones,* pp. 247 f.

74

of God, as prescribed in Lev. 10:11, but also Luke 4:16; Acts 13:14 f., 44; 15:21. The *dispensing of the sacraments* continues under the New Covenant with a change as to form, but not as to content: the sacraments are no longer Circumcision and the Passover, but Baptism and the Holy Supper. Under *invocatio ac celebratio* Gerhard understands all the other parts, briefly designated as "liturgy," such as hymns, confession, prayer, etc. (Ps. 22:23, 26; Acts 16:13). To this is added *the collection for the support of the poor* as another divinely commanded component part of the external service. (Is. 58:7; 1 Cor. 16:1, 2)

The method by which Lutheran Orthodoxy arrived at the elements of the public service is not the way taken by Luther, who did not consult the Decalog when dealing with the service. What was authoritative for Luther was the service celebrated by *Christ* with His disciples and directed by Him to be continued until His return; that is, the celebration of the Eucharist.[33] The Order of Holy Communion is "the one obligatory fundamental form of the Christian service."[34] But this involves "preaching" as well as "praise and thanksgiving for the grace of Christ."[35] Thus "the celebration of the sacraments according to the institution of Jesus Christ, the preaching of the Gospel, and praise of God in prayers and hymns"[36] make up the God-given substance of the liturgy. For this reason it cannot seriously be questioned that the divine service must take on an outward form. We may refuse with Luther to consider this a law, but that does not exclude the fact that it is supported by divine authority.

In the 17th century the "outward form" of the service is always traced to God's legislative authority. Activities of individuals, whether they be the invocation of God by word or gestures or the testimony to Christ in wider circles, are brought under the Second Command-

[33] WA 12, 206, 14: "We cannot deny that the Mass and the communion of bread and wine is the rite instituted by Christ." See also Vajta, *Theologie,* pp. 44 ff.; *Worship,* pp. 27 ff.

[34] Theodor Knolle, "Luthers Deutsche Messe und die Rechtfertigungslehre," *Lutherjahrbuch* 1928, p. 184.

[35] WA 30, II, 606, 14.

[36] Theodor Knolle, *Bindung und Freiheit in der liturgischen Gestaltung* (1932), p. 9. See also Peter Brunner, *Leiturgia,* I, 284.

75

ment; [37] actions by the assembled congregation are referred to the Third Commandment. Naturally, no distinct dividing line can be drawn. For the sphere of the congregation extends even to the gathering of two Christians who have come together in the name of Jesus, and hence to a private fellowship; while the public praise of God demanded in the Second Commandment has reference first of all to the individual, but becomes meaningful only in connection with the congregation.[38] Baier therefore combines the duties enjoined in the Second and the Third Commandments in one section.[39]

Nevertheless, the Third Commandment embraces a feature not really enunciated by the preceding commandments. The Pietistic conventicles did not lack outward forms of worship, and yet they could not lay claim to fulfilling the Third Commandment rightly, as understood by Orthodoxy; for they lacked a requirement of the Third Commandment that cannot be surrendered: the *character of publicity*. The right worship must be both private and public.[40] Externalism is not enough; it must be the externalism of the church. Brochmand, too, when discussing zeal for the name of God and its rightful use in connection with the Second Commandment, speaks only in general terms of "glorifying the divine name with word and life" and of "confessing God's name even at the extreme risk of life." [41] Only when dealing with the positive demands of the Third Commandment does he stress the ecclesiastical character of worship and expressly

[37] Gerhard, *Loci*, III, 55.

[38] Dannhauer, *Hodosophia christiana seu theologia positiva* (1666), p. 508: "A doxology is a virtuous act which extols God's name, that is, whatever utterance can be spoken about the Triune God, by reading, hearing, confessing, preaching, blessing, vowing, swearing an oath, singing, praying."

[39] He classifies: (1) the external use of the Word and the sacraments; (2) the confession of faith; (3) the glorification of God's name by outward prayers, praises, and thanksgiving; (4) the religious oath; (5) the pious Christian vow; (6) the religious fast; (7) keeping the Sabbath and other festivals. (*Theologia moralis*, p. 264)

[40] Balduin, *Tractatus*, p. 174: "The public exercise of religion consists in pious concern for the maintenance of true religion in any country, in keeping up the public meetings, in hearing the Word, in public prayers, in the use of the sacraments. The private form consists in domestic discipline, the exercise of piety among children and servants, in maintaining innocence of life, and in sweetest harmony of the household, so that they can worship God together."

[41] Brochmand, *Systema*, II, 32.

76

mention private devotion at home instead of attendance at church as a case of emergency.[42]

The constant and clear emphasis on this thought should not be esteemed too lightly. Though the derivation of external worship from Old Testament law is contestable, yet the Orthodox theologians had embedded the divine service so firmly in their system that influences threatening the church with disintegration could be effectively resisted. "Private worship" always remained a mere part of the service, which was essentially public and without which private worship could not exist, for the latter was and remained dependent on the Word heard in the assembly. In Hollaz it appears only in the fourth position among the duties pertaining to the holy day: "Private worship (cultus) of God consists in reviewing the Word that has been heard, study of the catechism, searching of conscience, confirming good resolutions."[43] Dannhauer speaks only of "external or public worship."[44] Hence also churchgoing, so often decried as "not doing the trick," is part of the divine command to conduct divine services.[45] Reading sermons at home cannot take its place. Sometimes psychological reasons on a par with the pedagogical significance of the

[42] With respect to worship the Third Commandment requires in substance: To hear the divine Word in the public gatherings of the church (Acts 15:12); to offer prayers with the church (1 Tim. 2:1 f.); to administer the sacraments or at least to witness their administration devoutly (1 Cor. 11:18, 19); to employ the whole day for sacred exercises held in public gatherings (Ps. 92:2; Acts 20:7) or, if that is not possible, at least to use the whole day for private meditation on the divine Word and the divine works. (Deut. 6:6, 7; Ps. 1:2 f.; Col. 3:16; Is. 38:13)

[43] Hollaz, Examen, p. 1005.

[44] Dannhauer, Collegium decalogicum, p. 553. He defines thus: "For as friends associate with friends to converse, so God with man through the sermon and other sacred acts, chiefly sacramental ones . . . Man speaks and deals with God through prayer."

[45] Heinrich Müller, Predigten, p. 33 f. (Sermon on Luke 2:41 ff.): "You ought to blush, you who excuse yourself with empty words by saying: 'I serve God in my house; there is the best church; there I can be most quiet and devout.' Ah, did not Joseph and Mary also have opportunity to serve God at home? The church at home is not to be despised. But the church in the town or village has also been built for a purpose. If you wish to be a member, cling to the body! He is not worthy of the name Christian who neglects the gathering of the Christians."

77

external service of God are urged for the hearing of the sermon,[46] sometimes there is merely a reference to the binding nature of God's ordinance.[47]

There is general agreement, then, that the divine service must also be "external." But as we have pointed to various reasons assigned for this necessity, so the nature of the outward form is likewise variously assessed. It is the will of God that the pious emotions of the heart should find fulfillment also in the bodily act of prayer; but details regarding words and gestures to be employed are left open.[48] It is similar in the case of ceremonies introduced for pedagogical reasons. They must be. But there is no direction from God as to their number, form, mode and manner, etc. In the case of the sacramental rites, however, the authority of the divine institution extends beyond the basic act; it touches certain external matters and affects liturgical formulations of seemingly secondary importance. Here strict obedience to what is written is indicated.[49] It is God's will to be apprehended in the possibilities offered by Himself. If this creates offence, it is not greater than the offence caused by God's will to meet humanity for salvation only in His incarnate Son, Jesus Christ.

God's recognition of our physical nature is not limited to this present age, as a sort of concession to our imperfect spirituality; it extends farther. We believe in the "resurrection of the body," and hence also that the redeemed will praise and glorify God in and with their glorified bodies.[50] Grossgebauer has this to say about the divine

[46] Dannhauer, *Theologia casualis*, p. 344: "The efficacy of the living voice is greater than that of solitary reading."

[47] Ibid.: "It is God's will that assemblies come together, and indeed on the Sabbath, whether the seventh day or Sunday. Hence, he who is not present on Sunday in the Lord's assembly, certainly sins."

[48] Dannhauer, *Collegium decalogicum*, p. 203: "There follows the external, liturgical worship, significant of the inner; necessary as a manifestation, free as regards acts to which no one is bound, nor bound not to do them, forever. Religious homage before the Godhead is commanded; it is free as to act or gesture: whether genuflexion, or prostration, or licking the ground."

[49] Ibid., p. 395: "Rites . . . commanded in Holy Writ as necessary, or prohibited, such as sacramental ones and idolatrous rites opposed to them."

[50] Althaus, *Sinn der Liturgie*, p. 244: "The liturgical form of the divine service has an eschatological meaning. It foreshadows future events and confesses the hope of the promised physical life of the new world."

service which gives praise to God especially through music: "No more beautiful harmony can be found than this" [that is, speaking to one another in psalms]; "it is nothing less than a type and foretaste of the eternal gathering in heaven." [51] The glorification of God, the real destiny of man, consists in external liturgical action; it will be our exclusive function in eternity when we have been relieved of all wearisome labor. [52] Our whole physical nature will share in this. With the eyes of our body we shall see God. [53] When the 17th-century dogmaticians speculate in all seriousness in what language the heavenly liturgy will be chanted, they record their conviction that in eternity, too, the praise of God will be uttered *by the mouth*. The Hebrew language, they think, might come into consideration; for the patriarchs used it, and we hear it in the Amen and the Hallelujah of the redeemed in heaven, Rev. 19. Or it is held possible in view of Phil. 2:11 that *all* tongues will praise God. Or, finally, that opinion seems to deserve the preference which attributes to the elect the knowledge of a language transcending all languages spoken on the earth. That earthly speech will cease is testified 1 Cor. 13:8. In his state of ecstasy (2 Cor. 12:2 ff.) Paul heard ineffable words, which seem to have belonged to the tongues of angels mentioned 1 Cor. 13:1. A typically scholastic problem! [54] Of greater weight is Brochmand's proof that the praises in heaven will be given physical expression. The demonstration operates partly with the argument already mentioned (that God wishes to be worshiped with soul and body) and partly with Scripture quotations possessing more or less validity. [55]

[51] Theophil Grossgebauer, "Wächterstimme aus dem verwüsteten Zion," *Drei Geistreiche Schriften* (1667), p. 194.

[52] Gerhard, *Loci,* III, 61: "We were not created originally for those servile works, that sweat of the brow, but for those works whereby we sanctify the Sabbath; and in eternal life, when we shall celebrate Sabbath after Sabbath, those laborious and servile works for the necessities of this life of servitude will cease."

[53] König, *Theologia,* p. 64: "The organs of that vision are partly the intellect (1 Cor. 13:12), partly the eyes of the glorified body."

[54] Cf. Dunte, *Decisiones,* p. 984.

[55] Brochmand, *Systema,* II, 649: "Will the saints in the other life praise God not only with mental but also with vocal speech? . . . Reason for the belief that there will be the use of vocal speech in yonder life is readily ad-

It cannot be maintained, therefore, that the spiritualism of Pietism and of the Enlightenment was prepared or initiated by Lutheran Orthodoxy. The position of both Luther and Lutheran Orthodoxy was characterized by an awareness of the necessity of a visible form in the divine service. This form was adhered to as the 17th century neared its close, partly in a conscious effort to ward off spiritualizing tendencies.

duced: because God is to be worshiped always by the whole man, with the body no less than with the faithful soul; because in Christ's transfiguration Moses, Elijah, and Christ engaged in conversation (Matt. 17:7; Luke 9:32); because Paul, when caught up to the third heaven, heard unspeakable words (2 Cor. 12:4); and finally because in Rev. 5:9; 7:9 ff.; 11:16; 13:10 very many doxologies and other utterances of the blessed are written down."

CHAPTER FIVE

The Essentials of Form

1. Church and Ministry

Our external divine service is a composite of divine institution and human formation. But these two factors must be kept strictly apart and differently evaluated. The relation of the two is roughly that of substance and incidentals. The error of limiting the divinely instituted substance of worship to the *inward* service of God has been discussed in Chapter 4.[1] The divinely given content of all worship is the offer of reconciliation through the Word and the sacraments. Man responds in faith by *hearing* the Word that is read and spoken and by receiving the proffered sacraments. Even in this external process the Evangelical understanding of divine giving and human receiving is reflected. No matter how manifold the means of communicating the divine Word may be, the normal way is the hearing within the *congregation*. "The Word whereby God engenders faith, the Spirit who works in and with the Word: these, according to the reformers, have been entrusted, not to the school

---

[1] The 17th-century dogmaticians saw very clearly at this point, much more so than many of the champions of a tendency to remove sensuous elements from the Evangelical service who appeal to Luther (thus Friedrich Flemming, *Die treibenden Kräfte in der lutherischen Gottesdienstreform,* 1926). The latter are right in opposing "the tremendous overevaluation of the expressive possibilities of formal liturgical language" (p. 86) that appeared in the older liturgical movement following World War I. But it will not do to call up Luther as a primary witness for the attenuation of everything visible and tangible in the divine service. See Vajta, *Theologie* pp. 26, 37 f.; *Worship,* pp. 15, 22 ff.

or the printery or the private library, but to the congregation of Jesus, to the invisible church which enters into view precisely because it proclaims and hears the Word . . . The Holy Spirit works through the Word on those who are assembled. An assembly, people gathered together, is the presupposition; that is, people gathered to hear the sermon." [2]

With these words the church is posited as the area in which alone the reciprocal giving and taking between God and men can take place.[3] It takes a necessary part in the substance of the liturgy. The salvation mediated to us through Word and sacrament does not become ours outside the church (extra ecclesiam).[4] The conduct of the divine service belongs to the domain of the church alone. The individual believer takes part in the external service only in so far as he is a member of the church and regards the divine service as a function of the church.

It is the duty of the *ministry* of the church to discharge the particular functions of the church service. This office is the earthly organ of the offer of reconciliation through the Word and the sacraments.[5] It is also the earthly beginning of the perpetual sequence of sending, preaching, hearing, faith, invocation, salvation (Rom. 10:13). Preaching the Word of Reconciliation is therefore not an act of Christians among themselves, left to chance and inclination, but is regulated by a standing office deriving its authority from God Himself.[6] Midway between the divine commission to preach and the actual proclamation this office has been erected as a representative of all, that is, of the church,[7] with the responsibility of seeing that the proclamation corresponds to the commission.

[2] Fendt, "Der reformatorische Gottesdienstgedanke," p. 29.

[3] Gerhard, *Loci,* V, 372: "The church is where the Word of God is being heard."

[4] Ibid., V, 279.

[5] See Ch. 2, n. 75.

[6] See Ch. 2, n. 78.

[7] Gerhard, *Loci,* VI, 36: "In a relation, the end has no place without a foundation. The office of the ministry is a relation, as it were, whose foundation is the divine mission and call; the end is preaching itself. Hence the end, that is, the proper, salutary, and God-pleasing sermon, has no place without the divine mission and calling as its foundation."

Questions about the substance of the liturgy can therefore be answered only from the previous knowledge that its administration has been handed over to the ministry of the church and must remain there in all normal circumstances. This does not imply any limitation of the means of grace by a principle that would superordinate the office of the sacred ministry. On the contrary, this office is a *ministerium,* a ministry of *service;* and its main duties are the preaching of the Word of God and the administration of the sacraments. Of course its sphere of duties is more extensive; it embraces the spiritual guidance of a congregation, the exercise of church discipline, the care of the sick and needy; the regulation of indifferent liturgical matters *(rituum ecclesiasticorum conservatio)* also belongs to it.[8] But its primary duty is carrying out the two liturgical activities ordained by God: the preaching of the Word and the administration of the sacraments.[9]

In all normal situations the demand must be made on the incumbent of the sacred ministry that he be rightfully called and ordained, and also that he be orthodox. Blameless conduct of life is also to be demanded as far as possible (1 Tim. 3:2 ff.; Titus 1:7), but not as an absolute condition.[10] The efficacy of the means of grace does not depend on the worthiness of the minister.[11] While exceptions to this rule [that is, that the sacraments are to be dispensed by the ministers] are possible in the case of the *sacramentum initiationis,* or Holy Baptism, in an emergency *(casu necessitatis),*[12] this cannot be

[8] Gerhard, *Loci,* V, 177.

[9] Calov, *Systema,* VIII, 309: "The holy ministry is an estate, instituted by God, of men called thereto, to proclaim the Word and will of God and to dispense the sacraments, also entrusted to the church of God, to the glory of God and the salvation of mankind."

[10] Quenstedt, *Theologia,* IV, 107: *"The causa ministerialis* is ordinarily a minister of the church who is called, ordained, orthodox and, if possible, blameless as to conduct."

[11] Gerhard, *Loci,* IV, 274: "Yet, if it happens that a minister who is secretly or openly not upright administers Baptism, we judge that his improbity and unworthiness detracts nothing from the completeness and efficacy of the Baptism, so long as he observes the essentials of Baptism."

[12] Quenstedt, *Theologia,* IV, 107: "Extraordinarily, in a case of necessity, also a minister who is heretical or notoriously impious may administer

conceded for Holy Communion, the *sacramentum confirmationis*.[13] Hence Orthodoxy evidently assumed different degrees of necessity for the sacraments. Quite different again are "cases of emergency," where there is not merely a temporary absence of the incumbents of the sacred ministry, but where a "gathering in the name of Jesus" in extraordinary situations finds itself altogether without their services. Thus, for example, "when some Christians are in prison for the sake of the truth, or are in peril on the sea, or are isolated among the Turks or under the papacy." [14] In such cases the church here present has the authority to confer the ministry anew in its own right.[15]

2. The Proclamation of the Word

Quite evidently the proclamation of the Word, to which we now turn, presents no special problems as to form. That it rests on the clear direction of Christ is beyond doubt (Matt. 10:5; 28:19). There

Baptism, or even a layman or a woman, provided that the words of institution are pronounced completely and nothing is altered in substance." Cf. Gerhard, *Loci,* IV, 149.

[13] Gerhard, *Loci,* IV, 277: "Baptism is the sacrament of initiation, whereby we are first joined to the church; therefore it is more necessary than the Eucharist, which is the sacrament of confirmation, concerning which in a case of necessity that quotation applies: Believe and you have eaten." V, 11: "Wherever water is available, Baptism can and should be administered even by a layman. But the use of the Holy Supper is not in the same degree of necessity; and hence, there being no regular minister of the church, that word of Augustine is in place: Believe and you have eaten." Gerhard sees another reason for this distinction in the fact that Jesus had Baptism administered by John and the apostles, but distributed the Holy Supper in His own person. Hence Baptism may be given for the pastor by proxy, but not Holy Communion. (*Loci,* V, 1. See also Calov, *Systema,* IX, 209 f.)

[14] Dunte, *Decisiones,* pp. 453.

[15] Ibid.: "In such cases a private Christian who has been appointed for it by others may perform the duties of the priest [pastor] and take his place. Every Christian has his own share and right in the office of the ministry and in all that pertains to the service of the church. To the entire church Christ has given the authority to forgive the sins of penitent sinners in accordance with God's Word and promise. The exercise of this power the church commits to certain persons. Now when no such person is available, the office returns to the church, which has the right of disposal; just as at the death of a vassal the fief reverts to the lord who granted it. If then the whole church has this authority, it follows that if but two or three agree in the name of Christ to entrust the administration of the sacraments to some one, this call is as valid as one confirmed by a large number of Christians."

is also the example of Christ, the apostles, and the bishops of the primitive church (Matt. 4:17; Acts 6:2). All that takes place in connection with the proclamation, whether it be active or passive, tends to the praise of God. The Word of God is read, read aloud ("the praise of reading," *doxologia anagnostica*).[16] Man gives the proper honor to God by listening attentively ("the praise of hearing," *doxologia acustica*) and, fully assured that the Word spoken to him is truth, by joyfully confessing this truth ("the praise of assenting," *doxologia homologica*). Then he is also capable of communicating the divine message to others in his own words ("the praise of the public testimony, or sermon"; *doxologia demologica seu concionatoria*).[17]

The sermon makes its demands particularly on the incumbent of the office of the holy ministry. We observed above that Word and sacrament are closely tied to the call to the holy ministry; conversely, the call to the ministry is contingent on certain prerequisites inherent in the nature of the public address of instruction or edification. Only he is able publicly to interpret and expound the Scriptures who has been endowed with the appropriate gifts of the Holy Ghost. Consequently, exposition of the Scriptures is reserved for men who have displayed the qualifications for the holy ministry, among which is also that of being "apt to teach" (1 Tim. 3:2; Titus 1:9).[18] Individuals who do not possess these qualifications may therefore not presume to expound the Scriptures in the public assembly of the congregation.[19] This is not the place for a delineation of the specific homiletical principles of Orthodoxy. Besides, superior to them is the point of view which governs and dominates the whole doctrine of

16 The book from which God's Word comes to us is not only Holy Writ but also the Book of Nature (!). (Dannhauer, *Hodosophia*, pp. 508 f.)

17 On this whole point, see Dannhauer, *Hodosophia*, pp. 507 ff.

18 Gerhard, *Loci*, I, 237: "This public exposition of the Scriptures in the congregation is by divine will assigned to the ministry."

19 Hollaz, *Examen*, p. 181: "We do not permit laymen to expound Scriptures in the formal meeting of the faithful. It is enough for laymen that, as they attentively and devotedly page through the sacred scroll, Scripture by itself opens up and displays the meaning of the Holy Ghost so that they may perceive it and apply it to themselves for their salvation."

worship — that the glory of God and the salvation of men are the ultimate goal and purpose.[20]

But the sermon is only one side of the proper proclamation of the Word. There must be proper hearing too, and the duty to hear applies to all men. This is in the first place supported by the command of God (Is. 8:20; Col. 3:6). Besides, external necessity demands such hearing of us; for our faith, and so our salvation, depends on the hearing of the Word (Rom. 10:14, 17). Moreover, hearing the Word contributes to our inner gain (Luke 11:28), and the holy act of listening to the divine Word becomes a dynamic for our conduct (Luke 10:42). Again, the expectation of the promised great reward and the fear of the punishment threatening all despisers of God's Word (Luke 14:24) may urge us in the same direction. Finally we are admonished by the example of the saints.[21] What is asked of us in the hearing of the divine Word is that attitude of receptivity which is the presupposition for the blessed work of the Holy Spirit within us.[22]

3. The Sacraments

The real problems of form do not emerge so much at the proclamation of the Word, the so-called "legomenon," as rather in connection with the "dromenon" of liturgical activity, the dispensing of the sacraments. Preaching and hearing the sermon are predominantly spiritual acts, while the external is largely a mere concomitant. But when the sacraments are administered, the dealing of God with men by means of external, visible forms is the accentuated characteristic.

First of all the concept "sacrament" must be clearly defined. Here

[20] Gerhard, Loci, I, 237: "All interpretation and application of Scripture is to be performed in such a way that God's glory is increased and the salvation of man promoted."

[21] Balduin, Tractatus, pp. 364 f.

[22] Müller, Predigten, p. 12: "The apostles were not idle in their meetings but waited for the promise of the Father and continued in petitions and prayers. It will not do to go to church, sit down, and leave the work to the preacher. No! We must do our part: pray that God would send down His Holy Spirit into our hearts; listen in steadfast devotion to the Word whereby the Spirit comes; have a yearning desire for His coming and longingly wait for Him to stir our hearts to holiness. The Spirit comes by prayer." (Luke 11:13)

it is of course to be understood in its specific sense. The term is sometimes used of sacred or secret matters in general. Thus the Incarnation (1 Tim. 3:16), the union of Christ with His church (Eph. 5:32), the calling of the Gentiles (Eph. 3:3), our redemption (Col. 1:26) are called μυστήριον in Scripture, which is rendered into Latin as *sacramentum*. Similarly the fathers designated every sort of mystery and more difficult doctrine as a sacrament. They spoke of the sacrament of the Trinity, of the incarnation, of the faith. In a narrower sense the term was used to describe the outward symbol of a sacred or heavenly matter, as the Seed, the Mustard Seed, the Pearl. These are "sacraments" or symbols of things heavenly in the parables of Jesus, Matt. 13:24, 31, 45. Augustine speaks of the sign of the cross as a sacrament. When speaking of the divine service, however, we take the term in its proper sense, namely, a divinely instituted act in which by means of an outward sign spiritual blessings are communicated. That the external holy matter does not merely symbolize but "is" at the same time the spiritual good, is within the area of Lutheranism everywhere the self-evident basis of liturgics as applied to the sacraments.[23] At times the concept *sacramentum* is even narrowed down to one essential part of the sacrament, that is, to the earthly element.[24]

This definition does not yet state what, in detail, belongs to the category of sacraments in the most special sense. The Roman Church counts seven sacraments; the Lutheran Church counts two. Chemnitz constructs an exact hierarchy of the forms of worship, from which he thinks it possible to elaborate the sacramental concept. He begins with the following preliminary statement of a principle: Parts of the Holy Scriptures, whether or not connected with specific rites, which carry with them the command and a promise of God are to be re-

[23] Quenstedt, *Theologia,* IV, 73: "The word 'sacrament' stands . . . in a most special sense for a sacred, hidden, symbolical matter which not only symbolizes but at the same time bestows the thing symbolized; or for a sacred act divinely instituted, ordained, and prescribed, in which, through an external and visible sign, invisible blessings are graciously offered, conferred, and sealed." See also Gerhard, *Loci,* IV, 138; König, *Theologia,* p. 231.

[24] Ibid.: "In this most special and proper sense, which is in place here, the term 'sacrament' is used either generally for the whole sacrament, that is, for the earthly and the heavenly matter, the sign and the thing signified; or specifically for one essential part of the sacrament, namely for the external element, sign, and symbol, that is, the earthly and visible part, as for water in Baptism or for bread and wine in the Holy Supper."

tained and to be treated and used in accordance with Scripture.[25] He makes the following detailed distinctions:

1) Rites that are expressly commanded by God and include New Testament promises of grace. With respect to the promise, it is to be noted whether it conveys the saving treasures of the Gospel to the believers
   a) by signs that are Scriptural and instituted by God, or
   b) by words only.

2) Other matters, which are indeed divinely commanded but which do not include particular rites instituted by God. They may carry a promise, but not that which aims at the appropriation and confirmation of free reconciliation by grace.

3) Rites having no express command of God and no clear promise of grace, which are of human origin and have been taken over from the fathers.[26]

It is clear that under point one we are dealing with that kind of "rite" in which either outwardly *(promissio vestita ritibus)* or inwardly *(solo et nudo verbo)* the grace of God is actually appropriated to us. Point two refers to the five "sacraments" which the Evangelical Church cannot recognize as such: absolution, ordination, matrimony, confirmation, unction. The lack of a *signum* but also the absence of a promise of grace in the New Testament sense are the reasons why Chemnitz cannot regard them as being on a par with Baptism and Holy Communion.[27] The third group comprises the "ceremonies" or "traditions," clearly to be distinguished from the "rite," which are to be treated as adiaphora.

Heading this hierarchy, then, is the sacramental concept, with criteria applicable only to Baptism and the Lord's Supper. This may create the impression that the sacraments of the New Testament have been deduced from an abstract major concept. In reality, however, the entire scheme is merely a supplementary effort to register the Biblical facts. Baptism and Holy Communion, which incidentally lie on different planes, cannot be inferred as necessary from a dogmatical

25 Chemnitz, *Examen,* p. 226.

26 Ibid.

27 Ibid., pp. 204 ff.

system. They are religious acts instituted by Christ.[28] That is their primary characterstic.[29]

Their second characteristic is the communication of heavenly, invisible treasures by means of earthly, visible signs.[30] *In the service, divine activity enters into our earthly limitations.* God is creator *(princeps),* origin *(causa),* founder *(conditor),* producer *(auctor),* introducer *(institutor)* of the sacraments. He uses them as "holy means" *(media sacra)* to offer men His grace.[31] The human action does not merely symbolize the nonvisible divine action but is drawn into its service. Man is entrusted with the tremendous responsibility of taking up and passing on the activity of God; hence the seriousness with which the 17th-century dogmaticians treat the doctrine of the sacraments. Even seemingly quite unimportant matters of form are discussed very carefully.

Furthermore, there must be a clear line of demarcation between divinely constitutive action and human ceremony that explains and helps to shape the action. Here we are plainly in a *borderland* admitting of no clear division as regards the authorship of the separate acts. For, after all, every rite commanded by God is executed by men who, just because they perform the earthly action, will in one way or another carry their own personality or a certain ecclesiastical ordinance into every act. But for this very reason it is necessary to

[28] Besides the divine command the example of the saints, the promised rewards, and the threatened punishments may also urge the proper use upon us. (Baier, *Theologia moralis,* p. 511)

[29] The number of the New Testament sacraments is also proved by the analogy of the two Old Testament sacraments (Hafenreffer, *Loci,* p. 560). Again, the blood and water flowing from the side of Christ are said to typify Baptism and the Eucharist; just as in 1 John 5:8 water and blood together with the Spirit, meaning the proclamation of the Word, form a triad. (Brochmand, *Systema,* II, 423)

[30] Brochmand, *Systema,* II, 404: "A sacrament is a sacred and solemn act, divinely instituted, in which God, through a regular minister of His Word and under an external element perceptible to the sense, seriously and with the aim of communicating offers to every user heavenly blessings promised by a certain word, but so that free forgiveness of sins, righteousness, and salvation are applied and sealed only to the believers." For further definitions see Hafenreffer, *Loci,* p. 549; Gerhard, *Loci,* IV, 219; Calov, *Systema,* IX, 88; Quenstedt, *Theologia,* IV, 77; Hollaz, *Examen,* p. 1041.

[31] Brochmand, *Systema,* II, 399.

89

be sure precisely which acts are ordained by God and therefore to be observed with the greatest exactness,[32] and which acts connected with the administration of the sacraments are permissible human additions. König — and following him also Quenstedt [33] — sets up a pattern fitting all sacraments, in which three essential factors appear: ". . . On the part of the minister, the consecration of the elements, which is done by reciting the words of institution; then also the very presentation (δόσις) of the sacramental matter; and on the part of him who uses the sacrament the λῆφις or reception." [34] This example shows with particular clarity that one must not foist upon the New Testament sacraments (and of course not upon those of the Old Testament) some overarching scheme. Quenstedt was doubtless thinking of Holy Communion in particular; hence his terms do not fit Baptism very well, to say nothing of circumcision.

Which, then, are these essential acts *(actus formales)?* As for Baptism, there is no direction from Christ except to baptize "in the name of the Father and of the Son and of the Holy Ghost" (Matt. 28:19).[35] This basic form was not lost under the papacy in spite of other superstitious ceremonies.[36] As regards the Lord's Supper, the following acts are indispensable according to Christ's example: taking bread, blessing and distributing and eating it; taking the cup with the fruit of the vine, blessing and distributing it, drinking, and declaring the Lord's death (Luke 22:19; 1 Cor. 11:24.).[37] What is stated of these Communion ceremonies applies also to the single ceremony at Baptism; they are inviolable to us because they belong to the essence of the sacrament.[38]

[32] König, *Theologia,* p. 233: "Essential acts are those without which the substance of the sacrament cannot remain unimpaired."

[33] Quenstedt, *Theologia,* IV, 75: "The basic nature of all sacraments is the complete external action round about the earthly and the heavenly matter of any sacrament."

[34] König, *Theologia,* p. 233.

[35] Gerhard, *Loci,* IV, 389.

[36] Balduin, *Tractatus,* p. 406.

[37] Cf. Gerhard, *Loci,* V, 248 f.

[38] Gerhard, *Loci,* V, 248: "Whatever ceremonies were used by Christ in the institution and administration of the sacrament as peculiar sacramental acts, these belong to the essence and integrity of this mystery and cannot be omitted without violating its completeness."

Over against the absolute necessity of these rites the relativity of all others is stressed. Yet differences exist also with respect to the latter. Thus admonitions to receive the sacrament worthily, the use of the Lord's Prayer and of other prayers relating to the institution, the chanting of psalms, thanksgiving, the pronouncing of the benediction to conclude the celebration are to be retained as salutary and helpful to devotion even though not commanded by Christ. Ceremonies indifferent in themselves, the *adiaphora,* form another group. Here belongs the use of chalices of gold or silver, of paraments, vestments, candles, Gregorian chants, the organ, etc. No objection can be raised against such things provided there is no contradiction to sound doctrine, no violation of consciences, no exaggeration and over-evaluation. But rites that add little or nothing to edification, like the ringing of little bells, dipping the consecrated host into the chalice, the use of unknown languages, saying the words of institution in a low voice; or rites that are even idolatrous or superstitious in themselves and run counter to the institution of Christ, such as withholding the chalice, offering the mass as an expiatory sacrifice, the invocation of saints, celebrating private masses, etc. — these are to be abolished at once.

Speaking of baptismal rites, Gerhard adds to those of divine and of human origin others for which he claims apostolic authority. The latter, he holds, while not necessary in the same sense as the divine rite of baptizing in the name of the Triune God, are nevertheless to be kept apart from purely human rites and to be carefully observed. Here belongs a statement on the meaning of the sacrament, exhortations, prayer, thanksgiving, etc. These are necessary because the sacraments are not mere indifferent performances *(nuda et otiosa spectacula),* but serve to strengthen faith and to explain the divine promise. With reference to indifferent ceremonies that the church has instituted in connection with Baptism, Gerhard makes a distinction similar to that already noted with regard to Holy Communion, including the strict demand for the abolition of superstitious rites, such as the exorcism of the baptismal water, and the like.[39]

A third characteristic of the sacraments is that they mediate the *presence of Christ* in a very special manner. Where the liturgy is in

[39] Gerhard, *Loci,* IV, 390.

progress, Christ is near with His presence. This is true also of the proclamation of the Word.[40] Where the church gathers to speak the Word and to use the sacraments, there Christ, the Head of the church, is also present. Hence the divine service provides "the absolute Christian occurrence" *(das christliche Ereignis überhaupt)*, as Asmussen calls the presence of God in Christ within the congregation.[41] But this occurrence takes place in a very special manner in the sacraments. It is not that they mediate more to us than God's presence; their peculiarity lies in the mode of this mediation. "If the Word of God, upon reaching our ears, no longer convinces us owing to our self-will and our fear, God does something more. Besides addressing Himself to our ears, He also appeals to our feeling, our taste, our eyes, so that we might trust Him and relinquish our self-will and our fears." [42] The 17th-century dogmaticians attempted to combine this miracle of the bodily presence with the concept of the heavenly element *(materia coelestis)* of the sacrament. It is the gift communicated to us in, with, and under the earthly elements. And its content is the perfect Trinity Itself.[43] That God lets Himself be found in a bodily way as well is the gracious mystery of the sacraments.

Which liturgical problems, then, are posed by the inviolable basic patterns of Baptism and Holy Communion as instituted by Christ? In the system of the 17th-century dogmaticians such liturgical questions arise both when the earthly element *(materia terrestris)* and when the essence *(forma)* of the sacrament are under consideration.

a. Baptism. The earthly material is "simple water, not mixed with other liquid; whether rainwater or even standing water, as long as it is not impure or foul." [44] The quantity, too, is a matter of indifference: "the earthly matter is only water . . . even if used in a very small quantity." [45] There is no mention of a special consecration of the baptismal water. Nor is the water to be subjected to

[40] Ibid., V, 373: "Christ is truly present in that gathering where the Word of God is heard."

[41] Asmussen, *Die Lehre vom Gottesdienst* (1937), p. 46.

[42] Ibid., p. 39.

[43] Calov, *Systema*, IX, 166.

[44] Ibid., p. 160.

[45] Quenstedt, *Theologia*, IV, 109.

92

other sorts of earthly influence (let the water be "natural and pure").[46] Brochmand knows of several reasons why water was appointed as the material for Baptism. First, this was to indicate the fulfillment of certain Old Testament prophecies which were referred to the water — Is. 12:3; 44:3, 4; Ezek. 16:9; 36:25, 26; 47:1; Joel 4:18; Micah 7:19; Zech. 13:1. Again, in view of the universal necessity of the sacrament its earthly element must be at the disposal of all (John 3:5). Finally, the analogy existing between water and the Sacrament of Baptism was to be expressed.[47] As regards the form, Baptism is generally speaking a washing or an ablution. It may be performed by dipping into the water (immersio), or by pouring (affusio), or by aspersion with water (aspersio). Actual liturgical practice adhered to pouring, in contrast to the primitive church. True, this form received ecclesiastical sanction only in the late Middle Ages, although it had been practiced long before. Whereas Luther was in favor of complete immersion,[48] Orthodoxy attempted a theological justification of aspersion, the mode which happened to be in vogue at the time. According to Gerhard,[49] the word βαπτίζειν signifies any kind of ablution, whether it be by immersion or aspersion. He held that a "washing with water" (lavacrum), as Baptism is called (Eph. 5:36; Titus 3:5), by no means always meant an immersion of the whole body, but could refer to the washing of single parts (Ex. 2:5; 30:18, 19; Mark 7:4; Luke 11:38, and often). New Testament accounts of baptismal acts also readily permitted the inference that pouring was the method used, partly because of the great number of persons involved (Acts 2:38), partly for reasons of propriety.[50] Besides, aspersion was a most appropriate symbol of the sprinkling with the blood of Christ (1 Peter 1:2) which cleanses us from all

[46] Hollaz, Examen, p. 1704: "By 'natural' water we exclude artificial, distilled, medicated, perfumed water; by 'pure' water, that which is muddy, full of sediment, such as water with lye, broth with particles of bread and meat, and the like."

[47] Brochmand, Systema, II, 426.

[48] WA 2, 727, 4 ff.

[49] Gerhard, Loci, IV, 305.

[50] Hollaz, Examen, p. 1078: "The candidate for Baptism, after laying aside his garments, used to go down into the river and, naked, be immersed in the water."

93

sin.[51] To Calov this question was an adiaphoron. Βαπτίζειν by no means necessarily implied immersion.[52]

Calov distinguishes an external and an internal "form" of Baptism, the former consisting in the pouring of water with the use of the baptismal formula: "I baptize thee in the name of the Father and of the Son and of the Holy Ghost." By the inner "form" he means that the earthly and the heavenly matter are one, and that the latter is bestowed with the water.[53] Gerhard's three essential parts of Baptism are water *(aqua)*, Word *(verbum)*, act *(actio)*.[54]

When dealing with the administrative element *(causa ministerialis)* of Baptism we are already entering the sphere of ecclesiastical law. The legitimate administrants of the sacrament are, as has already been noted, the incumbents of the office of the ministry; but this does not exclude that in case of necessity every Christian acquainted with the sacred ceremony, whether man or woman, performs a baptism.[55] Baptism by a heretic is valid because the efficacy of a rightfully performed baptism does not depend on the administrative element, but on the primary element *(causa principalis)*, that is, the Triune God (1 Cor. 3:7). The implacability of confessional polemics speaks from one of the "decisions" of Dunte, who recommends that a believing layman be called in rather than a Papalist or Calvinistic priest. For the former, a member of "the holy generation and royal priesthood" (1 Peter 2:9), is certainly to be preferred to a heretic.[56] Ultimately, however, even a baptism administered by an unbaptized person is valid, provided that all requirements are met otherwise.[57] For even John the Baptist had not been baptized.

[51] Gerhard, *Loci,* IV, 305: "1 Peter 1:2 notes the ῥαντισμὸν (sprinkling) with the blood of Christ, which is the effect not only of the ministration of the Gospel but also of Baptism, in which we are rightly said to be sprinkled with the blood of Christ for the forgiveness of sins. Therefore Baptism can be performed also by aspersion with water."

[52] Calov, *Systema,* IX, 288 f.

[53] Ibid., p. 225.

[54] Gerhard, *Loci,* IV, 301.

[55] Hollaz, *Examen,* p. 1071.

[56] Dunte, *Decisiones,* p. 455.

[57] Ibid.: "The quality of the person neither adds to nor detracts from the completeness of Baptism, if only the essentials are observed; and Baptism

All eventualities that might arise in connection with Baptism are carefully examined. In a welter of casuistics, things essential and nonessential rub shoulders. Is a baptism not performed in the name of the Triune God valid? What is to be done if baptism is unduly delayed? If the child should die meanwhile, can it be saved? In such circumstances, what is to be done with the parents? Is a baptism performed by an intoxicated pastor effective? Should and may one baptize children of noblemen with good wine or with rose-colored water? [58] The admissibility of self-baptism is denied because the baptismal formula would have to be changed *(ego baptizo me . . .)*, because the command to baptize presupposes the duality of baptizer and baptized,[59] because no one can be born of himself and hence not reborn of himself. However, for Orthodoxy the duality of the person who dispenses *(porrigens)* and the person who receives *(accipiens)* is a necessary condition only as regards Baptism. It is evidently not opposed to the essence of the Lord's Supper, which is a kind of feeding, if the dispenser and the recipient are identical. The fact that the instituting command ("Take, eat") has a different ring seems to remove the obstacle in this case.[60]

The object of Baptism consists only of "human beings who are living and who are not resisting, without discrimination as to race, status, sex, and age." [61] This definition includes pedobaptism, which was indeed the usual form; for baptisms of adults, that is, of former pagans, Jews, Mohammedans, or Anabaptists occurred so rarely that church orders mostly made no provision for such cases.[62] The stormy conflicts with the Anabaptists had agitated, in the main, the 16th century. Now the controversy was restricted again to objective statements of reasons and to the refutation of objections.[63] The necessity of infant Baptism was derived from the general need of redemption

is such as is He in whose name and power it is given, not such as he through whose ministry it is given."

[58] Balduin, *Tractatus,* p. 1061.

[59] Gerhard, *Loci,* IV, 292.

[60] See note 81.

[61] Quenstedt, *Theologia,* IV, 114.

[62] Graff, *Geschichte der Auflösung,* I, p. 309.

[63] Hollaz, *Examen,* p. 1082.

(John 3:5,6), from the general command of Christ (Matt. 28:19), from the universal promise (Acts 2:38,39), from the analogy with circumcision (Col. 2:11), from the special closeness *(aptitudo)* of children to the kingdom of heaven (Mark 10:14), and from the practice of the primitive church (Acts 16:15; 18:8; 1 Cor. 1:16).[64] Strong support for pedobaptism was also found in the assertion that infants can believe, which was based on Matt. 18:3,6 (and passim).[65]

b. The Lord's Supper. Bread and wine are quite unmistakably designated as the *materia terrena* (earthly material) (Matt. 26:26 ff.). The question why these particular elements were chosen is answered quite simply by Gerhard: "Because thus it pleased God *(quia Deo sic placuit).*[66] But bread and wine were already prefigured in the Old Testament: by Melchizedek (Gen. 14:18), by the manna and the water in the wilderness (Ex. 16:15; 15:25), by the showbread (Ex. 25:30), by the gifts of David (2 Sam. 6:19), by the feeding of Elijah (1 Kings 19:6). The heavenly matter, the body and blood of Christ, also has its types — in the tree of life (Gen. 2:9), in the Passover lamb (Ex. 12), in the flesh of the sacrifice (Lev. 8:31), etc.[67] There is also an analogy between bread and wine on the one hand and Christ's body and blood on the other. As bread is prepared from kernels of wheat, so Christ's body is, as it were, that grain of wheat which must fall into the ground to bring forth fruit (John 12:24). As wine quenches thirst and gladdens the heart of man (Ps. 104:15), so Christ's blood quenches the eternal thirst and refreshes the souls of men. (John 6:55)

The bread must be ordinary bread, it was held, inasmuch as it must be baked of flour and water. All other details regarding its composition, shape, quantity, etc. are indifferent. Similarly the wine must be genuine wine;[68] its particular kind is of no consequence.[69]

[64] Gerhard, *Loci,* IV, 370; Hollaz, *Examen,* p. 875.

[65] On this question see Elert, *Morphologie,* I, 261; *Structure,* p. 298.

[66] Gerhard, *Loci,* V, 12.

[67] Gerhard, *Loci,* V, 7.

[68] Thus water cannot replace wine, for instance in the case of teetotalers. That would be a violation of the fundamental sacramental principle. (Calov, *Systema,* XI, 164 ff.)

[69] Quenstedt, *Theologia,* IV, 177 f.: "The earthly matter is true bread in substance, made of flour and water; it does not matter whether it be leavened

Orthodox theologians were certain that such details were adiaphora, yet they sometimes preferred a particular view. Thus Gerhard favors unleavened bread;[70] Calov, to whom the question of leavened bread does not matter, insists — as does Gerhard [71] — on the use of pure wine, unmixed with water.[72] Hollaz has reconciled all possibilities by listing them side by side.[73]

The administration of the Lord's Supper consists (1) in blessing the bread and the cup, (2) in distributing the blessed bread and cup (δόσις), (3) in eating and drinking the sacramental bread and wine (λῆψις).[74] The consecration by the pastor is not a mere historical repetition of what Christ once did. It shows that the pastor is not acting arbitrarily but as the steward over the mysteries of Christ, that the bread and wine are by his act removed from mundane use to become the bearers of the body and blood of Christ. Besides, the consecration is a prayer that Christ would be present for us in these outward symbols, as well as an admonition to all communicants to come in a worthy manner.[75]

Between the consecration and the distribution there occurred, according to the Biblical account, the breaking of the bread. Does this belong to the substance of the Communion liturgy? Absolutely so, according to Reformed opinion, since the breaking of the bread indicates symbolically that Christ's body was broken for us on the cross. Besides, it is held, we are obliged to follow Christ's actions in every detail, as He has obligated us to do. The Lutheran conception dis-

or unleavened, oblong or round, etc. The wine too must be true natural wine, of whatever quality or quantity."

[70] Gerhard, *Loci* V, 14 f.

[71] Ibid., pp. 17 ff.

[72] Calov, *Systema,* IX, 300.

[73] Hollaz, *Examen,* p. 1108: "The earthly matter of the Holy Supper is true bread as to substance; it does not matter whether it be more or less, round or oblong, unleavened or leavened, of flour from wheat or rye or barley. The other is true wine as to substance, no matter whether red or white, neat or mixed with a little water." Cf. Graff, *Auflösung,* I, 183 ff.

[74] Thus Gerhard, *Loci,* V, 148; Brochmand, *Systema,* II, 452; Hollaz, *Examen,* p. 1120. Calov (*Systema,* IX, 338) combines consecration and distribution in δόσις.

[75] Gerhard, *Loci,* V, 151. Hollaz, *Examen,* pp. 1120 f.

avows the necessity of breaking the bread.[76] Jesus did break the bread, not to represent His death symbolically, but simply because the loaves were so large that they had to be divided for the purpose of distribution. In addition, a distinction must be made between the constitutive and the merely concomitant or accessory actions of Christ. If one wished to observe all the latter, among which the breaking of the bread is to be reckoned, one would be compelled, to be consistent, to celebrate the Supper at Jerualem, in the late evening, in an upper room, and in a company of disciples reclining at a meal. Nevertheless, the breaking of the bread may be retained, where it has been practiced, as a nonobligatory custom.[77]

While distribution and reception of the elements are commanded, the precise manner is not specified; it is left to the option of Christians.[78] Therefore it is optional whether the symbols are given into the hand of the communicants or placed directly into their mouths. Hence both the Roman Catholic Church errs, which strictly forbids the touching of the Eucharist by the hand of a layman or a woman, and also the Reformed Church, which declares it to be necessary that the Eucharist be given into the hand of the communicant.[79]

In the matter of self-communion, however, Orthodoxy was divided. When the Smalcald Articles say: "But to communicate oneself is something uncertain and unnecessary, and he who does so does not know what he is doing because he is following a false human opinion and invention unsupported by the Word of God," [80] they are referring of course to the Roman Catholic private mass with-

[76] Quenstedt, *Theologia*, IV, 216: "The breaking of the bread may be necessary for its distribution. Yet it is not an act essential to this sacrament, nor need it necessarily be performed in the very celebration of the Holy Supper. It is a free act, since it may be done also beforehand."

[77] On this question see Gerhard, *Loci*, V, 156 ff.; Balthasar Meisner, *Collegium Adiaphoristicum* (1663), pp. 154 ff.; Calov, *Systema*, IX, 342 ff.; Hollaz, *Examen*, p. 1121.

[78] Gerhard, *Loci*, V, 156: "In the administration of the sacraments, dispensing and receiving must be distinguished from the manner of dispensing and receiving. Dispensing is always necessary, for, like receiving, it belongs to the essence of both sacraments; but the mode of dispensing and receiving has been left to the liberty of the church."

[79] Ibid., p. 164.

[80] Smalcald Articles, II, Art. II, 8.

out a participating congregation. Lutheran theology is concerned with the needs of a pastor living at such a distance from a neighboring fellow-clergyman that it is difficult or impossible for each to administer the Sacrament to the other regularly. Nevertheless, the judgment of the Smalcald Articles exerted some influence on self-communion in the Lutheran Church. At any rate, one felt uneasy about it in the 17th century. The most favorable pronouncement is on the whole that of the Wittenberg faculty, which argued for the retention of self-communion, not only in cases of need but where it had been customary, and thought that no theological objections could be raised against the practice.[81] Gerhard, following Pelargus, declares against it, though he feels bound to concede exceptions in cases of need.[82] Similarly Calov, appealing to the Smalcald Articles, rejects self-communion "except in cases of necessity." [83]

With regard to the Lord's Supper, too, numerous questions of conscience engaged the attention of casuists: How is one to deal with unworthy communicants? In the absence of bread and wine, may substitutes be used? What is to be done with total abstainers? Is fasting before Communion necessary? Etc., etc., etc.[84]

Applying the principles mentioned before to the *Roman Catholic ritual,* one realizes where it runs counter to the Gospel insofar as it is represented as absolutely obligatory.[85] The liturgical differences

[81] Dunte, *Decisiones,* p. 464: "It would indeed be better if pastors received Holy Communion from one another. But if it has been customary in a church for years that at Holy Communion the pastor administers the Sacrament to himself, one cannot call the continuance of this custom wrong, lest those who have practiced it for years be burdened in their conscience and others are offended. For we do not see that it belongs to the integrity of the Sacrament that the dispenser be one person and the receiver another, since it is not a question of dispensing and receiving; and this may occasionally be done by one and the same person, other things being equal.

[82] Gerhard, *Loci,* V, 12. [Christopher Pelargus (1564—1633), professor of theology at the University of Frankfurt-an-der-Oder and *Generalsuperintendent* of the Mark, converted from the Lutheran Church to a moderate and irenical Calvinism.]

[83] Calov, *Systema,* IX, 299 ff.

[84] For example, Balduin, *Tractatus,* pp. 430 ff.

[85] Properly speaking, every item in the ritual of the Roman Catholic Church is declared to be unconditionally binding. This eliminates the concept of adiaphora. The division into prescriptive and directive rubrics (see

are mostly rooted in different doctrinal tenets. But in the case of the sacraments, where "the performance of the act takes precedence over doctrine in fact and in principle" (Elert), the corresponding false teaching originated from disobedience to the liturgical act plainly ordained by Christ. Generally speaking, disregard of the liturgical substance divinely given is characteristic of a great many heretical liturgical forms. The great distance separating the two churches appears with marked plainness especially at the Lord's Supper.

The first point of controversy lies in the Roman Catholic teaching of *Transubstantiation*. The entire New Testament is silent with respect to any transmutation of the elements. The ancient church likewise knew nothing of it. That bread and wine remain bread and wine, Orthodoxy stresses by distinguishing an earthly element *(res terrena)* and a heavenly element *(res coelestis)* in the Sacrament. Therefore every sort of adoration of the consecrated host, demanded by the Roman Catholic Church as ritual of worship *(cultus latriae)*, can be evaluated from the Evangelical point of view only as the idolatrous deification of a creature (ἀρτολατρεία). The adoration in spirit which is due Christ is certainly offered to Him in the Eucharist; it must not coincide with adoration of the consecrated element.[86]

The second unevangelical inference drawn from the doctrine of the Lord's Supper was the adoration of the "eucharistic Christ" *outside* of the liturgical act of celebrating the Supper. But the promise of His special presence applies only when the bread is consecrated, given, received, and eaten. When the words of the institution are indeed spoken over the bread, but the act is not continued according

Wetzer and Welte, *Kirchenlexikon*, X, col. 1343) becomes practically ineffectual in recent Roman Catholic liturgies. Cf. Ludwig Eisenhofer, *Handbuch der Katholischen Liturgik* (1932), 1, 51: "The distinction between prescriptive rubrics entailing a rule and directive rubrics merely offering nonbinding suggestions is to be rejected on the whole even though adhered to by some liturgiologists. Legislators of the church desiring liturgical uniformity had to aim at making all rubrics obligatory, since otherwise this unity would be gravely jeopardized and the gate would be wide open to arbitrary decisions, which would narrow or widen the circle of obligatory rubrics according to the inclination of individuals."

[86] Chemnitz, *Examen*, p. 321: "Let Christ be adored, God and man, in His divine and His human nature, who is present in the celebration of the Supper; but let the substance or appearance of the elements of bread and wine not be adored, lest we adore a creature more than the Creator."

to the ordinance, so that the substance of the Supper is cut off, there is no promise of Christ's sacramental presence.[87]

A third departure from the Biblical testimony consists in shifting the center of gravity from the reception (*sumptio*) to the continual *veneration* of the Sacrament of the Altar even outside of the Communion. The entire Roman Catholic liturgy furnishes evidence of this grave dislocation, by which the oral reception of the Eucharist was removed from the center to the periphery.[88] Or how could participation in the Corpus Christi festival be rewarded with indulgences of altogether 40,000 days, while no more than 400 are allotted to the act of receiving the Sacrament? [89] Again, it is not in harmony with the institution of Christ when the sacramental elements are reserved in a tabernacle, carried about in procession, or placed on exhibition, whereby intervals lasting for months are sometimes introduced between the consecration and the reception. Thus the Sacrament of the Altar is no longer an action, but a thing.[90] Even though it is possible to point to a few instances of such reservation for cases of emergency in the ancient church, this took place outside of the fixed liturgical order. Besides, the special reasons which the ancient church could plead for the practice at that time no longer exist. The consecration is bound up with the time and place of the Communion and with the presence of the communicants. For the words, "Take, eat . . ." are not addressed to the elements, but to the communicants.[91] Such a reservation was never a part of Christ's purpose.[92] The three sacramental acts are indissolubly connected as to place and time.

[87] Ibid.: "When the Words are indeed recited over the bread, but the action prescribed and commanded is not observed, or changed into some other rite, we have no promise of the presence of Christ's body and blood, as in His true Supper."

[88] Ibid., p. 325: "And that rite, invented by men, men are persuaded, is much more excellent and pleasing to God than if the Eucharist were distributed, received, and eaten and drunk in commemoration of Christ."

[89] Ibid.

[90] Quenstedt, *Theologia*, IV, 234: "It is proved that the Sacrament of the Altar is not an enduring thing, but an action."

[91] Chemnitz, *Examen*, p. 333. See also Gerhard, *Loci*, V, 180 ff.

[92] Quenstedt, *Theologia*, IV, 235: "The purpose of the consecration of the bread is its distribution; therefore its reservation is outside of this purpose and the intent of Christ's institution."

101

Another act of liturgical arbitrariness on the part of the Roman Catholic Church is the *withholding of the chalice* from the laity. All arguments advanced in support of this practice — that the words referring to drinking were meant only for the apostles; that with the bread Christ's blood was also received; that in John 6:48 ff. Christ spoke only of bread, etc. — cannot nullify the clear command of Christ.[93] Indeed, even the suggestion is declined that in some emergency, when one of the elements cannot be provided, at least the available one might be consecrated.[94] It is better to do without the Sacrament than to celebrate it in a mutilated form or with unwarranted substitutes! [95]

However, it is the Roman Catholic *offering of the mass as an expiatory sacrifice* that stands in sharpest opposition to the Evangelical Lord's Supper. For by it the basic idea of the Christian service is perverted. What man ought gratefully to receive is thereby placed under his power of disposition and used as a means for winning justification. This mass has nothing in common with the Christian mass; Hollaz calls it the idolatrous mass *(missa idololatrica)* in contrast to it.[96] Christian faith knows nothing of a continuing sacrifice in the strict sense, after Christ offered the *one* sacrifice once for all (Heb. 9:26). True, we, too, speak of every act proceeding from the holy communion with God — praise of Him and kindness to the neighbor (Heb. 13:15, 16) — as a sacrifice.[97] But this is a figurative extension of the original concept. In this sense one could call the Eucharist a sacrifice. Yet in the proper sense the mass can never be a "sacrifice." Apart from the fact that no word in Christ's institution of His Supper hints at such a purpose, as was also the understanding of the

[93] Ibid., p. 225: "Our Redeemer instituted the Eucharist under both kinds, bread and wine, and at the same time prescribed to all the use of both. Hence sacramental drinking is not free and indifferent, but necessary." See also Gerhard, *Loci,* V, 22 ff.; Calov, *Systema,* IX, 366 ff.; Hollaz, *Examen,* pp. 1130 ff.

[94] Quenstedt, *Theologia,* IV, 214: "Nor should one (element) be consecrated without the other on account of the lack of the other, since it would not be the complete Sacrament."

[95] Ibid.: "Where there is no bread and wine, the Eucharist cannot be celebrated."

[96] Hollaz, *Examen,* p. 1134.

[97] See p. 30.

102

primitive church, the distinguishing marks of the sacrifice, such as the slaying of the victim,[98] do not apply.[99] If this repetition of the sacrifice were necessary, the sacrificial death of Christ on the cross would have to be considered as incomplete and imperfect. Rome is consistent in ascribing to its sacrifice of the mass the power to atone for the sins of the living and of the dead. That this is a relapse into meritorious legalism, and that thereby the divine service ceases to be a grateful receiving and giving back, but becomes a calculating claim, requires no further explanation.[100]

The controversy with the *Roman Catholic* worship has thus been fully disclosed by dealing with the essentials of form, but the differences with the Reformed service have hitherto remained latent. The rituals in the Lutheran Church and in the Reformed Church seem to coincide, apart from certain peculiarities. But here, too, there are no doubt differences, for instance, in the conception of the sacraments, which do not appear as yet in connection with the fixed content of the liturgy as ordained by Christ. The discrepancy will be revealed in full measure in the discussion of the adiaphora.

It may be said of Lutheran Orthodoxy that it honestly endeavored "to exhibit the true Christian mass in accordance with the order and institution of Christ." [101] Even though their endeavors led these men into rigid formalism and at times into much hairsplitting, they nevertheless succeeded in erecting a protective wall against the disruptive influences emanating from enthusiastic subjectivism and later from self-willed rationalism.

[98] Ibid., p. 1135: "Whatever animate object is properly sacrificed, is slain and by death destroyed."

[99] Scherzer, *Kurtzer Weg und Handgriff*, p. 127: "Hence Christ when instituting the Holy Supper by no means offered a sacrifice, for this He did but once on the cross (Heb. 7:27; 10:14). A real and yet unbloody sacrifice is like a dream without sleep."

[100] See Calov, *Systema*, IX, 389 ff.

[101] WA 38, 247.

CHAPTER SIX

The Adiaphora

1. Theological Foundations

Although the basic content and the basic form of a proper external divine service are clearly indicated in God's revelation, it does not follow that every question which occurs to us when shaping our service must receive a direct divine reply. The Christian is not bound to a servile repetition of a divinely fixed and immutable order. (An attempt to do so would merely show the nonexistence of any order regulating the last detail.) It was otherwise with the legislation of the Old Testament, which left practically no room for human enterprise. Even the ceremonies required only for good order and edification, where freedom of choice obtains in the life of Christians, were removed from human disposition through the Ceremonial Law given by God.[1] The Christian of today has the duty, however, of interpreting the basic scheme given by God and to give it an articulated shape suited to conditions as they may exist. Compared with the essence of the liturgy, to be sure, only a relative importance can attach to such human undertakings. They cannot be obligatory in an absolute sense. Their distinguishing mark is that in all their variety they belong to the sphere of *indifferent matters*.

Such adiaphora, subject entirely to human judgment, are met with not only in the divine service. Greek theology knew of τὰ μέσα or τὰ ἐν μέσῳ κείμενα, including under this head whatever was not

[1] Hollaz, *Examen,* p. 1018: "God ordained ecclesiastical rites so that in the church everything might be done orderly and decently." (1 Cor. 14:40)

touched by a divine command or a divine prohibition. The Orthodox dogmaticians, too, designated as adiaphora quite generally all things that are neither good nor evil, but which may be used for good or for ill.[2] Meisner had in mind the most varied questions of daily life such as food, drink, clothing, marriage and celibacy, civil contracts, pilgrimages, etc. Strictly speaking, however, the concept of the adiaphora, which played an important part in the history of Evangelical thought, is narrower and concerns only matters liturgical. During the later period of Orthodoxy (about 1680) Pietism transferred the question of the adiaphora to the field of ethics (dancing, the theater, taking walks, the use of alcohol and tobacco, etc.). Orthodox dogmatics (even as late as Hollaz), on the other hand, always understands the term as referring to part of the worship ritual: the adiaphora comprise those ceremonies which are of human origin and consequently cannot belong to the essence of the liturgy. They never promote the salvation of men; their meaning is to promote order, dignity, and edification.[3] As examples are mentioned images, church edifices, festivals, holy days, church music, organs. With respect to Baptism we find: threefold immersion or aspersion, the place of baptism, the sign of the cross, the renunciation, exorcism; with respect to the Lord's Supper: the use of unleavened bread, the material and design of the vessels and the altar, the color of the wine, the breaking of the bread; with regard to the ministry, the issues of hierarchical order, difference in various vestments, private confession, etc.

a. One can reduce this welter of adiaphora to something like order by classifying them according to their relationship to the ministerial acts (the sermon and the sacraments). Baier notes a twofold relation: some are detached *(separati)* from these "divine acts" as independent actions, like for instance the ecclesiastical solemnization of marriage and the church funeral; others again are loosely connected with them, being additions *(superadditi)* to Word and Sacra-

2 Meisner, *Collegium Adiaphoristicum,* p. 10: "Which by nature are neither good nor evil, but which a person may use well or ill."

3 Ibid.: "Matters, whose use in the public administration of sacred things or in the private exercise of divine worship is indifferent, as not being in themselves part of divine worship and neither promoting nor hindering the eternal salvation of men, but instituted for the sake of good order and decency, add a certain dignity, with respect to men, to religion and ecclesiastical discipline."

ment. Thus to Baptism are customarily added the name-giving and exorcism; to the Lord's Supper, confession and also prayers and hymns and solemn rites like the lighting of candles.[4] Similarly Meisner differentiates between the divine acts (*divina* ἔργα) and the human incidental acts (*humana* παρέργα).[5]

The two relationships thus established between the essence of worship and the "ceremonies" are, however, not sufficient. The relationship remains too loose. The adiaphora are represented as something additional, as *adiuncta*[6] that may be regarded as completely indifferent not only as to their mode and manner but also as to their right of existence. Accordingly, one could imagine a divine service conducted, at need, without the slightest human aid in giving it shape. But that is impossible. There is a third relation between worship and ceremonies which is much closer and cannot be resolved into mere addition. Some human ceremonies cannot be added to and taken away from worship at will; even though they are adiaphora, they are indispensable if corporate worship is to assume earthly reality at all. Hence these human ceremonies are not something existing alongside of worship; they are rather the means through which the external divine service is carried out. A distinction was drawn in the Communion ritual between the δόσις and the *modus* δόσεως.[7] The δόσις as such is purely abstract; if it is to become empirical reality it must somehow be given a form by men. The result is the strange paradox that on the one hand the service cannot come into being without human ceremonies but remains in a sort of vacuum, while on the other hand human ceremonies must not be regarded as essential parts of worship.[8] This seems to place a tremendous responsibility on man, since all that he receives as substance divinely given is exposed to his subjective judgment; but he is relieved by the doctrine of the adiaphora, which assures him that his more or less happy

[4] Baier, *Theologia moralis,* Suppl., pp. 411 f.

[5] Meisner, *Collegium,* p. 14.

[6] See, for example, Gerhard, *Loci,* IV, 385.

[7] See chapter 5, note 78.

[8] Balduin, *Tractatus,* p. 1135: "Divine worship cannot be without ceremonies; and though the ceremonies are not part of the worship, they are yet its supports and ornaments."

106

efforts at finding the best form do not endanger the objectivity of that substance.[9]

There is, accordingly, some overlapping of the essentials and the nonessentials in the Christian service. This again is highly important for the doctrine of *Christian liberty*. Classic Lutheran theology speaks of Christian liberty only in connection with the adiaphora.[10] By doing this, however, it narrowed the scope of Christian liberty in an un-evangelical manner. As long as ceremonies are viewed only as something additional to worship, Christian liberty would extend only to the area formerly regulated by the Jewish Ceremonial Law. We Christians should then be unfree in the sphere of the Moral Law, which is still valid for us, and could only occasionally cross over into the narrowly limited sphere of liberty, which would then be identical with the sphere of liturgical adiaphora.

But the true Christian liberty has reference to all that we do, irrespective of whether it concerns worship or ceremonies. The definition of Meisner seems to contain the right concept of liberty; for he describes as the servitude that lies behind us the state of being bound to sin and to the coercion and enslavement by the Moral and the Ceremonial Law.[11] Yet this is followed at once by a modification; viz., liberation from the Law is not absolute, but it applies only in so far as the Law had a *negative* meaning for man. According to

[9] Mentzer, *Handbüchlein,* p. 94: "When the Gospel of Christ is proclaimed in newly discovered countries, a Christian church is gathered there even though much human opinion is sown at the same time, whereby the Word of God is darkened and sullied, but not destroyed. A pearl that is smeared with mud does not cease to be a pearl. Its beauty and luster are hidden; but one duly recognizes them by washing away the filth, so that its original brilliance is restored."

[10] Meisner *(Collegium)* entitles his first chapter "Concerning Christian Liberty and Adiaphora in General" *(De libertate Christiana et adiaphoris in genere).* Thus also Hutter, *Compendium,* p. 24; Brochmand, *System,* II, 520; Dunte, *Decisiones,* p. 726.

[11] Meisner, *Collegium,* p. 4: "This Christian or spiritual liberty is the undeserved release and manumission of fallen man, through Christ, from the tyranny of sin, and guilt of eternal death, the coercion and curse of the Moral Law, and the yoke and slavery of the Ceremonial Law. In it the faithful, joined to Christ by Baptism and renewed by the grace of the Holy Spirit, rejoice already in this life and then serve God spontaneously and gladly, with mind and body, in righteousness and holiness all the days of their life, to His glory, to the edification of their neighbor, and to their own salvation."

107

Meisner, our liberty is freedom (1) from the slavery of sin and of coercion, (2) from the Moral Law (but only with respect to the curse and condemnation of the Law and with respect to its importunate exaction and servile obedience) and from the wrath of God, (3) from the observance of the Ceremonial Law and the multiplex Mosaic rites.[12] This thought runs through all the 17th-century Lutheran dogmatics.[13] There Christian liberty never means the total "freedom from all human works, legal actions, and hence also from ecclesiastical ceremonies." [14] Obligation to the Law, in so far as it is to be evaluated positively and regulates also worship, cannot be relinquished according to Orthodox principles, lest all that pertains to God's legislative authority should collapse. There is an element of truth in this; it resides in the recognition that man can never be completely free, but is bound either to evil or to the God who reveals Himself in Christ. But a misconception as to the relation of Law and Gospel prevented Orthodoxy from stating clearly and boldly that the man bound to the Gospel is the man set free from the Law. If one thinks of the Law as represented by two concentric circles, of which the inner signifies the Moral, the outer one the Ceremonial Law, then Christian liberty extends only to the outer space, but not to the center itself. If the dogmaticians had at least placed stronger emphasis on the indissoluble connection of worship and ceremonies, the legally commanded worship would receive some rays of light from the liberty of God's children by way of the adiaphora. As it is, liberty is claimed only for things marginal and "nonessential." [15]

b. Adiaphora that are merely superadded to the worship may be conceived of as quite dispensable. Nevertheless, we find occasional references to the fact that it is impossible to give concrete form to the liturgy without drawing in adiaphora, as has already been mentioned.[16] There is a Scripture passage from which, it was believed,

12 Ibid., pp. 7 ff.

13 Cf. Gerhard, Loci, IV, 127: ". . . that Christian liberty is liberation from the coercion and curse of the Law, but not from true obedience to it."

14 Vajta, Theologie, p. 317; Worship, p. 171.

15 On Luther's position see Vajta, Theologie, pp. 317 ff.; Worship, pp. 171 ff.

16 See chapter 5, note 78; chapter 6, note 8.

the necessity of adiaphora must be deduced; viz., the directions given by St. Paul in 1 Cor. 14:26, 40. All insights and demands relating to our problem allegedly flow from this "apostolic aphorism." [17] Meisner even speaks of this passage as the general command (generale mandatum) supporting all adiaphora and ecclesiastical usages.[18]

Three important viewpoints are contained in this classic passage: decorum,[19] good order, and edification, and these are intended to be assured in the gatherings of the congregation by means of the ceremonies. But Orthodoxy attempts to derive more from this Pauline admonition than it actually contains. St. Paul's aim went no farther than to urge a dignified manner of arranging the divine services; it did not lie in his purpose expressly to issue a general authorization for the introduction of human ceremonies. Nor indeed can Meisner achieve his object of constructing from 1 Cor. 14 the criteria on account of which there *must* be ceremonies in the church.[20] He merely reiterates their purpose as already stated by St. Paul: "They are to make for decorum, promote good order, and serve edification." [21] But in his detailed exposition he no longer treats the question *whether* and *why* we may or must have ceremonies; he explains *what they*

[17] Meisner, Collegium, p. 23.

[18] Ibid., p. 25. Meisner occupies a rather isolated position with his formulation that ceremonies in the church are authorized by a "command," though only an apostolic one. According to Gerhard they do not rest upon an express command but were introduced by good counsel (Loci, VII, 31). Yet Gerhard conceded great importance to 1 Cor. 14:26, 40 as justifying all ceremonies not mentioned in the Scriptures in so many words. Hence the passage is of importance for proving the perfection of Scripture: "As regards ecclesiastical rites, although they are not mentioned in the Scriptures specifically, yet the genus is declared; for all things are to be done decently and in order, 1 Cor. 14:40, for edification, v. 26, without offense to the church, 1 Cor. 10:32." (Loci, I, 157)

[19] The Greek εὐσχημόνως is variously rendered in Latin. *Decorum* is the noun form of *decenter;* but the substantive *decus* is also found. The *honeste* of the Vulgate would demand the noun *honestas.* Several related concepts are united in the term.

[20] Meisner, Collegium, p. 13: "The apostle has noted certain matters derived from their useful purpose on account of which rites and ceremonies can and should be introduced into the church; and if they are confined within those limits, even an uncommon use of ceremonies in the matter of religion and in the interest of piety is advantageous."

[21] Ibid., p. 13.

must be like in order not to miss their purpose. Thus he believes that the demand of "decorum" excludes all theatrical pomp and show from the service and calls for a dignified simplicity. "Good order" is not only the reverse of all confusion and disorder; it also rules out an excessive number of ceremonies. And if ceremonies are to serve "edification," nothing else is meant than that the ceremonies must be attuned to the use of the Word and the sacraments; that they must not exist for themselves and their own glory, but kindle active piety.[22]

By offering only this comment on the Pauline injunction, Meisner unintentionally admits that the passage 1 Cor. 14:26, 40 cannot meet the expectations of Orthodoxy. The apostolic insistence on decorum, good order, and edification does not involve an absolute call for new human ceremonies in addition to what is divinely commanded. Nothing is said to the effect that Word and Sacrament require some orderly communication by means of ceremonies. For Christ's directions concerning acts of worship carry the requirement of sacred order within themselves. In brief, the necessity of ceremonies cannot be deduced from any Biblical command. Otherwise our vaunted freedom in the matter of ceremonies would be greatly limited, if only their "how" were subject to Christian liberty, but not they themselves. We are not obliged, but entitled to have them; and that not by virtue of a special divine fiat, but in Christian liberty.

Hence the argument from 1 Cor. 14:26, 40, which constantly recurs in the classic Lutheran theology, is only relatively tenable. The text merely gives guidance for the right execution of what we do in the service, irrespective of whether or not it is commanded by God. Paul is only expressing what should be self-evident in the church.

c. Ceremonies also have explanatory and auxiliary significance. As the external liturgical action serves to support what is inward and invisible, so the ceremonies render service to the external worship as supports *(adminicula)*, embellishments *(ornamenta)*, and aids *(subsidia)*. The sacraments are not "mute and idle spectacles"; and the ceremonies instituted by the apostles and also later by pious men

22 Ibid., pp. 14 f.

110

add their admonitory and explanatory voices.[23] They are there for the purpose of kindling reverence *(ad excitandam reverentiam)*.[24] Similarly the gestures employed with prayer, though in their nature indifferent, assist true devotion.[25] Indeed, ceremonies are even part of the proclamation of the divine Word; for this proclamation does not end with the sermon delivered from the pulpit. It embraces not only disciplinary, catechetical, and pedagogical measures, etc., but also "the praise of godliness by poor and rich . . . the edifying customs of the church in public gatherings . . . Will not the Holy Spirit operate also through these sacred means?"[26] For this reason it will not do to identify the divine service with the sermon. Grossgebauer rightly finds fault with people's way of saying that "they have been present at the sermon."[27] Although Grossgebauer has often been called a precursor of Pietism, his emphasis on the public and liturgically articulated service stamps him as belonging to Orthodoxy.[28] Finally, one of the most important functions of ceremonies is that they give visible expression to the abstract doctrines of the church and present the doctrinal content in a plastic and concrete form to the unlearned, who are incapable of following theological disquisitions. This appeared most strikingly in the age of the Reformation. "The main thought of the Reformation would have remained a theological opinion of the universities or an esoteric teaching of the most mature within [Roman] Catholicism, had it not begun to act as a leaven in matters belonging to divine worship."[29]

[23] Chemnitz, *Examen*, p. 262.

[24] Gerhard, *Loci*, V, 248.

[25] Quenstedt, *Theologia*, IV, 354: "During prayer also a bearing of the body is to be employed which attests earnest reverence for the divine name as well as true humility in the presence of God, and which assists the attention of the mind in this sacred exercise."

[26] Grossgebauer, "Wächterstimme," p. 14.

[27] Ibid., p. 190.

[28] Ibid., p. 217: "When psalms and spiritual hymns are sung, when the Lord's Supper is celebrated and God's people are honored; then we are also filled with the Spirit, we produce fruit, the death of the Lord works in us, we keep the spiritual Sabbath. This will never be accomplished by preaching alone, if the public service with its ceremonies after the manner of the holy apostles and the pious fathers is not again instituted."

[29] Fendt, "Der reformatorische Gottesdienstgedanke," p. 43. See also chapter 8, note 31.

111

What Georg Kempff wrote about hymns in particular applies to ceremonies in general: "They are not made by the church; they grow in it as a living expression of faith. They antedate all theology." [30] Hence it is not the business of theology a priori to lay down fixed rules for the elaboration of ceremonies; it must rather allow them to develop in accordance with their own laws of growth. Nonetheless it must observe this growth carefully, remove undesirable shoots, and urge moderation and order in harmony with the Gospel. There was much neglect of this in the Middle Ages. Within a few decades the Reformation brought about a tremendous process of purification which incidentally raised the question of the proper criteria for judging ceremonies. When in the 17th century these criteria were carefully and extensively expounded by Orthodoxy, the purpose was of course not to find the right viewpoints for setting up new ecclesiastical rites; for meanwhile the existing rites had long been domiciled. But the viewpoints of Orthodox dogmatics operated retroactively as a subsequent attestation that the sweeping reforms introduced in the Reformation century had been carried out with a sound instinct for what was right, so that the form of worship, as it appeared then with all its ceremonies, actually corresponded to Evangelical principles.

d. Which, then, are the points of view from which all adiaphora must be examined? Incontestably, the first place among all criteria is occupied by the Gospel, the center of all Scripture. Rites running counter to the Word of God must be abolished.[31] In a concentrated form we find this "center of the Scriptures" in the Confessions. To judge ceremonies by this standard is not altogether easy, to be sure.

[30] Georg Kempff, *Der Kirchengesang im lutherischen Gottesdienst und seine Erneuerung,* (1939), p. 6: "In all times when the church was conscious of its true nature there has been well-ordered church music. Church music was then aligned with the liturgy of the church. The liturgy, again, expressed the faith of the church; and it did so oftentimes before that faith had been fixed in confessional form. What was uttered as prayer from the deep experience of faith, and what was prayed in songs or sung as a prayer: all this was sanctioned by councils much later. For there were periods when there were confessions without confessional writings. The formulated Creed grew out of the living confession."

[31] Hutter, *Compendium,* p. 127: "First, let them not be impious, but of such a nature that they can be observed without sin. Whatever rites conflict with God's Word must be rejected as impious."

112

The critical principle becomes operative only after a violation. As long as ceremonies are as they should be, they are in a sphere that does not trouble faith. The Reformed Church made its task easier. It also knows of one criterion for the Scripturalness of ceremonies; viz., that they can be traced back directly to Christ. It does not recognize a province outside of the ceremonies instituted by Christ that nevertheless does not contradict the Word of God. Thus there can be no indifferent ceremonies. Yet it is in the nature of these ceremonies "not to be instituted by Christ"; for otherwise they would indeed be required of us.[32]

Despite our freedom to observe some ceremonies or others, we know that we have been directed to the Gospel as a fixed point of orientation. But this is not an ultimate authority handing down legal decisions on ceremonies under dispute. The judgment called for is that of *faith;* and this judgment must be constantly renewed and may vary from case to case (Rom. 14:5). Besides the judgment of faith there is also that of *love,* which knows that ceremonies exist not for their own sake but as aids for the neighbor (Rom. 14:15 ff.; 1 Cor. 8:12 ff.). Only when every offense is avoided, may the Christian use his right to deal with human ceremonies both freely and indifferently.[33] All other viewpoints must be subordinate to love, particularly also questions that arise in connection with ceremonies. "Love is the foremost commandment in the Law. All ceremonies are to serve love. If one must act either against love or against the ceremonies, it is better to adhere to love and to drop some of the ceremonies." [34]

However, this principle was not maintained fully in the question of the proper mode of observing the Sunday. This becomes plain when in connection with the Third Commandment cases are considered where cultic and ethical duties seemed to clash. It was ad-

[32] Meisner, *Collegium,* p. 30: "Whatever was instituted by Christ cannot be an adiaphoron, because it rests on divine authority and demands necessary observance; contrariwise, what is an adiaphoron was necessarily not commanded by Christ. Hence, since they would have indifferent Christian ceremonies instituted by Christ, they rather childishly demand indifferent things not to be indifferent — a contradiction in itself."

[33] Hutter, *Compendium,* p. 125: "Human traditions, except in case of offense, may be neglected and omitted without sin."

[34] Dannhauer, *Collegium decalogicum,* p. 34. Cf. Vajta, pp. 329 ff.

mitted that since the abolition of the Ceremonial Law works of charity and duties undertaken in cases of the utmost necessity must have absolute precedence.[35] This sounds as though the conflict between worship and ethics, found in the Old Testament and also in the life of Jesus, had been fully resolved by drawing a clean line of demarcation between cultic works and works of love, and that in favor of the latter,[36] so that we are released from personal responsibility. Still, in reality the precedence of works of love does not obviate the need of an actual moral decision that must be repeated from case to case.

Ceremonies must not only be in harmony with the Gospel; they must also be attuned to the human beings for whom they are to have validity. Hence a second criterion, which is of a purely human nature.[37] Whether ceremonies are profitable for the Christian, that is, whether they possess the virtue to assist, to enrich, to arrange, to beautify the course of the service: these are questions that must be answered by psychology and aesthetics. It is to these human considerations that Paul appeals with his admonition in 1 Cor. 14:40. To contend for the right form with strenuous energy is just as necessary as other good works are "necessary." It is a strange phenomenon that within the various currents of Protestantism the *moral* conduct of the regenerate man is stressed without fear of thereby calling into question the doctrine of Justification, but that with respect to *liturgical* action a peculiar paralysis develops from the appeal to the same doctrine of Justification, because a "work" is to be avoided at all costs. In the opinion of Orthodoxy, endeavors to arrange beautiful and dignified services belong to the category of good works, even though they are assigned the lowest place.[38]

Still another point of view was the nature of the adiaphora as

[35] Dunte, *Decisiones*, p. 251.

[36] Dannhauer, *Theologia casualis*, p. 376: "Matt. 9:13. I desire mercy; that is, I desire more the mercy of the Second Table than the external worship of the First Table. Otherwise, as regards internal worship, let the Second Table yield to the First."

[37] Hutter, *Compendium*, p. 127: "Let them be useful, that is, helpful toward tranquillity and good order in the church."

[38] Cf. Gerhard, *Loci*, IV, 4: "The fifth grade (of good works) comprises the ceremonies of the First Table."

such.[39] It is incompatible with the nature of an adiaphoron that it should be held to possess a special right of existence, or a special value or effect, or absolute necessity. Not only because of the very concept of "an indifferent thing" *(res indifferens)* but also in view of the Gospel, adiaphora must not be permitted to exceed their proper limits in this way. The constantly recurring formula that no adiaphoron may be associated with the "notion of essential worship, merit, or necessity" is also a corollary of the basic conception of divine service that has already been presented.[40]

On the other hand, there is a situation in which an indifferent ceremony can acquire decisive importance. In times of persecution, or more generally when opponents insist on the abolition or alteration of some ceremony as necessary,[41] it becomes a mark of confession *(nota professionis fidei).* Thus one may normally approve of either opinion with respect to making the sign of the cross, or the form of the Lord's Prayer; but in the cases mentioned one is obliged to hold to the form rejected by the opponent. Self-limitation of liberty may be required by *love* of the neighbor; but there are cases when it must take place on account of *faith.*[42]

The use of ceremonies is subject to a further limitation in that they are not left to the arbitrary decision of individuals, but that these ceremonies, in so far as they bear a public character, are reduced by the community to a definite order, to which the individual submits for the sake of love.[43] Such subordination is necessary also in the interest of the matter itself. To interpret liberty in ceremonies as boundless arbitrariness would be doing poor service to the cause

[39] Hutter, *Compendium,* p. 127: "Finally, that they do not burden consciences either by their excessive number or by a false notion of merit or of worship or of necessity."

[40] Cf. Meisner, *Collegium,* pp. 15 f.

[41] Balduin, *Tractatus,* p. 425: "Adiaphora become necessary if a change in them is undertaken rashly, without cause, and to the offense of the weak."

[42] Baier, *Theologia moralis,* Suppl., p. 416: "Although ceremonies do not by themselves have that power of signifying, they sometimes receive it by opinion or custom . . . Here, then, where ceremonies or adiaphora have become such marks, care must be taken lest by incautiously taking up such marks we deny our faith or at least seem to others to wish to deny it."

[43] Cf. Elert, *Morphologie,* I, 291; *Structure,* p. 332.

of formal worship.[44] The pronounced conservatism of Orthodoxy regarding the liturgy, which almost seems to militate against freedom in ceremonies, becomes intelligible at this point.[45] Let the liturgist exercise the same circumspection and faithfulness in ecclesiastical ordinances which he observes in those portions of the service which have been instituted by Christ! [46] For changes can be carried out only by the church as a whole; they are not within the scope of private, subjective judgment.[47] The pertinacious clinging to the use of exorcism is a typical example of this conservative trait. All this proves "that the heritage of the 16th century was faithfully preserved." [48] If, nevertheless, other tendencies are recognizable already in the 17th century, they must be held to be in conscious opposition to Lutheran Orthodoxy.[49]

2. The Most Important Adiaphora in the Judgment of Orthodoxy

a. We now turn to those adiaphora which were the subject of particular discussion in the period of Orthodoxy. As regards the ceremonies connected with the sacraments, minor questions that arose have already been treated in chapter 5. However, the use of *exorcism* at baptism was especially a burning question.[50] Its inclusion among

[44] Calov, *Systema*, IX, 268: "Order should not dominate, but serve the divine service."

[45] Balduin, *Tractatus*, p. 1035: "Rites of the church which were used of old and can be retained without offense should not be changed rashly. For such is the nature of rites that, although adiaphora in themselves, they become necessary through long use and custom of the church because they cannot be changed without evident offense to the church."

[46] Baier, *Theologia moralis*, Suppl., p. 412: "Concerning these acts, which by ecclesiastical law are different in different churches, the minister should be informed from the agendas and the customs of each church, and adhere earnestly and circumspectly not only to those divine rites, but also to these ecclesiastical acts."

[47] Ibid., p. 413: "The superiors will have to be approached — bishops, superintendents, consistories, etc. Where there are matters of public law, they should be settled by the public authority of the church."

[48] Graff, I, 66.

[49] Cf. Graff, I, 76.

[50] Balduin, *Tractatus*, p. 423: "Exorcism is that act in Baptism in which the unclean spirit is adjured, in the name of the Father and the Son and the Holy Ghost, to depart from this servant of Jesus Christ."

116

the Evangelical baptismal rites [51] had met with opposition especially in circles influenced by the Reformed Church. The opposition sprang from a different conception of the Sacrament of Baptism.[52] Consequently, when the bitter struggle against crypto-Calvinism began in the second half of the 16th century, the rite of exorcism became practically a mark of confession. The misgivings with which Reformed theology viewed this rite were not wholly out of place in so far as they concerned the form which Luther had used in his *Taufbüchlein*. In that form, however, exorcism did not survive within the Evangelical Church. Owing to the influence of Luther's authority, no attempt was made to abolish it; but it was invested with a new meaning which justified its retention.[53] Credit must go to Chemnitz for having cleared the way for the new understanding tolerable to Evangelical thought and of having prevented the inclusion of Luther's conception in the Confessions.[54] Thus exorcism, the

[51] Gerhard enumerates ten: (1) The reminder of original sin; (2) the name-giving; (3) the small exorcism; (4) the sign of the cross; (5) prayer; (6) exorcism; (7) reading from Mark's gospel; (8) the laying on of hands; (9) the Lord's Prayer; (10) the use of sponsors. (*Loci,* IV, 391)

[52] Dunte, *Decisiones,* p. 478: "The Calvinists would like to introduce a false teaching, namely, that children of Christians are led to Christ in the Christian church even before baptism, being sanctified even before birth; and that Baptism is no more than an external renewal and powerful seal of the covenant of grace in which they are already through the prayer of their parents. To introduce this teaching they so strongly urge the abolition of exorcism."

[53] See Johann Wilhelm Friedrich Höfling, *Das Sakrament der Taufe* (1846), II, 188 ff. A detailed account of Orthodox opinion on exorcism will be found there also.

[54] Georg Rietschel, *Lehrbuch der Liturgik* (ed. Paul Graff, 1951—52), II, 568, 577. [The author's words should not be misunderstood. The Book of Concord (Formula of Concord, Solid Declaration, Of the Summary Concept, 6) calls for the inclusion of both the Large and the Small Catechism of Luther "as they were written by him and incorporated into his published works," that is, in the case of the Small Catechism with the *Taufbüchlein* of 1526, which had been a part of the Small Catechism from 1529 on. The authority to omit the *Taufbüchlein* (and the *Traubüchlein*) was accorded to the individual princes and estates who signed the Formula not because of any theological objection on Martin Chemnitz' part but because it had become evident that this was the price of securing the signature of Elector Louis VI of the Palatinate, in whose domains the Heidelberg Catechism type of Calvinism had become established under his father and predecessor, Elector Frederick III.

117

efficacy of which was still strongly emphasized by Luther, became an adiaphoron to be regarded as not belonging to the essence of Baptism.[55] It is merely a "reminder and a testimony of the unspeakable spiritual captivity of the [unbaptized] infant in the realm of Satan, of the wretched condition to which we were brought by the fall of the first parents, of the saving power of Baptism, etc." [56] Exorcism does not rest on apostolic but on purely human authority; it possesses only significative but not effective virtue, even though a special effectiveness was sometimes ascribed to it.[57] Hence it must not be described as an essential or necessary part of Baptism. Quenstedt stresses the purely symbolical significance of exorcism even while pleading for its retention,[58] likewise Meisner [59] and Hollaz.[60] As reasons for the "fruitful" retention of exorcism Dunte states that it is "(1) a reminder that we are by nature captives of Satan but are liberated through Baptism; (2) a witness to the aim and purpose

In spite of this some Lutheran estates and theologians demanded an "unmutilated Catechism," and complete printings of the 1580 edition of the Book of Concord contain the *Taufbüchlein* — including both exorcisms — and the *Traubüchlein* on folios 170—173 (see *Concordia Theological Monthly,* XXIX, 1958, 10—13). For Chemnitz' own views, see his *Loci theologici,* pars III, *locus de baptismo,* iv (ed. Leyser, 1610, p. 161), in the light of which the implied contradiction between Chemnitz and Luther on this point disappears.]

[55] Chemnitz, *Examen,* p. 263.

[56] Gerhard, *Loci,* IV, 394.

[57] Ibid., p. 393: "Nor should an effective use of the exorcism be posited, as if the infant is liberated from the reign of Satan by the power of the very words, since this must be entirely attributed to the Sacrament of Baptism; but only a significative use. It cannot be denied that at times the pious ancients speak as if infants are delivered from the power of Satan by exorcism and breathing upon . . ."

[58] Quenstedt, *Theologia,* p. 169: "Exorcism is retained in our churches as an adiaphoron or an indifferent ceremony, useful to adumbrate the spiritual captivity of infants in the realm of Satan and the saving efficacy of Baptism, whereby they are set free from it." P. 171: "Granted that exorcism is an adiaphoristic rite and its nature such that it may be observed or omitted without hurt to conscience; nevertheless, it should not be abolished in those churches in which it has hitherto been in use."

[59] *Collegium,* pp. 81 f.

[60] *Examen,* pp. 92 ff.

of the office of the ministry (to oppose the devil, destroy his works, drive him away); (3) a confirmation of Christian liberty." [61]

Despite all this, faint undertones in classic Lutheran theology suggest that these men reckoned with the possibility of having to discard the rite. The reinterpretation had created a new situation. It was difficult to convince people that the ceremony meant something different from what it said. Spener admitted that the position of the church on the exorcism was in itself correct: "I do not deny that the sense which our teachers give the formula and in which our church uses it is true and agrees with the rule of faith." [62] Yet he also judged soundly when declaring: "The words as they read are so strong that the meaning which they bear in themselves is false and wrong." [63] This discrepancy between "gloss" and "text" [64] was felt also by the genuinely Lutheran dogmaticians, who concluded their disquisitions on exorcism by saying that, granted the consensus of the church, the rite could be discontinued or transformed into a prayer.[65] Further developments were far from favorable for the preservation of ceremonies; and it could be foreseen that this controversial and vulnerable rite would have to disappear.

b. Adiaphora connected with the celebration of the Lord's Supper include the sacred vessels, eucharistic vestments, liturgical colors, lights, candles, music, etc. Here also the Lutheran Church recognizes what has come into being historically, provided that it can stand before the forum of the Gospel and is not used superstitiously.[66] The mere fact that a certain ceremony is also Roman Catholic is not reason enough for its abolition. If the Reformed Church has the

[61] Dunte, *Decisiones*, p. 477.

[62] Philipp Jacob Spener *Theologische Bedenken* (1712), I 2,163.

[63] Ibid., p. 157.

[64] Ibid., p. 163.

[65] Hollaz, *Examen*, p. 1094: "The sense of the words is more appropriate though their sound is rather harsh. Since this rite is an adiaphoron, it can be abolished with the consent of the church, provided it be done without prejudice to the heavenly doctrine of the state of sin and the efficacy of Baptism. It can also be converted to a form of prayer, or also put forward and explained with words more consonant with the Scriptures." Cf. also Gerhard, *Loci*, IV, 394.

[66] Calov, *Systema*, XI, 161 ff.

ambition not to take over a single Roman rite, it must also do away with the use of the Lord's Prayer and of the Creed in the divine service. The debate on the legitimacy of using altars, for example, is very informative. The Reformed Church declined them categorically on the plea that no legitimate celebration of the Lord's Supper could take place where the sacrifice of the mass had been offered. Stryk also declares against them,[67] for Christ did not celebrate the first Supper before an altar. In reply Meisner points out that the offering of sacrifices is not the only meaning of the altar, but that it was always regarded as the place where prayers and benedictions were uttered, even as now. He admits that we can no longer speak of an altar in the strict sense of the term, since that would indeed demand the sacrifice as a complementary concept, unless one thinks of the spiritual sacrifices of Christians, their prayers and vows, as such. (Rev. 5:8)[68]

The time and the place for the administration of the sacraments are without question indifferent. There is no specific command of God as regards the *place* of either Baptism or the Lord's Supper. In principle, then, all possibilities are open. Practically, however, the proper place for Word and Sacrament is the church edifice where the congregation is assembled.[69] Since the service is and must be the business of the entire congregation, it is meaningful to adhere to the custom of the primitive church to have one fixed place of worship for all members of the congregation.

[67] Stryk, *De iure Sabbathi*, p. 134.

[68] Meisner, *Collegium*, pp. 188 f.: "We concede that we ought not have altars to sacrifice thereon; such sacrifices have ceased. But one thing may have several purposes. Altars were also for the purpose that prayers, blessings, etc. be uttered there. This use remains in our churches. It follows that our altars are not properly called altars because sacrifice and altar are correlated, each positing the other. I add that we also have spiritual sacrifices, viz., prayers and vows (Rev. 5:8), and the Holy Supper, which the fathers called a sacrifice (that is, a eucharistic one)."

[69] Reinkingk, *Biblische Polizey*, p. 84: "Although our great, incomprehensible God is not bound to any locality which the heavens cannot supply . . . yet it pleased His divine omnipotence, for the greater comfort of mankind, to provide for the consecration of certain places like tabernacles, temples, and churches, where His name is to be commemorated, hallowed, and celebrated in public, common, and populous gatherings, and where public divine service is held with especial reverence and devotion."

120

This observation no longer embodied an obvious truth toward the end of the 17th century. Pietism, which had begun to flourish, by its conventicles actively exploited the possibility of holding services almost anywhere. This would ultimately prove fatal to the concepts of both the church and the service. Thus, according to Stryk, Communion at home is in all circumstances as legitimate or justifiable as the celebration by the congregation.[70] Similarly, highly placed people in particular made efforts to have baptisms, marriage ceremonies, Holy Communion conducted for themselves in a private service. Apart from the fact that this retreat from publicity is not in harmony with the idea of the church, there was danger that the celebration in the family circle might detract from the solemnity of the occasion. Andreas Kesler, General Superintendent at Coburg, found it necessary to answer with an emphatic No the question "Whether it could be approved that noblemen and other prominent people had sacred acts such as the solemnization of marriage, the baptism of children, and the celebration of the Lord's Supper performed in their own houses."[71] He himself seems to have had unhappy experiences with baptisms at home. His drastic and terrifying account throws light on the conditions that had set in as a consequence of the long war; but at the same time it reveals the earnestness with which the Lutheran clergy opposed such a state of affairs even among the nobility.[72]

Still, the request to restrict sacred acts to specific places for the

[70] *De iure Sabbathi,* pp. 131 ff.

[71] Kesler, *Schriftmässige Erörterung,* p. 137.

[72] Ibid., p. 139: "It is certain and undeniable that at private baptisms, solemnizations of marriage, etc. abominable vices of the Epicurean devil are practiced. The poor parson must wait until the devil of drink has intoxicated his votaries to the point of insanity. He must wait and be patient until the devil of pride has dressed up his handmaidens, women and especially young women, like mummers and shrovetide fools with all kinds of stuff at their foolish best. After that, even if it be broad daylight, the mob gathers with the comedians for the baptism, let us say. After the Epicurean devil has given the sign, the preacher begins to read and to administer Holy Baptism; and while this is going on, one drunken sow laughs, another curses, a third performs fools' pranks, and so forth. After the baptism the pastor must hear the most shameless remarks, the most contemptuous mockery, the coarsest oaths, and keep silence. This is supposed to be a holy gathering, better than the one in public church. Truly, it is the devil's synagog."

121

sake of order was not made a law. Self-evidently Baptism and the Lord's Supper may be administered anywhere in cases of necessity.[73] Gerhard repudiates the legalism of Beza, who would not permit the dispensing of the sacraments at a private place even in emergencies. It must be clearly understood, however, that "church" in the sense of Matt. 18:20 is to be found not only within the walls of a church building. The proper place for receiving the sacraments is, first of all, the "Orthodox Church" *(Ecclesia Orthodoxa)*.[74]

The time for the divine service is likewise a matter of liberty. This refers to times of the year and of the day,[75] and does not exclude the observance of certain times as particularly suitable. The morning hours are recommended for the celebration of the Lord's Supper, because we are then most receptive.[76] But freedom as to time does not refer to the individual's attendance at Word and Sacrament in the course of his life. Here the rule is: Let a person be baptized as soon as possible; let him attend at Holy Communion and also at preaching as often as possible.[77] The direction that circumcision was to be performed precisely on the eighth day after birth is not valid for baptism; we are not bound by the Levitical ceremonies. While in the ancient church baptism was performed relatively late (after a due period of preparation for the candidate) and took place only twice in the year, at Easter and Pentecost, it is now the custom to remove infants at the latest on the third day after birth from the state of sinfulness *(status corruptionis)*.[78] People who dally

[73] Quenstedt, *Theologia*, IV, 184L "The administration of the Holy Supper may take place not only in the temple or the sacred edifice, but also in a private house in cases of necessity; for instance, on account of the sick, criminals about to be executed, decrepit old people."

[74] Ibid. See also Calov, *Systema*, IX, 408.

[75] Calov, *Systema*, IX, 270 f.: "For the saving power of Baptism any time is suitable, whether day or night, whether an hour or any moment of time, even the shortest."

[76] Gerhard, *Loci*, V, 243.

[77] Ibid.: "This food of life is to be sought and used by the truly pious rather often because Christ did not leave to us its free and arbitrary use but prescribed it to us with a definite command. . ."

[78] Gerhard, *Loci*, IV, 386: "In our churches the laudable custom is observed that parents bring their little ones to Baptism at once on the first or

in the matter of baptism thereby indicate "that they think little or nothing of inherited sin and natural corruption, of the devil's reign and might and power over the unregenerated little children, of regeneration and the efficacy of Holy Baptism; and that they regard this sacrament as a mere external ceremony to be observed according to opportunity and at will . . ."[79] In the ancient church it was customary for people to go to Communion daily at first, and later at least on the great festivals of Christmas, Easter, and Pentecost.[80] At present, it is stated, some desired Holy Communion on certain Sundays in the year, others desired it daily.[81] At any rate, this must be left to individual conscience.[82]

c. These principles are properly applied also to other adiaphora. Thus *prayer* must not be reserved for definite times (Luke 18:1 and elsewhere). The best place for the prayers of the individual is some particular locality removed from the noise of humanity (Matt. 6:6; Mark 14:32, 35; Acts 10:9); for public prayers the gatherings of the congregation are the indicated occasion. There are special promises not only for prayer in the quiet chamber but also for prayers within the congregation.[83] The posture assumed by the person who

second or third day of birth, or also have them baptized without delay then and there when they are born, certainly if on account of weakness there seems to be danger of death."

[79] Kesler, *Schriftmässige Erörterung*, p. 140.

[80] Quenstedt, *Theologia*, IV, 185: "As to the frequency of the reception, in the primitive church the Christians at first used to communicate daily . . . Christ would have its frequent use at least, and so we should go to Holy Communion rather often, indeed at least three or four times a year. Canon XVIII of the Council of Agde reads: Laymen who do not commune at Christmas, Easter, and Pentecost shall not be considered or reckoned as Catholics."

[81] Calov, *Systema*, IX, 407.

[82] Gerhard, *Loci*, V, 243: "How often this sacrament should be taken every year, cannot be prescribed definitely and by some general rule, but must be left free for the approval of each one's conscience and for his piety."

[83] Brochmand, *Systema*, II, 494: "Yet on this account prayers which are poured out in the large gathering of the saints are by no means to be omitted; partly because it is the express direction of God's Spirit that we are not to forsake our assemblies (Heb. 10:25), partly because the Lord has bound Himself by a special promise to hear prayers made in the public gathering (Matt. 18: 17 ff.; 1 Cor. 5:4 f.), partly because Christ said (Matt. 21:13; John 2:16 from Is. 56:7): "My house is a house of prayer," and finally because we read that the apostles went into the temple to pray (Acts 3:1; 21:16)."

prays is likewise indifferent. Quenstedt enumerates seven possibilities.[84] Each one may take up the attitude which his spirit suggests. At public prayers, of course, one should curtail this liberty for the sake of order and accommodate oneself to the outward form adopted by the community.[85]

While the Roman Church insists on certain *festivals* as by the command of God,[86] and the Reformed Church rejects them as being prohibited by God,[87] 17th-century Lutheran dogmatics assigns to them their rightful theological place by counting them among the adiaphora. Festivals, too, have their "edifying" import: When we remember the deeds of the apostles and of our teachers, we do so only to the glory of God. Since the practice of that time was free from misuse, the observance of festivals might continue with freedom.[88]

The demand for the recognition of *certain localities and places as holy* is also to be rejected. Of course the erection of houses of worship in connection with the requirement that Christians come together for worship is unavoidable.[89] Such edifices should be as beautiful as possible in structure and appointments.[90] God Himself wills it.[91] Nevertheless, the judgment whether a church building ful-

[84] Quenstedt, *Theologia*, IV, 354: "(1) Raising hands and eyes toward heaven, (2) beating the breast, (3) standing, ... (4) lying prone, (5) bending the knees, or kneeling in adoration, (6) folding the hands, (7) baring the head (to be understood of men only)."

[85] Balduin, *Tractatus*, p. 243.

[86] Brochmand, *Systema*, II, 44: ". . . that certain days besides the day of the Lord must of necessity be observed and that these are in and by themselves holier than other days."

[87] Ibid.: ". . . that the celebration of festive days is not only not commanded in the Word of God, but is on the contrary comdemned, so that he who observes those festive days brings back Judaism."

[88] Calov, *Systema*, XI, 166.

[89] Brochmand, *Systema*, II, 45.

[90] Reinkingk, *Biblische Polizey*, p. 87: "Christian devotion does not forbid, but rather suggest, that church edifices are built imposingly, finished beautifully, adorned with historical paintings and statues, and also kept neat and clean, in honor of the divine service."

[91] Ibid., p. 88: "Ex. 25 ff.; 1 Kings 7:13 ff. What the all-wise God Himself ordained for the honor and praise of His holy name, cannot by itself displease Him or prevent Christian devotion. As Christianity spread, pious rulers, emperors, kings, princes, and lords also erected beautiful and costly

fills its proper purpose as a place for worship must not be pronounced on the basis of external splendor and ornamentation. Besides, we must not for the sake of adorning our churches neglect the poor, who are the living temples of the true God.[92]

The mediating position of the Lutheran Church, which is based on complete freedom in such matters, appears also in the question of *images*. It does not, like the Reformed Church, categorically forbid the use of religious images,[93] neither does it tolerate the veneration of images which is customary in the Roman Church. Both iconoclasts and iconolaters miss the meaning of images as "indifferent things" (*Mitteldinge*).[94] It is interesting to note that here, too, the area of Christian liberty is made to coincide with that of the ancient Jewish Ceremonial Law. Adiaphora do not involve the Moral Law.[95] Like all else that subserves worship, images are relegated to the sphere of the nonreligious, or ceremonial, veneration (*cultus civilis vel ceremonialis*).[96]

Fasting is also brought under the head of worship in classic Lutheran dogmatics.[97] It must never be made a law for Evangelical Christians; neither must consideration for Roman Catholics be urged

basilicas, churches, and chapels and adorned them splendidly; and though in time there came abuses like the tricking-out and venerating of carved, cast, or painted images, yet such abuse cannot and must not abolish the right use of ecclesiastical art."

[92] Brochmand, *Systema,* II, 48.

[93] Meisner, *Collegium,* p. 48: "Christians may have what is not forbidden by a moral law; and since images are not forbidden by any moral law, it is lawful to have them."

[94] Quenstedt, *Theologia,* IV, 372: "The controversy about images is twofold, and both are very old: the one about making and having images, the other about venerating them. The former we have with the Calvinists, the latter with the Papists. Without contention, but rightfully and after the example of the ancient church, we call the former iconoclasts and iconomachists, the latter iconolaters."

[95] Mentzer, *Handbüchlein,* p. 225: "The Moral Law states that one must not make images in order to worship them, for that is forbidden in the First Commandment. The Ceremonial Law concerned the Jews only, who were forbidden to have images because they were inclined to idolatry and lived among idolatrous heathen."

[96] See p. 44.

[97] See chapter 4, note 39.

125

as a reason for fasting, since they might otherwise feel insulted (1 Tim. 4:3; Titus 1:15).[98] When practiced voluntarily, it was considered wholesome and advantageous;[99] on penitential days it was a self-evident custom in the period of Orthodoxy.[100]

The *burial of the dead,* too, was examined by Orthodoxy with reference to its theological foundation.[101] The funeral is not a mere liturgical matter; it is connected with the general history of civilization. Naturally, then, the church rendered this duty of love to its members from its very beginning. For this duty Lutheran theology found many points of contact in the Scriptures; for instance Gen. 23:4; Deut. 34:6; 2 Sam. 2:4, 5. As regards ceremonies, it declared that misuses must be avoided, both those of Rome (consecration of cemeteries, the meritorious character of the funeral rites, sprinkling graves with holy water)[102] and their own (excessive pomp). Funeral ceremonies are regulated by the same principles as all rites in general. But the church cannot lend dignity and comfort to all obsequies with its ceremonies. It must refuse its rite to heathen and to obstinate heretics and criminals. Children of Christian parents who died before receiving Baptism constitute an exception, according to 1 Cor. 7:14. The bitterness of confessional polemics is revealed by the statement that "the corpse of a Calvinist" can never be interred with Lutheran rites. If suicides are refused Christian honors, it is still more impossible to pronounce the enemies of the true church blessed.[103]

[98] Dunte, *Decisiones,* p. 727.

[99] Balduin, *Tractatus,* p. 491 f.: "Fasting in itself is not worship of God, because the kingdom of God is not meat and drink, but righteousness and peace and joy in the Holy Ghost, and he who serves Christ herein is pleasing to God and accepted (Rom. 14:17, 18). Yet it is not forbidden or altogether foreign to the worship of God; it helps much to promote it, and hence has illustrious testimonies and examples in Scripture."

[100] Graff, *Geschichte der Auflösung,* I, 331 ff.

[101] See, for instance, Gerhard, *Loci,* VIII, 54 ff.

[102] Ibid., pp. 56 ff.

[103] Dunte, *Decisiones,* p. 964: "Those who have taken their own life are not buried with ceremonies because they have lapsed from the comfort of the true faith, as their deed proves. Much less are they to be interred with Christian rites who drink up the hellish poison of deceitful doctrine and die the eternal death. And how could the Calvinists ask it, who malign our ceremonies, exorcism, altar, font, vestments, organ, music, unless they retract,

In contrast to the "stiff-necked," however, mildness must be observed in the case of such as "err in simplicity of soul or are misled." [104] A church funeral, or any funeral at all, may never be said to be necessary for salvation. Not the interment but the faith of the departed is decisive.[105]

Finally, a word on the view taken by Orthodoxy of liturgical *language*. One of the main liturgical demands made by the Reformation was the conduct of services in a language understood by all. But it is also known that Luther pleaded for the retention of the Latin language on account of the young.[106] Hence there were efforts especially in city churches to have the fixed liturgical parts chanted or spoken in Latin, and that, too, because in part no unexceptionable German translations were as yet available.[107] Yet the tendency was toward the gradual elimination of Latin, even though many theologians made efforts to retain it. Balduin still defended the custom of having Latin prayers and hymns in large city churches at high festivals.[108] Meisner also was unwilling, for pedagogical reasons, to surrender this adiaphoron.[109] It is probable that scholars were led to champion the retention of Latin not exclusively for pedagogical rea-

admitting that they did and are doing wrong thereby? At many Calvinistic places the dead are carried to their graves in deep silence; no attempt is made there to compose funeral ceremonies. Why should they want it otherwise than at such places?"

[104] Ibid., p. 971: "These latter ones, as stray lambs, are to be buried in all patience out of Christian love with the customary ceremonies. For in such people, who err in simplicity and ignorance, the Holy Spirit usually performs His work in the hour of death, so that the errors to which they had consented through deception are through the fear of death consumed like stubble and are forgiven."

[105] Hollaz, *Examen*, p. 1223: "If they die in true faith, there is no doubt about their salvation."

[106] WA 19, 74. Cf. Apology, XXIV, 3.

[107] Graff, *Geschichte der Auflösung*, I, 167 ff.

[108] Balduin, *Tractatus*, p. 1137: "If anyone objects to the custom of our churches, where sometimes, especially on solemn festivals, collects and public prayers and hymns are heard in the Latin idiom, he must know that this does not happen everywhere, much less in the country, but only in larger cities, where our youth study languages in the schools and where if not all, yet some of the hearers can say Amen."

[109] *Collegium*, p. 63.

sons but also because of a predilection for that language. Those who opposed the use of a foreign tongue in the services appealed to 1 Cor. 14 and argued that the whole congregation could respond with an Amen only to what it understood (v. 16). The unanimous praise of God *(concorditer et uno ore)* was possible only if all could join in. The Israelites had not thought of singing in other languages than in Hebrew, neither did the Greek and the Latin churches act otherwise. To the objection that 1 Cor. 14 referred only to the sermon, which must be in the mother tongue, but not to prayers and hymns, the reply was made that it was not to the sermon, but to prayers and praises that the people were to say Amen.[110] Brochmand expressly disapproves of the use of a foreign language in prayers.[111] But the use of the mother tongue does not help if the pastor employs a careless, faulty pronunciation.[112] The purely technical requirement of clear, intelligible speech is not the least adiaphoron in the church of the Word.[113]

d. A special problem is posed by the *sacramental ceremonies,* that is, the sacred acts which are held to be sacraments in the Roman Catholic Church but cannot be recognized as such by the Evangelical Church: ordination, solemnization of marriage (or matrimony itself), penance (or confession), confirmation, extreme unction. Orthodoxy simply counted the first four with the adiaphora, since they were not instituted by Christ and hence are not "essential" for the service.

Ordination, accordingly, is not a constitutive but a declarative act. According to the classic Lutheran conception, the actual conferring of the rights and duties of the office *(approbatio,* also *vocatio)* takes place by a canonical procedure; in relation to it, ordination is only the solemn public recognition of this rightfully existing status, taking the form of a ceremony with the laying on of hands and prayer

[110] Dunte, *Decisiones,* pp. 899 f.

[111] *Systema,* II, 494.

[112] Quenstedt, *Ethica pastoralis,* p. 649: "Experience testifies that a faulty pronunciation moves the minds of the hearers not at all or little, but that a proper and precise pronunciation adds life and spirit to the speech . . ."

[113] Ibid., p. 648: "Let a clear, distinct, pleasant, and dignified mode of speech be used, suited to the person speaking, the subject treated, and the person hearing." P. 657: "Let him sedulously avoid the monotone, continual shouting, persistent murmuring, a querulous tone, and sing-song."

(publicatio approbationis).[114] From God's viewpoint, there is no need for this ceremony; but there are weighty earthly reasons supporting it. Hence this rite should not be relinquished: "First, on account of those who run without having been sent the vocation requires a public testimony; and ordination is nothing but a public testimony whereby the fact of the vocation is recognized, witnessed, and confirmed as regular, Christian, and godly. Second, by this rite the office is committed to the person on behalf of God and the church and entrusted to him with public witness. Third, the called person is bound by the ordination as by a public vow to be faithful. Fourth, the church is thereby directed to hear its pastor as speaking in God's stead. Fifth, by the act of ordination the entire church is exhorted to commend the office of the called person to God in earnest prayer." [115]

In connection with this subject thought is given to the ceremonies used at ordination, the imposition of hands and the anointing.[116] In the Roman Church they are sacramental signs, whereby a supernatural power of consecration is communicated to the ordinand as an indelible character *(character indelibilis)*. Orthodoxy rejected the unction as unscriptural and gave a new interpretation to the act of laying on hands: it is a purely symbolical act and is applied so that it may be publicly shown and attested (1) that the present person has a regular call to the sacred ministry; (2) that he is dedicated henceforth to conduct the service; (3) that the divine order was observed in appointing this minister; (4) that God approves, endorses, and takes pleasure in this work; (5) that God is being asked to give and confirm the gifts the minister needs for his office; (6) that God is being besought earnestly for His blessing and for success." [117] According to the witness of Augustine the imposition of the hand is

[114] Balduin, *Tractatus*, p. 1032: "Ordination is nothing else than the public and solemn confirmation of the call, so that all may be certain that this person did not wrest the ecclesiastical office to himself, nor enter it somehow like a thief or robber, but entered by the right door. It is an act of the whole church, though one particular person performs it in the presence of the whole ministerium, 2 Tim. 1:6."

[115] Dunte, *Decisiones*, p. 657.

[116] Gerhard, *Loci*, VI, 109 ff.

[117] Kesler, *Schriftmässige Erörterung*, p. 5.

129

nothing but praying over a human being.[118] But since the imposition of hands, understood as prayer, can of course be repeated, it cannot establish the (unrepeatable) Roman Catholic sacraments of ordination and confirmation.[119] In the Lutheran Church it is used also at baptism, absolution, the solemnization of matrimony, and confirmation, without being regarded as necessary or essential.[120] By designating the laying on of hands as an "indifferent ceremony" all has been said that needs to be said.[121] If it is repudiated as a sacramental sign, one of the chief conditions for a sacrament of ordination is lacking, that is, the external sign;[122] and consequently ordination is not a sacrament. Yet Gerhard would by no means have this custom dropped which goes back to the days of primitive Christianity.[123]

All these thoughts aim largely at demonstrating that ordination is not a sacrament. But although it is not a sacrament, the question remains whether it may then simply be relegated to the realm of

[118] Chemnitz, *Examen*, p. 296: "What else is the laying on of the hand than praying over a man?" [Chemnitz is speaking only with reference to confirmation in this passage.]

[119] Ibid.

[120] Dunte, *Decisiones*, pp. 658 f.: "The imposition of hands is a rite in ecclesiastical ordination, not strictly necessary but traditional . . . The object of this ceremony is not to confer anything as though by some magic power."

[121] Kesler, *Schriftmässige Erörterung*, p. 6: "Note in connection with this ceremony (1) that it is used not of necessity, as if it were a sacramental sign ordained by God Himself, since no command can be shown from the divine Word; but in Christian liberty as an indifferent ceremony, which nevertheless dates back to the apostolic church; (2) that it is not a rite to which God has bound His grace, or which produces spiritual effects, but a ceremony of the church reminding us of many divine operations; (3) that it is a ceremony which indeed could be omitted, but which need not be omitted; and which may and should be retained as a good reminder, for the sake of order and unity, and not to foster offensive innovation."

[122] No rite, not even that of Baptism and the Lord's Supper, is a sacramental sign by itself, but only by Christ's institution. The conjunction of a special rite (such as the imposition of hands) and of a divine promise (like that given to prayer) does not yet constitute a sacrament. "To make a sacrament, it is not enough that any free external ceremony be used indifferently together with prayer in the bestowal of any divine benefits. What is required is a definite element to which by divine institution is joined the promise of the grace of the Gospel" (Gerhard, *Loci*, IV, 253).

[123] Gerhard, *Loci*, VI, 97.

nonessential ceremonies whose sole function is to serve beauty and order. Certainly in ordination the emphasis does not rest on an outward symbol. It rests on the *word* of the church that orders, blesses, and sends; the word which, as in absolution, is spoken to a man personally and which, as the word of the Gospel, belongs to the unrelinquishable substance of the service. According to the testimony of Orthodoxy, however, this word of blessing has not merely the significance of a wish, but even though cast in the form of a prayer it *mediates* as a genuine *gift* the grace of God to him who is blessed.[124] This gift can be received aright only through faith; it cannot be accepted as the decree of some church authority; and therefore this word of blessing is spoken rightly only in the service. But then the so-called sacramental signs belong to the essence of the divine service after all; not indeed as sacraments, but as a special form of the proclamation of the Word.[125] Justifiable opposition to the Roman Catholic doctrine of the sacraments caused Orthodoxy to minimize the importance of these "sacramentals" *(sacramentalia)*.

Similar considerations apply to the remaining indifferent ceremonies: marriage, confession, and confirmation. The ecclesiastical *solemnization of marriage* is first of all the acknowledgment before the congregation of the situation created by the consent of the nuptial partners and the parental assent. A marriage does not cease to be such merely because of the lack of the blessing of the church.[126] That

[124] Gerhard, *Loci,* V, 148: "The divine blessing always has the matter itself and the effect conjoined with the words, because God is activity of the purest and most potent kind *(purissimus et potentissimus actus),* so that His benediction is benefaction. . . . When human beings bless each other, they ask in prayer for each other all good gifts from God; and this benediction likewise becomes effective for them by divine grace if it proceeds from a pious man, or if it is pronounced in the name of God and by His order and command."

[125] Cf. Brunner, *Leiturgia,* I, 200 ff. (on the Salutation and the Benediction).

[126] Gerhard, *Loci,* VII, 240: But even without the blessing of the church, we have sufficient actually operating and unencumbered causes of matrimony. For the legitimate consent of competent persons can be given, legitimately expressed in external words, to an indissoluble way of life, although the blessing of the church is not added; and this matrimonial consent is sufficient to bring about that indissoluble union, since matter and form are there. Hence the blessing of the church is not the essential form *(forma)* of wedlock, nor some kind of prerequisite absolutely necessary for its essence."

131

the ecclesiastical solemnization of matrimony is nevertheless something more than an adiaphoron is not explicitly stated by the great works of Orthodoxy, although a number of faculty opinions express this view.[127]

To speak of *confession* is to introduce the distinction between private and general (public) confession. It is questionable whether the former is to be included under worship; for it does not have to have a fixed liturgical form, and it lacks public character.[128] Yet Orthodoxy speaks of it as a "ceremony" to be retained: "Confession[129] is not absolutely necessary, but it is an indifferent thing *(res indifferens)*, an adiaphoron; yet it is a very useful and edifying ceremony and custom of the church that should by no means be abolished."[130] This statement plainly allows the inference that lively discussions for and against private confession had taken place. Yet no objections were raised against the matter itself; it was rather the manner in which it was conducted, and in fact had to be conducted on account of the large number of penitents, that raised grave scruples. Private confession did not founder on the rock of theological opposition; it came to grief because of its alleged impracticability. In the 18th century it disappeared and merged into the general confession; a development which, as Graff correctly observes, would have taken place even without the rise of Pietism.[131]

Public (general) confession takes place either in special prayers of the divine services or in special confessional services.[132] It has been in existence together with private confession since the 16th century. Its use together with the celebration of Holy Communion became established even though Luther denied the theological neces-

[127] Rietschel-Graff, II, 713.

[128] Cf. Graff, I, 374.

[129] Dunte was thinking of private confession, for he had previously put the question: "Why one should not drop private confession as it was customary in the Lutheran churches."

[130] Dunte, *Decisiones,* pp. 418 f.

[131] Cf. Graff, I, 378—382.

[132] Gerhard, *Loci,* III, 252: "Public confession is that whereby the whole community, the voice of the minister leading, confesses its sins and seeks forgiveness for them, whether ordinarily in the daily prayers or in extraordinary public calamities, present or impending."

sity of this connection.[133] If one is to be reconciled with one's brother before bringing one's gift to the altar (Matt. 5:24), how much more do we owe it to the community of brethren to be reconciled with them before approaching the Table of the Lord.[134] But nowhere do we read of a necessary connection. The Pietistic depreciation of a confession "before the church" is traceable already in Grossgebauer, who writes, "Confession is of two kinds: the one is made to God in secret, the other before the church. He who comes to the confessional penitently already has forgiveness of sins before God; if he is impenitent, the absolution of the priest will avail him nothing." [135] This only accelerated the disintegration of private confession.

The theological significance of *confirmation,* too, was still rather obscure in the 17th century. The rite itself had at that time been accepted in many parts of Germany; on the other hand, it was practically unknown in other Lutheran regions. Its beginnings extend back to the time of the Reformation. Bucer had first introduced it in Hesse in 1539.[136] From there it spread in all directions and found its way into various church constitutions, though there was no unanimity as to its essence and its form. Yet it shared one basic purpose in large measure: that of catechetical examination previous to the first communion. This basis was supplied by Martin Chemnitz, who had offered in his *Examen,* in contrast to the Roman Catholic doctrine of the sacrament of Confirmation, the true Evangelical conception of the rite. The latter embraces the following: (1) Instruction on the meaning of Baptism, including the renunciation, (2) public confession of the confirmands, (3) examination in the true faith, (4) admonition and pledge to avoid all heretical opinions, (5) exhortation to remain in the baptismal covenant, (6) public prayer for the confirmands, with the imposition of hands (yet without superstition).[137] In this form, Chemnitz thinks, the Evangelical confir-

133 Cf. Brunner, *Leiturgia,* I, 377.

134 Gerhard, *Loci,* V, 239.

135 "Wächterstimme," p. 159.

136 Cf. W. Maurer, *Gemeindezucht, Gemeindeamt, Konfirmation* (1940), pp. 43—107. Maurer regards the Hessian confirmation as a synthesis of Lutheran and humanistic thought, no longer tenable in the face of our present-day difficulties with confirmation.

137 Chemnitz, *Examen,* p. 258.

mation is nothing but the ancient rite cleansed of Roman superstition; and he earnestly advocates this proper use as profitable not only for the youth, but for the entire church.[138]

All this is quite close to Bucer's form of confirmation, which also contained the elements of catechetical instruction, examination, and intercession with the laying on of hands. In this form confirmation extends beyond the borders of the worship service. The liturgical act involved lies in the "imposition of hands without superstition," whereby the Roman understanding of the laying on of hands as a sacramental sign is repudiated and the true meaning of the act is referred to prayer. But prayer could, on account of the promise attached to it, also be called a sacrament according to the principle enunciated by Melanchthon in the Apology.[139] Such prayer becomes, even when addressed to God as a petition of men, God's act of benediction upon men.

The work of Chemnitz remained basic for most orders of confirmation used in the 17th century. Orthodox theology was rather reserved over against the rite. Gerhard in his *Loci* contented himself with a refutation of the Roman sacramental teaching, for he had searched Scripture in vain for either a special institution or a special promise. Moreover, he had nowhere found an indication that one of the apostles had anointed baptized Christians with oil in order to equip them in this manner for their spiritual battle against Satan.[140] So, too, we find no detailed, positive treatment of Evangelical confirmation in the dogmatic works of Hafenreffer, Calov, Brochmand, König, Quenstedt, Hollaz; they all rest content with the repudiation of the Roman view of confirmation as a sacrament. This does not exclude that they defined their position on the question of Evangelical confirmation in occasional writings; but it is nonetheless remarkable that they did not deem it necessary to include even a casual reference to this rite in their voluminous systems.

[138] Ibid., p. 259.

[139] Apology, XIII, 16. [Actually, however, of the seven sacraments of medieval Western Christendom, confirmation and extreme unction are precisely the two to which Melanchthon does *not* concede the designation "sacrament"; he describes them merely as "rites received from the Fathers" (Apology, XIII, 6).]

[140] *Loci*, IV, 252 ff.

134

The Pietistic conception of confirmation made its first appearance with Grossgebauer, who in his widely circulated *Wächterstimme* urged its general adoption not only for the sake of the children, but also of adults. "For intelligent people know well how strongly such holy ceremonies affect the heart!" [141] He sees the connection between Baptism and confirmation in this, "that after the reception of the Sacrament of Baptism there is also need of a heart converted and enlightened by the Word of God." [142] Confirmation and conversion in the sense of the Pietists are thus wrongly coupled and regarded as supplementary to Baptism. But these thoughts became effective only in the 18th century, when confirmation thus understood became popular throughout Germany. Its theological precipitate may be found in a work by Pfaff, a thelogian of the transition period, *De confirmatione* (1723). His view has exerted a determining influence up to the present time.

Confirmation cannot be accepted today simply as a historical phenomenon. Its right of existence and its meaning must be derived directly from pedobaptism and the Lord's Supper. A mere reinterpretation of the Roman sacrament as undertaken by Orthodoxy will inevitably lead to a depreciation whereby confirmation is wrongly assessed as an inconsequential rite *(ritus indifferens)*.

Extreme unction has no place whatever in the Evangelical Church as an act of worship. Mark 6:13 does not speak of the institution of a special sacrament, but of the miraculous healing of the sick, which had a singular significance limited to the time of the primitive church. In James 5:14 f. it is likewise a question of healing the body *(sanitas corporalis)* by the anointing. There is no mention of an extreme unction to be administered only to the *dying,* so that thereby they receive remission of sins in a special way. The prayers of those who are present for the increase and strengthening of the sick person's faith is a natural expression of Christian faith, but it does not constitute another sacrament.[143]

In recapitulating, we come to the conclusion that the attitude of

141 Grossgebauer, "Wächterstimme," p. 55. The factor of subjective emotion emerging here had already influenced Erasmus. Cf. Maurer, p. 47.

142 Ibid., p. 69.

143 Gerhard, *Loci,* IV, 253 ff.

Orthodox theology toward the "ceremonies" was preponderantly critical and negative. There was no need for theology to be anxiously concerned that the services should be beautified by edifying ceremonies according to the injunction of the apostle Paul in 1 Cor. 14: 26, 40. An order of service richly adorned with ceremonies had been taken over from the time of the Reformation as a fixed institution. To this fact the church orders of that time bear eloquent witness. These men were appreciative of their wealth and rejoiced in this treasure. An arbitrary squandering of this wealth was always most sharply condemned by Orthodoxy. Yet the time of rising Pietism was to show that, while the negative dogmatic principle, whereby the existing ceremonies were examined as to their justifiability, can remain intact as a principle, it can be so radically applied [144] that finally nothing is left except what is found in our liturgies at the beginning of the 19th century, the meager remnant of a service that had once been so richly diversified. In this situation the negative-dogmatic principle was not powerful enough to bring about a revival of the old richness of form. When Löhe faced the task of reconstruction, he felt bound to draw attention to this deficiency.[145] Hence we of the present time cannot simply operate with the repetition of classic Lutheran principles. In our days the Lutheran liturgy is still one arrived at by subtraction *(Subtraktionsliturgie)*;[146] and the low ebb to which it sank in the 18th century compels us to ask very seriously whether the surrender of "indifferent" ceremonies does not somehow affect also the substance of the Christian service. If this is the case, we are not at liberty to use the magnificent feeling of superiority toward the ceremonies which distinguished the Lutheran Church of the 16th and 17th century, and which at that time was

[144] Cf. Stryk's basic theses on ceremonies in general (*De iure Sabbathi,* pp. 106 ff.), which with the exception of the seventh ("even good rites must sometimes be done away to avoid superstition," p. 111) could stand in every good Lutheran dogmatic work, with the subsequent discussion of individual rites (pp. 112 ff.), in which all are practically rejected in the end.

[145] Wilhelm Löhe, *Der evangelische Geistliche,* II (Stuttgart, 1876), 216: "I for my part cannot find a trace anywhere of the application of a Lutheran principle in compiling our Lutheran liturgies, except the negative dogmatic one." Cf. Hans Kressel, *Erneuerung des lutherischen Gottesdienstes* (1937), p. 8.

[146] Wilhelm Thomas, *Liturgische Bewegung,* p. 272.

justified, as a cloak to cover the liturgical indifference prevailing in wide circles today. The strength for a revival will be gained only in part from a restoration of old forms. Lutheran theology today is confronted far more with the task of letting the fundamental principle of Christian worship, the doctrine of justification, spelled out by Orthodoxy, work itself out positively in the liturgical renovation also in the "ceremonies." [147]

[147] An admirable example of how to develop anew from the Gospel the principles for giving form to the adiaphora is Peter Brunner's treatise "Divine Service and Art" ("Gottesdienst und Kunst," *Leiturgia,* I, 291 ff.). Although described as an "attempt," it signifies a triumph over the negative-dogmatic principle.

CHAPTER SEVEN

The Theological Evaluation
of Music

1. Music and the Gospel

As employed in the Lutheran service, music, like all the other arts, lies in the area of the adiaphora. As far as Orthodoxy is concerned, the question whether music is to be used in the service, and if so, what kind of music, lies on the same plane as questions pertaining to the nature of Communion vessels, Eucharistic vestments, paraments, etc.[1] The refusal of Reformed theology to acknowledge adiaphora leads to the serious consequence of excluding music from the service. It is remarkable that Zwingli, though highly gifted musically, could draw his theological conclusions so inflexibly. That Zwingli erred in spite of his iron consistency was felt already by Calvin, who could not ignore Biblical examples and Biblical admonitions to sing and to make music in praise of the Lord. Since the primitive church had edified itself by singing psalms, Calvin thought that he might or should introduce at least the singing of psalms (or of metrical versions of psalms) in unison by the congregation. Yet he did not abandon his critical position toward the Old Testament exhortations, found especially in the Book of Psalms, to glorify God by means of music. To him this

[1] Gerhard, *Loci,* V, 249: "Such ceremonies are: using gold and silver patens and chalices in the administration of the Holy Supper, decorating the holy table with paraments, putting on special vestments, lighting lamps and candles, using Gregorian music and organs, chanting the words of institution, etc."

appeared strictly analogous to the ritual of sacrifices in the Old Testament, and hence a mere adumbration of what was to be done under the New Covenant "in spirit and in truth." According to this view, external music-making would be adherence to the external worship of Judaism.[2] In actual practice, however, Reformed church music was not for long frustrated by these unevangelical principles. The 4-part psalm tunes of Goudimel, which at first had been cultivated only in schools and academies, gradually made their way into the public services of congregations in the 17th century. The revival of polyphonic music led to the hesitant use of instruments. A modest place was again assigned also to the organ. However, distrust over against music has not disappeared from Reformed theology to the present day.[3]

[2] Cf. Reinkingk, *Biblische Polizey,* p. 89: "There are people, among them, John Calvin, who believe that music and what is mentioned and commanded of it in the Old Testament belongs to the Jewish ceremonies; and that, if we practice music within Christendom, this would harmonize with our divine services just as well as if one were to hark back to incense, lanterns, and other shadows of the Law in order thereby to trick out our services. As may be seen from his [Calvin's] comment on the 33d Psalm of David, v. 2, and on Ps. 81, he considers it foolish to apply to the time of the Gospel what the prophet and king David writes there and elsewhere about musical instruments and hymns of praise, and thus to use the shadows when dealing with reality."

[3] Erik Wolf, *Musikalischer Gottesdienst?* col. 132: "It is asserted that thanksgiving and praises *must* be expressed by means of 'a voice exalted in song.' Apart from the fact that one cannot see why the Word that is sung should be 'exalted' in contrast to that which is spoken, there is no evidence for this in Holy Writ. Christ *spoke* as a natural man to natural and mostly simple people, in simple, clear, and *sober* (by no means 'hymnic') words. The prophets of the Old Testament did not *sing* their message of judgment and grace before deeply stirred men; they *spoke* it to them plainly, unmistakably, and clearly. . . . None of the Gospels report that the disciples sang with Christ" [the author should convince himself of the contrary from Mark 14:26!], "but on the contrary, that they listened to His speech and handed it down as faithfully and simply as possible. The most important passage dealing with the first divine services of the New Testament church is Acts 2:42 ff., where the basic order of congregational life is exhibited for all future generations. Here we read of fellowship, doctrine, the breaking of bread, and prayer, but not of the cultivation of music. . . ." Col. 136: "The practice of alternation in hymn presentation is very disturbing to devotion. The attention of the congregation is constantly being diverted and directed to subordinate matters. By such 'liturgical' interpolations the entire service increasingly becomes a strenuous concert performance, little conducive to

The evaluation of music proceeding from Lutheran quarters has an altogether different ring.[4] Music is of course subject to theological delimitation as an adiaphoron; but within those limits its manifold possibilities are to be utilized to the full. Lutheranism is not driven to search for Biblical commands or prohibitions; for music is a spontaneous activity of life, inherent in God's creation, and needs no apology. This appears plainly from the manner in which the praise and glorification of God in eternity is constantly and ingenuously referred to as singing. Scripture itself represents the worship of eternity as adoring and jubilant song.[5] Fellowship with the angels will consist in uniting our voices with theirs in the praise of God.[6] Music is the direct effect of the praise of God (δοξολογία θεοῦ).[7]

It is not from eschatology only, however, that music derives its vindication. Music is most eminently qualified to achieve the aims and the proper function of the adiaphora: to serve the need of order, beauty, edification; to set faith aglow in human hearts; to comfort the sorrowing.[8] Thus one finds "Christian music" mentioned alongside

composure within. The 'mutual rivalry' in praise is expressed much more beautifully by clear, heartfelt, reflective congregational singing of the chorale than by the multiplication of selected and separate choral devices."

[4] Cf. G. Kappner, *Sakrament und Musik* (1952), pp. 63—76. In his presentation of the 17th-century musical Communion service we see the classic Lutheran views on music translated into practice.

[5] Calov, *Systema*, XII, 357: "We shall see God as He is, love Him intimately, and praise Him eternally, chanting without end the Thrice Holy of the Seraphim and of the four living creatures with the utmost joy (Rev. 4; 5; 7; 12; 14; 15; 19). For we shall then be joined to the harmonious universal angelic choir and shall sing perpetually: Holy, holy, holy is Jehovah Sabaoth, the Lord God of hosts. Holy, holy, holy is the Lord God omnipotent, who is, who was, and who is to come." Brochmand, *Systema*, II, 632: "Eternal life consists in the perpetual glorification of God and the Lamb. For this is the united song of the saints."

[6] Gerhard, *Loci*, IX, 354: "It is certain from Scripture that the angels exclaim incessantly, 'Holy, holy, holy' (Is. 6:3). With them the blessed will form one chorus and will with united voices praise God unceasingly and endlessly."

[7] Dannhauer, *Theologia casualis*, p. 333.

[8] Meisner, *Collegium*, p. 220: "What about the fact that music serves to increase devotion, to restrain the evil spirit, to recall the human heart from sadness and sorrow, and also to impress the things heard more firmly upon the memory?"

141

of "medicine," "the association of honest people," and "a moderate draught of wine and amusement" as external means for "driving away sadness and melancholy." [9] Self-evidently not every sort of music will meet these requirements. Let music be without levity and lasciviousness! If it remains true to the purpose of rightly expressing the pious attitude of the heart, it will not fail to display the dignity demanded of it.[10] Dannhauer requires of music that it be "sacred, glowing with love, humble, dignified, the praise of God sung by the voice of men and instruments with becoming grace and majesty"; he contrasts with it "profane music, which is unspiritual, frivolous, proud, irreverent." [11]

2. The Danger of Misuse

But the kind of music that has no place in the Evangelical service must be described a little more closely. Brochmand would not only reject all lighter music, but considers even serious music that is not connected with the Biblical Word as unacceptable for the divine service.[12] This leads us to the fundamental problem of church music

[9] Dunte, *Decisiones,* p. 909: "Because he [the devil] is a gloomy spirit, he cannot bear music, as we see that the melancholy devil was driven from Saul by the harp of David, 1 Sam. 16. Paul urges singing in such a case, Col. 3:16. Aristoxenus said that the human soul was music; and Aristotle (*Politics,* Bk. 8, Ch. 5) calls music the medicine of sadness. We see this with little children. If they will not keep quiet, one puts into their hand something that produces a tone or a note, and they keep still. Or, if they will not go to sleep, one sings them to sleep with some lullaby. The deeply spiritual 'Our Father, Thou in heaven above,' the joyful 'Dear Christians, one and all, rejoice,' the heartening 'A mighty Fortress is our God,' the comforting 'We all believe in one true God' can dispel much sadness. Dr. Luther said at Coburg, after suffering much anxiety: 'Let us, to spite the devil, sing in four parts the 130th Psalm, From depths of woe I cry to Thee, etc.''

[10] Meisner, *Collegium,* p. 220: "Words of advice about music: Let all levity, and sensualism be absent. On the contrary, let gravity and a pious intent of the mind prevail, which does not contemplate and pursue bare harmony but devoutly fits and joins to it the inmost desires and emotions. For unless a ready spirit is joined to the turns of the voice and a vigilant and fervent heart to the varied words, we weary God and ourselves in vain with that melody. For not our voice but our prayer, not musical chords but the heart, and a heart not clamoring but loving, sings in the ear of God."

[11] Dannhauer, *Hodosophia,* p. 511.

[12] Brochmand, *Systema,* I, 50 f.: "Although we also disapprove of wanton songs, even the sweetest, and think that they should not be permitted either publicly or privately; and although we judge that even serious tunes,

in general: When are we dealing with "Christian music"? Only in the case of vocal music strictly guided by the Word? [13] May musical instruments be used? May instrumental music by itself claim a place in the service?

As regards purely vocal music, provided the text is either directly Biblical or poetry bearing the character of the Biblical Word, Orthodoxy unhesitatingly took up a positive attitude, just as this form soon gained admission into the Reformed Church, at first as a unison song but later also as part-song. For music as singing has abundant witness in Scripture.

There is also much mention of instrumental music, and no lack of admonitions to use it to the glory of God. One weighty voice was raised within Orthodoxy, however, which declared instrumental music to be incompatible with the Evangelical praise of God. It was that of Grossgebauer. Not that he was an enemy of music; he knew its power and would have it placed, as the men of old had done, entirely in the service of edification.[14] What was decisive for him, however,

if not set to religious words, are not fit for the house of God; nevertheless, we cannot disapprove in the house of God, the singing of hymns whose contents are taken from Holy Writ; for God's Spirit approves such hymns both in the Old Testament (Ps. 150:4) and in the New Testament (Eph. 5:19)."

[13] Grossgebauer shows that the mere setting to Biblical words is no protection against misuse: "Just as the world now is not serious, but frivolous, and has lost its quiet devotion, so hymns are coming from Italy to Germany in which the Biblical text is torn apart and chopped into small pieces by the rapid movements of the throat. These are the 'happorethim' of Amos 6:5 ['Who sing idle songs to the sound of the harp' (RSV)], who can sustain their tones and sing falsetto with their voices like songbirds. Then begins an ambitious screaming together to see which of the birds can sing best and most evenly. Now it's Latin, now it's German; few understand the words; and what is understood does not stick." ("Wächterstimme," p. 208). One must not forget that these "songs from Italy" point to the influences that were prominent in the men who emerged from the Italian school of music: Hassler, Schuetz, Praetorius, Schein, Franck. Bach himself would not have escaped Grossgebauer's condemnatory judgment.

[14] Grossgebauer, "Wächterstimme," p. 194: "The divine influence seeks and desires a quiet Sabbath of the heart. The holy men of God did not despise the external means whereby the Holy Spirit operates to collect the distraught senses, to reduce them to quietness, and to speak His Word to the previously tumultuous but now quiet soul. Therefore the church employs psalms, hymns of praise, and spiritual songs. Thus the Sabbath of the soul can at last be attained." It is noteworthy that the spiritual songs are not

was that music should be rendered by "the living human voice." This had been the custom of old; and the introduction of precentor and choir in addition to simple singing, and of antiphonal singing in general, had greatly enriched the service.[15] In the opinion of Grossgebauer the decline began when the singing of psalms became the prerogative of the clergy and the people were offered organ music instead. The organ pipes seemed to him to be emblematic of a dying Christianity which indeed still gives forth a sound, but which utterly lacks inner spiritual emotion.[16] Since the reduction of church music to priestly chanting and organ playing was a typically Roman feature,[17] he held that this defect must be remedied in the church of the Reformation. While a beginning had indeed been made to have the congregation again take a larger part in the singing than previously, Grossgebauer thought, the professional musicians still carried things with a high hand in the services. Besides, one could never be sure

taken for what they are really intended to be, that is, prayers of petition and thanksgiving; they are evaluated merely as a psychological sedative: only the soul that is quieted thereby is thought to be capable of gaining from the psalms their inherent meaning.

[15] Grossgebauer felt the charm and beauty of responsive singing with a fine sensitivity. "Be that as it may, there is some mystery of nature about this alternative singing. For when I always sing with the crowd, I hear myself no more than the others and grow weary through the constant strain; I am not encouraged and fired by the others. But if I can with Augustine sing in the congregation in such a way that I pause a while, take breath, and hear the other words of the other chorus, my spirit is the more quickened by the beautiful words. Thus is fulfilled what Paul urged: Speak to one another in psalms." ("Wächterstimme," p. 203)

[16] Ibid., p. 205: "And so that people had something to see and hear in their assemblies, the pope had pipes of wood, tin, and lead foisted upon them instead of psalms, thus causing a great noise, and had them persuaded that God was being praised thereby. These organ pipes are nothing but living images of a dead Christianity, in that they indeed make plenty of noise but have neither heart nor spirit nor soul. Thus he made the people mute and deaf, so that they can neither praise God nor hear His Word; but that, deafened by the sound of the organ and the strange magnificent music, they might be moved to admiration and have their ears tickled."

[17] Ibid., p. 206: "No matter who is responsible for the organ and music in the church, certain it is that it was of great aid to the Roman clergy, together with the Latin psalms, to put a bit into the mouth of the church and to make it dumb, so that the pope alone might speak and say what he liked."

whether their music was performed to the glory of God or to their own glory.[18]

But whereas Grossgebauer's position in the matter of all instrumental music was primarily negative, Dannhauer could see no reason for excluding from the praise of God musical instruments, which are after all creatures of God. He appeals to Old Testament and New Testament exhortations to make music.[19] Yet in the end the representatives of the two opposite views reach the same result. Dannhauer, too, has no use for music without a text;[20] he strongly warns that, when instrumental music is combined with singing, the human voice must not be beaten down by the loud noise of the former. Let people bear in mind the example of David, who had the singers march at the head of festive processions and placed the instrumentalists behind them! The same order ought to be observed also in the case of "mixed music."[21] Even Grossgebauer does not remain faithful to his ideal of a capella singing. If it is a question of instituting a "reasonable service," the singing that comes from the heart

18 Ibid., p. 208: "Hence, alas, organists, choirmasters, flutists, and other musicians, many of them unspiritual people, rule in our city churches. They play and sing, fiddle and bow to their hearts' content. You hear the various noises but do not know what they mean; whether you are to prepare for battle or go your way. One chases the other in their concertizing manner, and they contend in rivalry to see who can perform most artistically and come closest to the nightingale."

19 Dannhauer, *Theologia casualis*, pp. 333 f.: "Let every spirit praise the Lord, hence also the spirit of inanimate things. Indeed, there ought to be no creature which we do not use to the glory of God. Doubtless Adam in the state of innocence also used musical instruments; hence it is not sin to use them. Hence Paul admonishes us to teach and exhort one another not only with hymns and songs, but also with psalms, Col. 3:16. But a psalm has reference to the psaltery, a musical instrument so called from stroking (*palpando*), because it used to be struck."

20 Ibid., p. 334.

21 Dannhauer, *Collegium decalogicum*, p. 532: "Such a mixture is unlovely and useless. The simple human voice is doubtless sweeter than any lifeless pipe or string; but the pipe overwhelms it, the string drowns it, so that it can scarcely be heard. It is useless and fruitless, for it obscures the sense of the song so that the church cannot know what is being sung and cannot respond with Amen. This fault was already noted by the apostle in the church at Corinth, 1 Cor. 14. Hence the roles would more correctly and more delightfully be interchanged and that order observed to which David points, Ps. 68:26."

may well be supported by disciplined instrumental music. Only the instruments must never sound alone.[22]

At any rate, instrumental accompaniment of singing has its full right of existence in the Lutheran Church. The notion that the music employed in the divine services of the Old Covenant was merely typical of the "singing and making melody in the heart" characteristic of the New Testament did not gain entrance in the strict Reformed version. The typological meaning of Old Testament music was not denied. The playing on stringed instruments and the sound of the psaltery are now "the inward sacrifice of praise and the joy of the mind of the Christian." [23] But Calvin was not consistent. He must either interpret the music of the Jewish service as purely typological, and in that case banish singing together with instrumental music from the church; or else, if the typological sense of the Old Testament is but one aspect among several, all actual music-making is justified.[24] A curious instance of how music was used as a symbol for the contexts of faith is presented in Saubert's sermon for Cantate Sunday, 1623.[25] He declares that the imperative "Sing unto the Lord a new

[22] Grossgebauer, "Wächterstimme," p. 218: "If one were to lead the congregation in singing psalms and spiritual songs by means of the organ and strings and use the instruments to encourage it, that would not be bad. It would be doing what is written in Ps. 150: 'Praise the Lord with the sound of the trumpet, praise Him with the psaltery and harp.' When the congregation praises God the Lord with mind and mouth, one may well use also trumpets and psaltery and harp. But if these instruments are to praise God, and the congregation of God is mute and deaf, that would be mere noise and reprehensible praise. The Scriptures do not address organs, strings, trumpets, psaltery, and harp when they say: 'Praise the Lord!' but the church of God is exhorted to praise His great deeds and great glory."

[23] See Ch. 8, n. 14.

[24] Johann Arndt, *Vier Bücher vom wahren Christentum* (1722), p. 393: "These various choruses and instruments (that is, trumpets, psaltery, harps, cymbals), on which different psalms were played in the Old Testament as part of the external ceremonial service, are now a thing of the past; now our heart, spirit, soul, mind, and mouth have become God's trumpet, psaltery, harp, and cymbal. Hence St. Paul writes Col. 3:16, 'Sing and make melody to the Lord in your hearts.' This is not to be understood as though one were not to praise God in the assembly or at home with a loud voice or with other musical instruments; no, St. Paul means that all this is to be done with devotion, spiritually, from the very heart instead of its being mere outward sound and show."

[25] Johann Saubert, *Seelen Music* (no date; no paging).

song" does not refer merely to ordinary music; while this also pleases God, "we cannot take comfort in it in the face of judgment." Instead, he prefers to produce a sort of music which "all of us together, young and old, rich and poor, are not only to learn but also to pursue and practice all the time of our lives." There follows an allegorical treatment *(tractatio allegorica)*. The "conductor" for this spiritual music is God the Holy Ghost, who has composed the music (meaning Creation and Regeneration), who assigns the parts (1 Cor. 12:4), "who indicates the key" (that is, to heaven), who gives the pitch for the tune,[26] who beats the time correctly, who directs the whole choir,[27] and finally sings a part Himself — alto, because He is the Highest *(altissimus)*. True faith sings the bass part;[28] prayer carries the melody;[29] tenor corresponds to the godly Christian life. "If ordinary music is very effective, the bodily harmony of the Holy Ghost, of faith, of prayer, of a godly life is far more effective." The sermon ends with a plea for inward and *outward* music. (Eph. 5:19)

The use of Lobwasser's Psalter became a controversial point that was much debated. As is well known, Ambrosius Lobwasser (1525 to 1585), professor at Königsberg and a good Lutheran, translated the Psalter of Beza and Marot into German in order to introduce the Reformed psalm tunes in the German churches. In the judgment of Dunte, Lutherans had at their disposal so many beautiful and pure hymns as to have no real need for these versified psalms and their tunes, though they were not at all bad in themselves.[30] Dannhauer

[26] "Like one who gives the pitch to the chorus and takes care that it be neither too high nor too low, so the heavenly Conductor helps our infirmity."

[27] "The Holy Spirit provides tempo and rhythm for us, that is, governs our lives."

[28] "The voice called bass has its name from the fact that it is the foundation and basis of the other voices. Thus faith, too, is the foundation of all virtues in men."

[29] "You know, beloved, that in ordinary music the treble is a bright, shining voice, which soars high and is set according to the bass. In the same way prayer shines brightly; it lifts distress and tribulation out of the heart and takes them up to God on high. But blessed prayer must also be directed by faith and be founded and based on it in such a manner that we do not pray only with the mouth and the display of outward gestures but that we turn to God with our whole believing heart."

[30] Dunte, *Decisiones*, p. 899: "Although not all of Lobwasser's hymns are to be rejected or despised (for the man had his gifts; and since he follows

concedes the use of the Lobwasser Psalms only to those possessed of discriminating judgment [31] and therefore wishes to have such use restricted to home devotions. For there was danger, he thought, that Calvinism itself would soon follow where these Calvinistic hymns had gained an entrance.

Like all adiaphora, music is subject to abuse. It cannot fulfill its true purpose if it fails to meet with receptivity in the hearers; or if it is regarded and practiced not as ancillary to the Gospel but for its own sake as an independent art. Thus Mengering poses the following questions in his *Scrutinium conscientiae:*[32] "Whether in church, before and after the sermon, you really exercised your devotion with the Christian congregation and helped to sing the spiritual songs and hymns of praise, or read in your prayer book during the playing of the organ; or whether you entertained other thoughts, gazed at the organ loft, and were too lazy to open your mouth in the praise of God. Whether you attended church only for the sake of the beautiful music and organ playing; and whether you visited now this parish church and now that because you knew that a choir would be there and good music would be heard." [33] For some organists at least, church music seems to have been a welcome opportunity to earn money or to practice mischief. "They attended at the masses and the idolatrous services of the Papists, served them with their organ playing, and helped to beautify and deck out the mass business. Or, to spite the precentors, they tuned the organ off pitch, or gave out the wrong clef, and thus deliberately and frivolously caused dissonance and cacophony." [34] But all this is no reason for slighting music itself.

Pietistic aversion to music appears very plainly in Stryk. Naturally he joined Grossgebauer at once and complained that organs were being installed at great cost in every village church, "as if God were to be

a better method than the French composers Marot and Beza, he could well have served the church with his compositions), yet because there is no lack, God be praised, of truly Lutheran and other pure hymns, I judge that we can do without Lobwasser's hymns, all the more since, in the spirit of Calvin, he does not refer to Christ the psalms treating of Him."

[31] *Theologia casualis,* p. 334: "Who are endowed with right judgment."

[32] Excerpts printed in Schröder, *Zuchtposaune,* pp. 393 f.

[33] Schröder, *Zuchtposaune,* pp. 393 f.

[34] Ibid., p. 402.

worshiped with noise and not in spirit and in truth." [35] He roundly pronounced sentence of condemnation on contemporary church music. [36] He disapproved even of the Lutheran chanting of lessons and collects. [37]

3. The "stile nuovo" (New Style)

Admittedly, we are facing a much more difficult problem when dealing with music than is presented by any other adiaphoron. For not only does it present a multiplicity of forms, but the theological judgments passed on it are even more diversified. The judgment of Pietism was to a certain extent legitimate; for in the 17th century music had actually undergone a profound change which in the eyes of Pietism meant degeneration. The attitude of the Orthodox theologians toward music was throughout determined by the Netherland school, just as in the case of Luther. All their statements regarding music are in the main concerned with the Dutch school. Luther often praises the beauty and the value of music with glowing words by referring to very specific examples. Orthodoxy follows him; but one looks in vain for a reference to contemporary music.

When at the beginning of the 17th century the "stile nuovo" came in from Italy, the revolutionary significance of this music, whose "monody" reflected the subjectivism and individualism of the Renaissance, was at first not properly grasped by contemporary theology. Men tried to judge the new music by the old standards. Orthodox dogmatics was content, on the whole, with a Biblicistic undergirding of music. As to the value of music in its own right, one was glad to be able to appeal to the authority of Luther, [38] who had assigned to music "the place next to theology." [39] Of course these criteria soon proved inadequate. The retreat from polyphony, the growing im-

[35] Stryk, *De iure Sabbathi,* p. 121.

[36] Ibid., pp. 121 ff. He describes the church music of his time as "(1) contrary to the genius of the New Testament church, and not agreeing with the example of the primitive church; (2) superfluous; (3) useless, as not promoting but impeding divine worship; (4) superstitious, while men imagine that the glory of God can be promoted in this wise."

[37] Ibid., p. 125: "The gospels and epistles of the apostles are not hymns; why then are they sung like hymns?"

[38] Cf. Dunte, *Decisiones,* pp. 901 ff.

[39] WA, Tischreden 6, 348, 17 ff. (No. 7034).

149

portance of concert music, the progressive development of independent instrumental music especially in connection with the cantatas and in works for the organ: all this should have compelled a reexamination of the problem of music, particularly also music as such, in the service of worship. Instead of that, the fundamentally reactionary attitude of Pietism now came into the picture, directing itself against the secularization of music; while Orthodoxy, using the standards outdated by the development of music, attempted to salvage what could be salvaged.[40] But the composers of the time of Orthodoxy had advanced far beyond the musico-theological conceptions of that epoch.

We are thus confronted by the remarkable fact that the real pinnacles of Orthodox church music, that is, Schütz and Bach, no longer satisfied the strict theological presuppositions of classic Lutheran dogmatics. If one were to apply the standards of classic Lutheran theology, which could of course not lay claim to any special musical competence, to the development of Evangelical church music, one would have to describe as its crest or summit the polyphonic music that flourished at the close of the 16th century (for example, Seth Calvisius, Johannes Eccard, and, in spite of all new Italian influences, especially also Michael Praetorius). This vocal music, which proceeds from the Word and allows only a discreet instrumental support, corresponds to the ideal of church music as set forth by the old dogmaticians. Incidentally, Winterfeld, too, was of the opinion that the culmination of Lutheran church music must be fixed at the turn of the 16th and 17th centuries.[41] If those principles were adequate, then all music set to Biblical texts, provided it is unobjectionable as music and strives to do justice to the textual content, hence also the religious music of 19th-century Romanticism, would have to attain the Evangelical ideal. But the music of Bach, including his "wordless" music, is far more profoundly related to the worship service than the emotional "pious" songs of later ages.[42]

[40] Fred Hamel, *Johann Sebastian Bach, Geistige Welt* (1951), pp. 58 ff.

[41] Cf. Graff, *Geschichte der Auflösung*, I, 280.

[42] Oskar Söhngen, "Zur Theologie der Musik," *Theologische Literaturzeitung*, 1950, No. 1, col. 19: "Religious music is peculiarly 'vocal' even when not joined to the Word. Thereby it has a mysterious relation to human life-breath. It seems to us that wordless church music can be legitimately explained

A thorough discussion of music as a problem for theology was undertaken only in very recent times.[43] So much is certain that we cannot simply appropriate the musico-theological utterances of Ortho doxy and apply them to the situation of today. One cannot blame classic Lutheran theology for being so much taken up with the practice of its contemporary church music that the musico-theological principles which it laid down could no longer satisfy later generations.

Today we occupy an altogether different vantage ground, from which we can define the nature of music in a comprehensive manner. The insights which we have gained from the course of both the history of thought and the history of music of the last centuries must therefore necessarily be drawn into all musico-theological considerations. This does not mean that the position of Lutheranism toward music will be in principle different from what it was before; but the lines of demarcation over against all misuse of music will have to be drawn more distinctly.

only from this viewpoint, and that for the theological interpretation of these connections we need the categories of the *verbum externum* and the *verbum internum* and of their deep correspondence."

[43] See the musico-theological dissertations of Edmund Schlink and René Wallau.

PART THREE

The Relation
of Essence and Form

The subjects treated so far — "The Essence of the Divine Service" and, as its external embodiment, "The Liturgical Form of the Divine Service," including the liturgy itself as it appeared to 17th-century Lutheran theology — suggest the need of clarifying the reciprocal relation between "essence" and "form." This relation presents one of the main problems for the right understanding of the divine service. For the relation between these two factors is of a dynamic nature in this world of ours. It is not a quiescent theory; it must constantly be established anew and be put into practice in our devotional life. The Lutheran Church of the 17th century was threatened by a twofold danger: (1) The danger of isolating the "essence" or the "form" and playing off the one against the other; (2) the danger that owing to the incursion of manifold mystic ideas a form of worship might be chosen that would ignore and set aside this relation as irrelevant.

First it must be shown how arduous was the struggle to preserve the right relation between essence and form in the setting of the 17th-century ecclesiastical reform movements (Chapter 8). Then the defense against an unevangelical mysticism and the theological vindication of an *unio mystica* that is proper to the Evangelical service will have to be presented. (Chapter 9)

153

CHAPTER EIGHT

The Tension Between Essence and Form

1. How the 17th Century Posed the Problem

The "service of God" *(Gottesdienst)* as the faith-directed attitude of the man who is justified by Jesus Christ and the "liturgy" *(Liturgie)* as the concrete expression of this attitude of faith are in the relation of a tension which dare never be resolved in this life, lest the essence of the Christian divine service be falsified. This tension, already mentioned occasionally, lies in the fact that on the one hand the service requires the liturgy for its completeness and indeed cannot become reality without it; but that, on the other hand, in our world the liturgy is related to "worship in the spirit and in truth" as the conditional is to the unconditional, and that the unconditional always strives to be rid eventually of its conditional and limited expression or fixation. The credit for having demonstrated this tension in Luther's views on the divine service belongs to Allwohn.[1]

This tension also explains Luther's position in the matter of worship, which seems to be contradictory in itself. Luther was obliged to accommodate himself to the situation of the moment and to the degree of maturity he found in the Christians who came into contact with his reforms of Christian worship. Most noticeable is the change of course to which he was driven by the events of 1522.[2] It was characteristic of the troubled Reformation decades that, to meet some

[1] Adolf Allwohn, *Gottesdienst und Rechtfertigungsglaube* (1926), p. 68.

[2] Cf. Allwohn, p. 76.

155

specific need, a certain feature in the relation between divine service and liturgy had to be placed in the foreground.

In the age of Orthodoxy the situation was simpler; the lines were more clearly drawn. The Evangelical liturgy had acquired a relatively fixed form. Two dialectic principles concerning the relation between worship and liturgy could be included in the theological system. One of them we have already met (Chapter 4): true service of God understood as pious devotion of the heart urgently tends toward embodiment in the liturgy; a human, and yet in the main divine, necessity causes the inner process to be fulfilled in the outward act. An absolute need of the external — such is the verdict of all Lutheran thinking directed against unrealistic spiritualization. The consequences in worship practices are obvious. A rich unfolding of all liturgical possibilities, a church order relevant to every last member, a permeation of the public life by the devotional life which is inconceivable to people of the 20th century — such were the characteristics of the liturgical situation within the Lutheran Church of the 17th century. One must never lose sight of this. Despite all negative statements, the positive note asserting that external worship is very much in order comes through unmistakably.[3]

At the same time, however, these negative statements were meant to stress that only one side of the relation between divine service and liturgy had had the floor and that the tension had thereby been resolved. Every isolated liturgy inescapably incurs the danger to which all one-sidedness is exposed: it monopolizes our horizon; it begins to grow autonomous and to separate from its foundations; it gets to be independent, an opus operatum. Hence a retrogressive movement set in to emphasize the other principle; and this is the real theme of the 17th-century *reform movement* with respect to the service of worship: people recalled the conditional, tentative nature of all liturgical actions

[3] Grossgebauer, "Wächterstimme," p. 5: "The *form of godliness* is there, but where is its *power?* Is it not being denied?" P. 213: "Since all men, even the worst scoundrels, desire that it should be well with them here in time and yonder eternally, it is no wonder that *the Lord's Supper is received so frequently* and made an idolatrous service." Johann Saubert *(Psychopharmacum pro Evangelicis et Pontificiis* [1636], p. 82) applies a complaint of Mathesius to his time: "Things are going according to the saying, Where God's Word is spoken most prolifically and most purely, its contempt is greatest and the worst punishment most imminent."

and harked back to the genuine, essential presuppositions of the divine service. Such a retrogressive movement may pursue either of two courses. It may either ignore the insights which had been gained previously and were then one-sidedly overemphasized, and may go to the other extreme; and that means in our case, regard the completely "desensualized" service as the ideal pattern, whereby the necessary tension would also be removed. Or it may, while retaining the one viewpoint, attempt to bring the other into the proper relation thereto, and then to let the two thoughts correct each other in living interaction. In the first case there is a relapse into mere spiritualism, which simply depreciates the bodily form for the sake of the spirit; in the second case the physical form is preserved intact, but is assigned its proper place as the consequence of what is spiritual.[4]

Both these ways were taken by the voluminous 17th-century literature dealing with reform. Hence the great difference in the reforms envisioned. The individual demands set up may sound very much alike; but one must inquire carefully what manner of spirit animated the author. It is often impossible to obtain a true picture of him from his reforming proposals alone; these proposals must be judged by his basic attitude. However well-intentioned and plausible these proposals may appear, if their final aim is the dissolution of all external forms, they fail to recognize the Lutheran tension between "liturgy" and "divine service" and must be declined. That is why Löscher, though at a time when the fronts were already plainly drawn, championed a clear-cut distinction between the concepts "to reform" and "to improve." If the latter is the continual duty of the church, corresponding to the struggle for sanctification of the individual, then "to reform" signifies the revolutionary change of such basic doctrines as have proved false and deceptive.[5] Accordingly, attempts at reform

[4] Balduin, *Tractatus*, p. 144: "The inward worship of God has its seat in the spirit of man and is the foundation of all outward reverence and honor which are shown to God by men in words, deeds, and gestures."

[5] Löscher, *Timotheus*, I, 722: "That there is a great difference between the Christian upbuilding and improving which are incumbent upon every Christian, especially the teachers, according to their calling, their powers, and given circumstances, and the reforming for which God raises up and equips with exceptional gifts particular men, is self-evident. The former is always necessary, and a congregation always needs building up although the condition

157

in the period of Orthodoxy require examination as to whether they sprang from honest concern about current abuses, or merely from opposition to Lutheran teaching.[6] One movement, which eventually was to prevail and which was supported by the forerunners of Pietism, recognizably began with Johann Arndt but could maintain itself in the 17th century only as an undercurrent. The real thrust of the reform movement came from the representatives of Lutheran Orthodoxy themselves. Naturally enough, it is often difficult to keep the two movements apart; so much so that one can identify some men, as for example, Grossgebauer, with either the one or the other tendency. In the 17th century it was often not quite clear to what extent thoughts of reform stemmed from the Lutheran faith and how far they sought to introduce other ideas. There is perceptible in this period a certain groping and questing, as becomes particularly plain to our view from the altogether dissimilar appraisals of Johann Arndt, who cannot apodictically be classed with either one of the two groups.

However much actual conditions called for these endeavors at reform in the 17th century, which by the way were not limited to the sphere of the divine service, the manner in which they were implemented seems to contradict Lutheran principles. The pathway now leads *from without to within*. The "good work" is there; now the right inner attitude is to be added. Roman Catholic theology consciously pursues this way, whereby the opus operatum is made the pedagogical point of departure; and the reform literature of the 17th century follows it. The reverse way from without to within may have been necessary inasmuch as it was conditioned by the historical situation, but theologically the "inner worship" always has priority.[7] There can never be a question of letting the pedagogical way "from without inward" stand as a second and equally valid possibility. It is not

is good in the main; the latter takes place only when there is thorough corruption and the whole cause must be placed on a different footing."

[6] Lutheran theology of the 17th century did not work out this conceptual distinction between "reform" and "improvement." Cf. Hans Leube, *Die Reformideen in der deutschen lutherischen Kirche zur Zeit der Orthodoxie* (1924), pp. 37 f.

[7] Balduin, *Tractatus,* p. 174: "External worship is nothing else than the exercise of true piety in which, from the abundance of the heart, the mouth speaks, the hands work, the whole body is made useful for God." Cf. n. 4.

enough to have the feeling of the heart adventitiously join the "work." The way from within outward must needs be taken, even though it be only a reaction. What now proceeds from the movement of the heart may indeed bear a great similarity to the opus operatum; yet the two are radically different. For the one work is dead, the other is alive.

2. The Worship of the Individual

Harmony of heart and deed: this is the decisive theme of the demand for reform of the divine service. It is a demand directed not to the divine service but to *man* taking part in it. Here we meet the question as to who is the true *subject* of worship.[8] It has already been indicated (Chapter 5) that only the church, that is, "the believers within the area of the church," can be the subject of the divine worship. If we dwell on this first with regard to the *individual*, all has really been said with the one word "believer." For faith means the integration of the whole person, the unity of heart and deed. The service of God must be "a living fruit from the good tree of the Christian state" (Fendt).[9] Every external ceremony which we use asks of us devotion within.[10] Although Tarnow voiced the complaint that God was being invoked only with the mouth, he did not go to the opposite extreme of demanding that God be adored not with the

[8] Cf. chapter 3, 1, a.

[9] Müller, *Predigten,* pp. 62 f.: "True worship must have its origin not in the outward but in the inward man. Outward without inward worship is pure idolatry. God is a Spirit and wants to be worshiped in the spirit; He looks at the spirit and judges all works according to the heart. Again, our sacrifice is to be a reasonable service; we are to live thus outwardly that every reasonable man can judge by the appearance that true faith is in our hearts. Although reason cannot see or know the inner man as he really is, yet it is to recognize its image." Lütkemann, *Harfe von zehn Saiten,* on Ps. 34, pp. 14 f.: "Our tongue is like a bell. If it is to sound to the glory of God, the rope must be drawn by the heart. Our mouth is like a pipe. If piping and singing are to be a praise of God, the breath must come from the soul. The tongue cannot praise God without the heart, and when the heart is full of praise, the mouth cannot keep silence."

[10] Dunte, *Decisiones,* p. 143: "And this ceremony must rightly be founded in the heart, so that there may be agreement between inner devotion and outward gestures. Here is the dividing line between true piety and hypocrisy."

159

mouth but only with the heart. The "inner worship" does not do away with the praise of the mouth.[11]

Arndt, on the other hand, manages to convey the impression that everything external could be omitted, as long as all is right within. Not that he engages in polemics against the existing divine services. His demands, which aim at the deepening of the inner spiritual life, are completely evangelical. Still, one cannot miss the spiritualizing undertone that ultimately all liturgy is superfluous.[12]

The cleavage of opinion is usually revealed by the interpretation of John 4:24. The text is often construed as showing a contrast between inward adoration and outward forms of worship; and to make the latter seem abhorrent, it is slandered and called legalistic. This reduces the situation to an either-or. Yet the 17th-century dogmaticians knew that the text merely demands the right inward presupposition for all service of God as the evangelical characteristic not only of worship but also of Christian ethics. Doubtless classic Lutheran theology also misapplied this Johannine text by using it to support the doctrine of the invisible church: since no one knows who really "worships in spirit and in truth," and hypocrites also worship

[11] Paul Tarnow, *De novo evangelio* (1697), p. 31: "They had this external worship of God, which is comprehended in calling upon God's name and was performed by the majority only with the mouth, by very few with the mouth and the heart."

[12] Arndt, *Vom wahren Christentum,* p. 86: "Our divine service of the New Testament is no longer external with typical ceremonies, prescriptions, and laws; but inward in spirit and truth, that is, in the faith of Christ because by Him the whole Moral and Ceremonial Law has been fulfilled — temple, altar, sacrifices, mercy seat, and priests. Thereby we also enjoy Christian liberty, redeemed from the curse of the Law (Gal. 3:13) and from all Jewish ceremonies (Gal. 5:1), so that by the indwelling of the Holy Ghost we can serve God with a willing heart and spirit (Jer. 31:33; Rom. 8:14), and our conscience and faith are bound by no human commandments. But the true, spiritual, inward Christian worship includes three parts: (1) Right knowledge of God, (2) right knowledge of sin and repentance, (3) knowledge of grace and of the forgiveness of sins." P. 91: "You understand, then, that true worship is in the heart, in the knowledge of God, in true repentance, whereby the flesh is mortified and man is renewed in the image of God. For thereby man becomes a holy temple of God, in which the inward service is performed by the Holy Spirit: faith, love, hope, humility, patience, prayer, thanksgiving, praise, and glory of God."

160

externally, the true church is "invisible." [13] While in the present context the visibility of the church is not in question, this argument admits that they who worship aright also do something *external and visible*. Not inward prayer but true prayer is referred to in John 4:24. Lutheranism's insistence on "worship in spirit and in truth" implies no antiliturgical bias.[14]

But where the Spirit is absent, all outward activity is a mere mechanism which is its own reward. The bigger and more important this mechanism is, the more people hope to achieve by it. Even prayer was debased into a mechanism and then drawn out to great length.[15] Christ did not condemn all long prayers, but only such as

[13] Gerhard, *Loci,* V, 311: "The true church, properly so called, consists of true worshipers. But the true worshipers cannot be recognized by human eyes, because the true worshipers worship in spirit and truth. But the eye cannot judge who they are that worship thus, since the hypocrites do the same so far as outward appearance is concerned. Therefore the true church, properly so called, cannot be seen."

[14] Lütkemann, *Harfe,* on Ps. 33, p. 5: "On the festive days of the Old Covenant the divine services were enhanced by the music of strings and pipes. It is not improper to do something similar today. But one must consider that the true praise of God does not consist in the external sound. That is why God said through His prophets: Put away from Me the noise of your songs; for I do not care to hear the playing of your harps. God would be worshiped and praised in spirit and in truth. There is no doubt, therefore, that by the music of strings and the sound of psalms God's Spirit here demands the inward sacrifice of praise and the joy of the mind, inasmuch as the believing soul feels God nigh and also praises and glorifies Him before others, whereto Paul incites us by saying: Sing and make melody in your hearts to the Lord." Cf. Ch. 3, n. 76. Gustav Mensching, *Die liturgische Bewegung in der evangelischen Kirche* (1925), p. 21: "Against this desire for form, men from the Evangelical Church like to raise the objection that Evangelical worship is worship 'in spirit'; but that spirit is antithetical to form and excludes it as a human addition. Over against this it must be stressed that, for instance, the word of the Lord in John 4:24 by no means states that the worship of God must take place in the human spirit by means of pure, unseeing thought and contemplation of God, as the word is unquestionably often understood. The 'spirit' here spoken of can be none other than the Spirit of God Himself, without whom no worship is possible. But this Spirit is indifferent to the form into which the act of worship is cast."

[15] Leonhard Fendt, *Der lutherische Gottesdienst des 16. Jahrhunderts* (1923), p. 58: "Jesus taught that prayer need not be long in the case of those who are always in communion with the eternal Father; but here this mutual fellowship is to be created or maintained by prayer. Here, then, prayer is plainly a means, a mechanism, whereas with Jesus it is a spontaneous singing

were made long in the hope of increasing their value.[16] Another step, a short one, leads to meritoriousness. Where the mechanism has grown important, calculation sets in. No one can read merit from another man's inward heart and mind. Just because that is impossible, the "old Gospel," which is concerned with the attitude of the heart, with the faith, precludes all man's own merit. But, thought Tarnow in view of bad experiences of that day, a "new Gospel" had arisen in accordance with which it was possible to attain God's mercy and eternal salvation by the mechanism of worship.[17] It is not the mere existence of outward worship that carries with it the idea of meritoriousness; this notion arose because this worship lost its foundation and thus became a mechanism.[18] The harm that results from such a performance of the service without inner participation is brought home to us most impressively at the Lord's Supper (1 Cor. 11: 27-29).[19] Holy Communion becomes idolatry not only through the

of the heart, even though it be a swan song. With Jesus prayer is the product of the religious attitude of the heart; with this later age the religious attitude of the heart is the product of prayer."

[16] Brochmand, *Systema,* II, 493: "At this point we must avoid βαττολογία, or the vain babbling of long and numerous prayers poured forth without serious thought and emotion of the heart, as also without living faith." Dunte, *Decisiones,* p. 897: "[Prayer is] unacceptable not because of its length, but on account of unbelieving, unspiritual babbling, and because the hope of being heard is based on the length of the prayer and the number of words."

[17] Tarnow, *De novo evangelio,* p. 16: "The old Gospel . . . is the doctrine about the mercy of the Father, the forgiveness of sins, and eternal salvation through faith in Christ; but the new . . . is the dogma about the mercy of God the Father, the remission of sins, and eternal salvation to be obtained by the outward worship of God."

[18] Ibid. p. 17: "The new and false gospel is a vain belief about Christ or an opinion about the grace and mercy of God, not learned from the Word of God but from the secret counsel of the Prince of Darkness through his agent, the Serpent . . ., in which he promises immunity for guilt and sins and eternal salvation to all who exhibit outward worship of God and profess the true Christian with the mouth but deny him with the heart, and who in that vain persuasion decide that all blessings promised only to true and constant believers pertain also to themselves, though they practice not an inward but only an outward and simulated repentance."

[19] Ibid., p. 23: "Then they are convinced that they are in heaven, and as a pledge of their opinion ask that the Lord's Supper be given them, and receive it like dogs and swine. But who of the great and powerful of this earth would admit into his hall and to his table those who are conspicuous by all vices from sheer wantonness?"

falsification of the object (adoration of the consecrated host), but also through the insincerity of those taking part. According to Grossgebauer, "the miserable people" made an idolatrous service of Holy Communion by "seeking their welfare in the external work, attending from habit or to please others, without hunger and thirst, without wisdom and awe."[20] Heinrich Müller thought of this process of turning worship into a mere mechanism as already penetrating to the very heart of the divine service. The sacraments, the office of the ministry, the office of the keys had petrified into dead works. "Christendom of today makes dumb ecclesiastical idols of the baptismal font, the pulpit, the confessional, and the altar, and takes comfort in external Christianity while denying its inner power."[21]

Hence *hypocrisy (simulatio)*, already specifically exposed by Jesus (Matt. 15:8 ff.), together with that sin of manner, self-chosen worship (ἐθελοθρησκεία, *superstitio*),[22] is here put forward as the gravest fault of the worshiping subject. According to Schröder, "Christianity of the mouth, or hypocrisy," was the greatest evil of his time.[23] Hypoc-

[20] Grossgebauer, "Wächterstimme," p. 72.

[21] Müller, *Predigten,* p. 145. In the 152d devotion of his "Geistliche Erquickstunden," he writes "on the idolatry of hypocrites": "Christianity of today (he is speaking of hypocrites as the explanatory text shows plainly) follows four dumb church-idols: the baptismal font, the pulpit, the confessional, and the altar. It finds comfort in external Christianity: being baptized, hearing the Word of God, going to confession, receiving the Lord's Supper; but it denies the inner power of Christianity. . . . But is it not Anabaptist error to call Baptism, Word, confession, the Lord's Supper 'dumb church-idols'? Well, is there no difference between Baptism and baptismal font, sermon and pulpit, going to confession and the confessional chair, Holy Communion and the altar? The Anabaptist does away with the right use of baptismal font, pulpit, confessional chair, the altar; I am striving to do away with the false trust of hypocrites, which fastens and founds itself upon these articles." In accordance with their principle *abusus non tollit usum,* the Orthodox theologians did not, of course, consider the inference often drawn later; viz., that abused ceremonies must cease together with the abuses. (Cf. Ch. 6, No. 144.)

[22] See ch. 3, 1 b.

[23] Schröder, *Zuchtposaune,* pp. 70 f.: ". . . that many, yes most people of our time perform the outward worship only from custom etc. and attend to that alone, without the intention of receiving faith from the hearing of the divine Word and amending their lives. This does not mean that we reject, in the manner of the Enthusiasts, the external divine service, churchgoing, hearing the Word, attending at confession and Holy Communion, etc. God

163

risy is not only an invisible dissension between heart and mouth; it becomes manifest in the discrepancy between our liturgical actions and our ethical conduct, the latter being truly the fruit of our heart. Arndt writes as follows: "It is mockery and wickedness . . . to honor God with the mouth and to dishonor Him by conduct." [24] The pastor, too, may incur the danger of turning his sermon into a mechanism. With this "professional preacher" (Allein-Prediger) Grossgebauer contrasts the true "steward," who is not merely concerned with delivering a sermon, but who through the sermon and in addition to the sermon intends to discharge his steward's office faithfully.[25] The right sermon can spring forth only from a heart that is filled with the love

forbid! It is God's Word; and the holy sacraments are also the means whereby God creates and preserves faith in the hearts of men. He who despises them, despises God Himself, falls into gross errors and finally (if he continues thus) into hell. Understand this of him who trusts entirely in externals and uses these means not in accordance with God's will, but after his own carnal notions, without calling upon God to be enlightened and moved thereby, without the earnest desire for faith and a Christian life to the glory of God, for which He has ordained them."

[24] Johann Arndt, Paradiesgärtlein (1722), Preface, p. 1. It is noteworthy that Arndt directly afterwards, in order not to jeopardize the unity of worship and ethics, again merges cultic action with ethical action: "A holy life is the best and most powerful prayer" (Preface, p. 1). Brochmand, on the other hand, under the Second Commandment requires "the glorifying of the name of God both with the voice . . . and in life." (Systema, II, 32)

[25] Grossgebauer, "Wächterstimme," p. 12 f.: "Your professional preacher says much; the steward speaks and acts. By his professional preaching the professional preacher brings it to pass that the Word is no longer esteemed as the Word of God; the steward adds impressiveness to the Word and shows in his stewardship which person is in life and which in death. The professional preacher is usually a sounding brass and a tinkling cymbal, even though he speaks with the tongue of men and angels; the steward gives witness to the spoken Word and would rather suffer death than knowingly administer the mysteries of God's kingdom contrary to the will of God in the case of this or that person, whoever he may be. The professional preacher preaches much and persuades the people that, where much is said, there St. Paul's word is fulfilled, 'Let the word of Christ dwell among you richly.' The steward narrows down his preaching and says openly that mere preaching does not achieve as much as people imagine. The professional preacher glories in ornate sermons and considers his work completed with his preaching. But the steward holds stewardship to be his proper work; and after preaching he will say that he has finished only one half of his work, unless important parts of spiritual stewardship are to remain undone."

of God.[26] It must be stressed, though, that the subjective insincerity of the incumbent detracts nothing from the objective validity of his official acts.[27]

We are confronted with hypocrisy also when the right attitude is indeed present, but when an act is performed that is not compatible with it. This occurs when believing Lutherans, either not to attract attention or to avoid persecution, take part in ceremonies opposed to the Gospel.[28] For in the first place clear Bible texts testify that one cannot serve two masters (Matt. 6:24; 2 Cor. 6:14 ff.; 1 Thess. 5:22);[29] secondly, the discrepancy between spiritual and external participation is reprehensible, for it is a lie;[30] and finally due consideration of the neighbor enters in decisively (1 Cor. 10:34). For this situation comes under the same judgment as the demand that indifferent ceremonies be reintroduced to please the adversaries: "By this hypocrisy the enemies of the Word are mightily strengthened, when they see that one begins to give way; the orthodox believers are plunged into doubt whether it was right to abolish such and similar abominations, all the more since the common people are more taken up with externals than with doctrine and the divine service itself."[31] Should one nevertheless be obliged by circumstances to take part in papalist ceremonies (here the reference is especially to the attendance of Evangelical princes at religious services at the imperial court), the inner dissent from the proceedings should be

[26] Gerhard, *Loci,* I, 341: "His sermon is born from love and desire of the Supreme Good."

[27] Gerhard, *Loci,* IV, 152: . . . "the Gospel is efficacious, with whatever purpose it is proclaimed."

[28] Dunte, *Decisiones,* p. 206: "When the church is under severe pressure, should it not be permissible to show honor to the mass, to images, etc. and thus to serve idols, if only the heart remains pure?"

[29] Ibid.

[30] Dannhauer, *Collegium decalogicum,* p. 397: "By this very act you lie, since the intent of the mind is contrary to the ceremonies of the body; and add that it is rightly called idolatry not to worship God with the whole heart and all powers. For as He is the Creator of the body as of the mind, He demands worship from both parts, without any spiritual adultery."

[31] Dunte, *Decisiones,* p. 605.

expressed in every way legitimately possible.[32] The mere presence at alien worship is not forbidden. Scripture offers us the example of Elijah (1 Kings 11:23 ff.), of Daniel (Dan. 3:12), of Paul (Acts 17:16,23). Quenstedt thought that there was no harm in for once seeing these "awful abominations and superstitions" with one's own eyes; one could then reject them all the more confidently.[33]

To resolve this contradiction of heart and mouth is our constant duty. But this contradiction will cease in eternity, when the praise of God will emanate from the fullness and totality of our being.[34]

3. The Worship of the Community

If we now look at the church as a whole, insofar as it is the subject of worship, we must say that on this topic, too, there were lively debates toward the close of the 17th century. There was general agreement of course that the church must be the prerequisite for the true divine service. Only opinions differed greatly about the concept of the church. Lutheran theology felt constrained to place special emphasis on the concept of the ministerial office; the rising Pietistic thought laid the greatest stress on the universal priesthood of all believers.[35]

The controversial question whether the church is a purely objec-

[32] Quenstedt, *Theologia,* IV, 383: "The orthodox man should either stay away altogether from the sacred rites of infidels and heretics, especially the Papists, or, if he wishes to be present at some time or is constrained to do so by reason of his office, he must take care not to seem to agree with them; thus, that he does not conform to them as regards external worship, shows no respect to the mass-idol, does not fall on his knees before images and statues, does not beat his breast during mass like the Papists, carries no rosary, etc. But better let him declare his dissent in some manner, by words or signs."

[33] Ibid.

[34] Gerhard, *Loci,* IX, 354: "The glory of God is rightly referred also to the internal blessings of eternal life which are common to the whole person, that is, the souls and bodies of the blessed. For that praise will not be produced only in the mouth, as in this life many approach God with their lips while their heart is far from Him (Jer. 29:13; Matt. 15:8), but it will proceed from the very depths of the heart. As the heart and the flesh of the blessed rejoice in the living God, so also the heart and the flesh of the blessed will burst forth into praises of God."

[35] See Johann Georg Engelhardt's comparison of Spener's *Pia desideria* with those of the anti-Pietists, *Zeitschrift fuer historische Theologie,* XV (1845), 157 ff.

tive institution or a religious-ethical fellowship is almost as old as the church itself. The Reformation had recognized that the truth lay in a proper synthesis of both thoughts (Augsburg Confession, VII). If one accepts this Lutheran concept of the church, then the legitimacy of the divine service depends just as little on adherence to the Roman Church, which claims to be the one true external church organization, as a gathering of those "who earnestly want to be Christians" is in itself sufficient to establish that legitimacy. Over against Rome the boundary was plainly visible; to draw the border-line against sects and groups was often much more difficult. The danger from this side became the greater, the more their ideas spread within the church itself. As the age of Orthodoxy came to its close, however, this very danger became acute through the Pietistic conventicles within the Lutheran Church. Senescent Orthodoxy had failed at first, when Spener championed his *collegia pietatis,* to recognize this danger. One of the few theologians to raise their voice against it at once was Balthasar Mentzer, Jr., who denied all Biblical justification to "private gatherings." Neither the saying of Christ about the two or three gathered together in His name (Matt. 18:20), he held, nor the fact that in the early centuries of the Christian church divine services were conducted in private dwellings, could justify organizing a church within a church *(ecclesiola in ecclesia).*[36] Mentzer indeed recalls that, strangely enough, Luther occasionally spoke favor-

[36] Balthasar Mentzer, Jr., *Kurtzes Bedenken von den eintzelnen Zusammenkunfften* (n. d.; 1st ed., 1691), p. 299: "First, then, there is in the Word of God no account whatever that Christ our Lord instituted or commanded, besides the gatherings of the church, such individual and private gatherings as are now being arranged and introduced by some. And neither Dr. Luther nor any Evangelical theologian has, as far as I know, found the institution of such private gatherings in the texts which are adduced in support, Matt. 18:16, 19, 20; but they regarded them as a gracious promise of Christ, given to His disciples and believers of the time, not to mind their small number but to be assured of His gracious help and aid nevertheless . . ." P. 301: "In the apostolic church, when the Christian doctrine was planted and spread and there were no public houses of worship, there was need of meeting for divine service in private houses, as the apostolic history witnesses But after the time of the apostles, and after the period of persecutions by pagan emperors and tyrants (when they had to hold their services in chasms and caves, obeying God rather than human government), when the Christians were at liberty to worship God publicly, there is no report of such separate meetings as being instituted by Christ and commanded to Christians."

ably of such narrow communities.[37] But such thoughts were and are, Mentzer thinks, foredoomed to failure.[38] If they were now to be realized, then the hitherto unfounded reproaches of the Papalists would be only too well justified.[39]

Later, when the effects of the thoughts embodied in the conventicles were in plain view, it was Löscher who once again pointed out the unbridgeable distance between the Lutheran service and the Pietistic conventicles.[40] The Lutheran Church had always emphasized that one could not be satisfied with merely attending the public service of a Sunday.[41] Keeping Sunday holy means, according to Dil-

[37] Mentzer was probably thinking of Luther's suggestion in his "German Mass", 1526; WA 18, 75.

[38] Mentzer, *Kurtzes Bedenken,* p. 302: "Dr. Luther cites a few texts aiming at this matter; but that was at the beginning of the Reformation, when necessity demanded such unusual gatherings. These texts do not fit the present condition of the church. Besides, Dr. Luther could not carry out his plan, as he himself admits; and that for the very reasons which obtain with us today. Yet Luther's proposals went beyond what is now ventured by those who like such separate conventicles; and when these men fear that those proposals might cause a schism or split in the church, they themselves confess that Dr. Luther's suggestions do not suit our present conditions . . ."

[39] Ibid.: "The Papists have for a long time placed us Evangelicals into the same category with the Mennonites, Anabaptists, and other Enthusiasts, although impudently and mischievously. But if these private conventicles were to be introduced, they would all the more consider themselves justified in their slander, because we should begin to do what was customary with those others but not hitherto approved by us."

[40] Löscher, *Timotheus Verinus,* I, 787: "Moreover, it was never the intention of our church and our theologians to condemn all exercises in Christian piety that take place outside of the public service. On the contrary, it has always been urged that fathers and mothers should get experience in reviewing the sermons, Bible hours, etc. with their children and servants. It has also been admitted that it is profitable if more Christians, though always in the presence and under the leadership of an orthodox ordained teacher, gain more knowledge in spiritual matters and meet for that purpose. But here is the rub, in the main: whether the instruction is to remain as stated, or whether something additional is permissible and profitable; viz., that one not called thereto acts as a spiritual teacher in the gathering, admonishes those present, and proclaims the Word of God. This is what we deny and the opponents affirm."

[41] Kessler, *Schriftmässige Erörterung,* p. 50: (1) On the holy day sincere Christians should first of all come to church and attend the service; for this is the chief purpose of the holy days . . . (2) Therefore we will also read God's Word at home, study theological books, praise and bless God with

herr, "praying before the sermon, preparing for it by reading the Holy Scriptures, singing devoutly with the congregation, following the church prayers with silent devotion, attending to the sermon with close attention, thoughtfully going one's way after receiving the benediction, repeating the sermon at home with one's family, and jotting down the most important points." [42] Speaking of the external sanctification of the Sabbath, Dannhauer enumerates among other matters: a sacred review and catechesis of what has been heard, a private doxology, holy beneficence, a holy life.[43] If with most dogmaticians the exposition of the Third Commandment extends only to public gatherings for divine worship, the reason is that this is felt to be the distinguishing feature of that commandment. And rightly so! For the *public* service is, in principle and reality, the instituted gathering for the purpose of worship. The "unofficial" service at home and the proclamation of the Word of God from man to man are, for the most part, the object of the Second Commandment.[44] But it can never be conceded that the worship conducted in private circles may take the place of the public service and be regarded as necessary in the same manner.[45]

We are again committed to the statement, therefore, that it is not enough to examine proposals of reform by themselves; they must be scrutinized also with respect to their spiritual paternity. The distinguishing trait is the position over against the ministerial office. How controversial a production, for instance, was Arndt's *Wahres Christentum!* The reader could register glad assent in part, but he could not ignore latent dangers. Thus the approval which the book

hymns and psalms, as the Jews did on their festive days. (3) Also, we cultivate spiritual devotion and take pleasure in theological thoughts, putting aside the earthly things which plague us on workdays."

[42] *Augen- und Hertzenslust, d. i. emblematische Fürstellung der sonn- und festtäglichen Evangelien* (1661), p. 188.

[43] *Hodosophia,* p. 513.

[44] Cf. Gerhard, *Loci,* III, 55.

[45] Löscher, I, 788: "This first error is followed by a second, namely, that such *collegia pietatis* [conventicles] are held to be necessary in and by themselves. This cannot be admitted, even when they are at their best. There may be certain conditions making necessary such exercises outside of the public worship here and now; but one cannot go beyond that. Hence it is wrong to allege, as Dr. Spener taught, that the *collegia pietatis* are necessary."

enjoyed in the Lutheran Church differed from that which it evoked, for example, from spiritualizing circles. Like his Lutheran colleagues, Saubert praised the book most highly. He found that it completely safeguarded the true Christian "intent," which to him consisted in "rightly indicating and urging sincere Christianity, or the exercise of faith and the practice of true righteousness, against all hypocrites and Epicureans." [46] On the other hand, this devotional book of Arndt's was viewed with some suspicion because it was so highly esteemed by the sectaries, especially the Weigelians. Yet the misuse to which these men doubtless subjected the book did not prevent its proper use. As long as the reader did not share "the contempt of the public ministry" [47] practiced by the Weigelians, the study of the book could only prove profitable.[48]

We have, then, fixed two important viewpoints when dealing with the proper subject of worship. The first pertains to the individual Christian, who is to worship God in spirit and in truth. Here the implied antithesis to spirit is not the body, but what is lifeless, dead, and a mere thing. Truth, on the other hand, finds its opposite in lies and hypocrisy. Hence the "form" must be in constant motion toward the essence of worship. This characterizes the themes which, in manifold variations, recur continually in the literature of Lutheran Orthodoxy insofar as it busies itself with the "service of God." The second aspect directs us from the individual to the sum total; the individual with his activity of worship has been placed in a community, in the church. Only there the liturgy experiences development and fulfillment. Now the direction is reversed; the way leads from the "essential," from the experience of faith, to the concrete embodiment of the liturgy. Thus the individual is also constantly being directed to the community. The "individual" and the "congregation" are interdependent. Since Christ has entrusted the means

[46] Saubert, *Die Neue Kreatur* (1625), p. 5.

[47] Ibid., p. 8.

[48] Ibid., pp. 9 f.: "But you, dear Christian people, who adhere to our public exercise of religion, diligently attend services, in addition have read Mr. Arndt's widely mentioned book on True Christianity and similar writings on genuine godliness, and have thereby amended your life and been edified to life eternal; continue boldly thus, you will not be sorry for it. Do not bother about those who abuse what is good . . . Polycarp Leyser says: In sum, the book is good if only the reader is good."

of grace to the church, that is where the individual finds salvation. On the other hand, the liturgy of the congregation is meaningless if it is not supported by the inner spiritual life of the individual believer, which is to find its proper expression in all ceremonies.

It can justly be asserted that classic Lutheran theology correctly grasped and presented this condition of reciprocal tension. The responsibility for the actual conditions affecting the conduct of divine worship in the 17th century, no matter how greatly they stood in need of improvement, cannot be laid at the door of a theology which allegedly had lost touch with life and was consuming itself with Scholastic bickerings. The horrible confusion resulting from the Thirty Years' War was by no means the slightest cause of the chaotic conditions in the church at that time. And the great merit of the Orthodox theologians appears exactly at this point. They were not entirely absorbed in the elaboration of their great systems. With keen insight they recognized the deficiencies of devotional life and the resultant responsibilities for church practice; they insisted that their thoughts should become the living property of all. They did not permit the tension pervading the Christian worship to remain abstract theological wisdom but by their reforming proposals furnished the best object lesson how this tension should be translated into active Christian life. As far as the teaching on worship and the life of worship is concerned, the adverse criticism which pronounced Orthodoxy ineffectual is certainly unjustified.

CHAPTER NINE

Worship and Mysticism

The true subject of worship can only be the Christian as a member of the body of Christ. As has been stated, one may err in defining this subject through some error in defining the church. In whatever way the concept of the church had been falsified, however, its community character was always maintained in some form or other. But there is a form of piety which, deliberately setting aside the idea of a community, centers its interest on what takes place between God and the soul. It does so not merely in the sense in which the Reformers recalled the individual to the conviction of his accountability and ultimate loneliness before God; it also denies in principle the hyperpersonal unity which is the new creation of God's grace. Detached from all earthly ties and connections, it seeks contact with the Divine. This form of piety, briefly called "mysticism," presents no uniform picture; it comprises the most diversified types. But one of its main and unfailing features is its essentially unsocial character. A second feature common to all mystic currents is the cancellation of the subject-object relation by man, who finds all things in himself and himself in all things.

The Christian faith must come to grips with this type of piety, which is represented in almost all religions; it will in fact do well to ask whether it is itself the bearer of mystic ideas. Heiler, for instance, sees in mysticism and in "prophetic piety" [1] the two main types of

---

[1] Friedrich Heiler, *Das Gebet* (1918), p. 216: "Mysticism is passionless, passive, quietistic, resigned, contemplative; prophetic piety is passionate, active, demanding and desiring, ethical."

173

personal piety, which are of course also reflected in Christianity.[2] To this extent mysticism is not a fixed magnitude that can enter into a clear relation, whether of a positive or a negative kind, to the Christian faith. It must be judged from case to case according to the form in which it may appear. Moreover, insofar as mysticism grew from the soil of the Christian church, it is subject to manifold fluctuations. One cannot fail to see the vast differences that characterize the mystical systems of the Areopagite, Augustine, Bernard, Eckhart, the Victorines, and Angelus Silesius, to cite but a few names.

1. Mysticism and the Mystic Union

To inquire into the importance of mysticism for the Orthodox Lutheran teaching on worship is quite in order, for there is much talk about an Evangelical mysticism of the 17th century. Just as the period of Orthodoxy is frequently interpreted as the "Middle Ages" of the Evangelical Church, so men think that they can see the two forms of medieval theology, Scholasticism and mysticism, fully developed also on the Evangelical scene. If it is true that in this era a mystic movement seized upon the Evangelical churches, this could not possibly have remained without effect on the concept of divine worship. For the fundamental thoughts of mysticism, as outlined above, are in strong opposition to the Lutheran conception of the divine service as presented here.

It is an incontrovertible fact that the 17th century was stirred by currents of mysticism in a highly exceptional measure. But — and this is decisive for our problem — these streams ran *alongside* of the church and mostly in conscious opposition. Although Luther had been influenced very definitely and fruitfully by medieval mysticism, yet he drew an incisive boundary, even in the early stages of the Reformation, between his work and that of the Enthusiasts (Müntzer, Karlstadt, Schwenkfeld, Franck), who by their "spiritual mysticism" endangered the doctrine of Justification. It is common knowledge that the position of Orthodoxy over against the Enthusiasts was no less critical.

It would nevertheless be illusory to suppose that the ideas of mysticism, which at that time were in the very air, did not somehow

[2] Ibid., pp. 212 ff.

creep into the theology and piety of the church. We must, however, draw a clear dividing line between the official theology of the church and the devotional literature of the time; for the latter was naturally far more accessible to alien thoughts than theology, which was strictly bound to tradition. Then again one cannot let the thoughts met with in devotional literature weigh as heavily as the propositions of ecclesiastical dogmatics. For in the former there reigns a certain mobility and freedom which often overlooks the boundaries of dogmatic correctness. That is simply rooted in the nature of things. Still, it cannot be accepted without question. Löscher also notes that in recent years the opinion had gained ground "that the paraenetic [hortatory] form of teaching permitted some statements which would not pass the acroamatic [academic] test." [3] What is said by way of admonition, he adds, should not be taken as seriously as what is presented thetically and antithetically; nevertheless, the two should agree as far as possible.

It appears to be true, then, that the entrance of mystic thought took place first of all by way of Lutheran devotional literature. Paul Althaus, Sr., has pointed out in his valuable *Forschungen zur evangelischen Gebetsliteratur* how the influence of mysticism was exerted. Above all, he thinks, the causes of this influence are not to be sought in a special affinity of Lutheranism for mysticism. They are far more external than it appears at first, inasmuch as the importation into Lutheranism of Augustinian-Bernardian medieval mysticism — for these are the types of mysticism in question — is to be explained by the history of literature. Between Roman Catholic and Evangelical devotional literature there "exists a state of reciprocity, a formal literary exchange . . . which finally assumes such dimensions on the Evangelical side that the prayer books are quite overgrown with Roman productions." [4]

Two remarks are in place here: first, that Althaus sees in the inroads of mystical material an overgrowing of Evangelical piety by foreign, non-Evangelical elements; second, that these mystic, Romanizing influences in the 16th century affected first of all books of devotion and prayer. With regard to the church collects contained in

[3] Löscher, I, 34.

[4] Althaus, Sr., *Forschungen zur evangelischen Gebetsliteratur*, p. 64.

the Lutheran agendas of the 16th century, for example, Althaus himself reaches the conclusion that they "maintained their Evangelical character with exceptional stability." [5] In this context Althaus did not draw theology in the narrow sense into the area of his research; hence the verdict as to how far Lutheran theology of the 16th century succumbed to heterogeneous elements remains open. Yet Althaus establishes the fact that the theologians took little part in the preparation of devotional books intended for private use. "As for the 'theologians' who acted as leaders (in preparing devotional books), it is to be remarked that we relatively seldom meet among them professional scholars. Among the great theological scholars of the 17th century only Johann Gerhard really comes into consideration as the author of popular devotional writings." [6] For Luther's time, he states, the present problem was not relevant.[7]

This view of "mysticism in Lutheranism" as a foreign body entering in by way of devotional literature in post-Reformation times must of course affect the judgment on Orthodox teaching of the mystic union. This doctrine, adopted by the 17th-century dogmaticians as a special step in the order of salvation (ordo salutis), would then be a result of the mightily growing mystic thought. As viewed by mysticism, to be sure, it would be "only a feeble precipitate, bereft of its content." [8] Still, that would not alter the fact that the theology of the 17th century also yielded to the universal current of mysticism and accommodated itself to it.

We should then have to ask whether this new element in its doctrinal system did not make necessary a sweeping correction in the worship of Orthodoxy. For if we are here dealing with the same mysticism as in the devotional literature, with a mysticism, that is, which by its nature is quite incompatible with the Lutheran concep-

[5] Ibid., p. 222: "The history of Lutheran collects in the 16th century shows preponderatingly a process of continuous appropriation and elaboration of traditional material."

[6] Ibid., p. 8.

[7] Ibid., p. 63: "While the problem of 'mysticism in Lutheranism' does not yet come into question for the previous period, it begins to unroll itself to our gaze from the fifties forward."

[8] *Die Religion in Geschichte und Gegenwart* 2d ed. (1927—32), IV, 353 (Bornkamm).

tion of the service, especially with its community character; then either the Orthodox view of the service must have suffered a fundamental change, or an inner contradiction in the Orthodox system must be revealed.

Neither the one nor the other is in reality the case. Because of the way in which the Orthodox teaching of the *unio mystica* is encountered, it detracts nothing from the Lutheran concept of worship. This is not because these mystical ideas were perhaps devitalized for theological use and were no longer dangerous in their harmless form; no, the reason is simply that the teaching of the *unio mystica* is of purely Lutheran origin. There is no need to demonstrate its growth from Luther's own convictions. That has already been done very thoroughly.[9] All critics of the *unio mystica* doctrine look upon the "mysticism" of Luther and the "mysticism" of Orthodoxy as two separate, incompatible entities. Thus Koepp admits an independent mystical activity of Lutheranism; but he thinks that it died in the 16th century and that therefore "the poisonous digitalis of the splendid foreign magic flower had to be administered to the degenerating heartbeat of Lutheranism."[10] There is a grain of truth in this statement. If one were to sum up all the mystical thoughts ever written in the age of Lutheran Orthodoxy — and, note well, by men who thought that they were standing firmly on the ground of their own church — Luther, too, would probably not withhold his criticism. But one must not hold the teaching of the *unio mystica* responsible for all such exaggerations and distortions, which in part flowed directly from Jesuit sources. On the contrary, a protest must be raised precisely in behalf of this doctrine; for it is not what it has so often been suspected of being — "mysticism" in the customary sense of the term. The name may in a certain way justify this understanding; but the 17th-century dogmaticians expressly describe it as having been derived from *mysterium* (Eph. 5:32).[11] The accent rests on *unio*.

[9] Elert, *Morphologie*, I, 135 ff.; *Structure*, pp. 154 ff. See also Scholz, *Fruitio Dei.*

[10] Wilhelm Koepp, "Wurzel und Ursprung der orthodoxen Lehre von der unio mystica," *Zeitschrift für Theologie und Kirche,* New Series, II (1921), 171.

[11] Hollaz, *Examen,* p. 928: "This union is called mystic because it is a stupendous mystery that the unmeasurable, infinite God dwells in the

A "union" of God and man is doubtless a feature common to the *unio mystica* and to mysticism; but the profound differences dare not be overlooked.

But the Lutheran doctrine of the mystic union did not originate from medieval mysticism, either through formal literary influence or on account of an essential affinity. The common root of both lies in the numerous statements of Holy Writ (especially in St. John) about the indwelling of God in the believers. Without question, Roman Catholic mysticism was in the course of historical development nourished by other, extra-Biblical sources. That is why the Evangelical doctrine of the mystic union, proceeding from the Scriptures, is uniquely hedged about against every possibility of misunderstanding. It states that this union of man with God is brought about only through the means of grace, the Word and the sacraments; that on the part of man there is no corresponding psychological technique, but only faith; that it is a matter not of working but of receiving. And because the mystic union, like all other steps in the *ordo salutis,* is bound to the means of grace administered by the *congregation,* a wrong individualism disruptive of the community is also excluded. Thus the *Meditations* of Gerhard are in the main based on the mystic relation between God and the individual soul, but he strongly emphasizes the idea of the church, pointing out that the blessings of God are granted to us only in the church.[12] Finally, another characteristic feature of mysticism, that is, its elimination of the I — thou relation, of the confrontation of God and man, is likewise sternly repudiated in every presentation of the *unio mystica.*[13]

human heart. It is called spiritual because it is effected by the Holy Spirit, who graciously dwells in the regenerate not in a carnal and corporeal but in a supernatural manner."

[12] Meditation 23: "The Spirit of Christ is not outside of the body of Christ. Great indeed are the blessings of God in the church, but they are not open to all. It is a closed garden, a sealed fountain. No one sees the beauty of a closed garden except he who is in it; so no one knows the supreme blessings in the church except he who is himself in it."

[13] König, *Theologia,* pp. 211 f.: "The essence of this union does not consist in the mere harmony of emotions, nor only in the gracious operation of the Holy Spirit in the believers; nor in a transubstantiation or conversion of our substance into the substance of God and Christ, or vice versa; nor in consubstantiation, as when two substances become one; nor in joining external units into one hypostasis or person, so that the believer in Christ could say:

All such defining statements, designed to safeguard the Evangelical-Biblical understanding of the *unio mystica,* unfortunately cannot prevent some foreign mystical piety from snatching up the Evangelical thoughts and using them in a manner that vitiates their true origin. This is usually done by drawing false conclusions from the union of man with God — a fact of faith. People expect to repeat this fact as a psychic experience by intense concentration. What pertains to faith is made a matter of reflection and emotion.

The transformation mostly begins when we pass from the cool air of dogmatics to that of devotional literature, which is often rather hot and humid. Simultaneously with the change from the theoretical to the devotional approach a change of the object under consideration takes place. When Johann Arndt enjoins "entering into oneself, yes, into God," he means not merely the quiet meditation of the soul but the constant effort of the mystics to be immersed in God, for he writes: "That is why he (Tauler) so often said that it is in one's inner depths that one must in a pure state have, seek, and find God and His kingdom. That means: What Holy Writ and its right explanation treat externally, that must be found so in deed and in truth in the depth of the heart. That requires retreating into one's own inner depths. And the more we withdraw from the world into ourselves, the more we enter into God, our eternal origin." [14]

If Orthodoxy is to be blamed at all, it should be faulted not for providing the doctrinal form for the *unio mystica* thoughts of the Reformation but for its frequent lack of the critical discernment to recognize that a brand of mysticism foreign to the Gospel was infiltrating in the guise of piety born of the *unio mystica.* Thus Saubert praises the glory of this doctrine but at the same time protects its transformation as represented by Arndt. [15] It is not surprising that in

I am Christ; Christ eats and drinks through me, but in a close and ineffable joining of the substance of the believer with the substance of the Trinity and the human nature of Christ, without extension or contraction of the divine or the human essence, the united extremes remaining essentially distinct even in the midst of the state of union."

[14] Arndt, *Vom wahren Christentum,* p. 492.

[15] Saubert, *Neue Kreatur,* p. 6: "The union of the believers with Christ (often praised by M. Johann Arndt in his books) is an exalted, excellent doctrine, at which almost all Scripture aims. For to what other end is God's Word preached and are the holy sacraments used than that thereby we should

the later stages of Orthodoxy a man like Löscher had no use whatever for mysticism, which had become a peculiarity of Pietism. He
accepted Arndt, believing "that his heart was upright with God and
the truth of the Gospel"; but that he had unfortunately taken over,
not only from the mystical writings of Luther but also from those of
the Enthusiasts, matters which greatly diminished the value of his
books. "Since now the books of Arndt have met with very general
favor, these defects have likewise been propagated more than one
would have supposed; and many a one has, after the weakness of
mankind, taken them more seriously than the good." [16]

Löscher's verdict, then, not only extends to the un-Lutheran mystical aberrations but includes what Luther thought he could safely
appropriate from the mystics. Therefore, he believed, the root of
the evil of mysticism was to be looked for in Luther himself; for
although he had later admitted his errors, his followers had retained
them. He writes: "We cannot even absolve the highly meritorious
and sainted Chemnitz of all human weakness." [17] A closer examination of Löscher's criticism reveals that the mysticism which he attacks
does not really touch the *unio mystica* at all but is connected with the
doctrine of Original Sin. It concerns the spark of the soul, the good
in man, "which," it is alleged, "(1) was created with him; (2) which
is of God; (3) which sin and Satan did not touch and could not touch
even in the deepest fall; (4) which must be resuscitated after having
been suppressed, lulled asleep, and as it were shriveled up by the gross,
animal ways of sinners; (5) yes, which by its rise and victory accom-
plishes regeneration." [18] Here are thoughts, it is very evident, "in
which nature and grace are hideously confounded" and which are
totally foreign to the mind of Luther. Not until near the end does

be united with God by Christ in the power of the Holy Spirit, so that we
in Christ and Christ in us should live, rule, reign, dwell, work, as in John 17
the Son of God earnestly and powerfully implores His heavenly Father?
Herein lies the highest dignity and glory of God's children in this life and
their highest comfort that they have God and the whole realm of God in
themselves, etc. From this source flows true godliness and divine, holy life
within; for they who are led by the Spirit of God are God's children, and
they who have not the Spirit of Christ are not His."

[16] Löscher, I, 37.

[17] Ibid., p. 32.

[18] Ibid., p. 496.

Löscher find it necessary to add that the corrupt mystics teach so ineptly about Christ in us (they call Him the mystic Christ) that some use the doctrine as a cover for their deism; while others teach that He communicates the divine being to the pious, and also that from His humanity, by virtue of the heavenly body and flesh which they attribute to Him, He provides for the skepticism or imagination of man a new garment of light." [19] Löscher admits the soundness of teaching the *unio mystica* but warns against drawing non-Biblical consequences.[20]

2. The Mystic Union and the Presence of Christ at the Divine Service

The doctrine of the *unio mystica* needs special safeguarding. Yet there is no need to stop with a negative delimitation; the positive lines, too, must be drawn. For this doctrine is not, as Albrecht Ritschl has it, "a mere luxury; perhaps harmless, perhaps harmful." [21] Particularly if we view it in relation to worship, a basic thought common to both can be gained which especially stresses the closeness of the mystic union to the divine service. It is the thought of the *presence* of the Triune God. According to Asmussen, the presence of God through Christ in Christendom is "the absolute Christian occurrence." [22] It becomes reality in the gatherings of the Christians, in

[19] Ibid., p. 522.

[20] Ibid., p. 524: "If they are pressed, they take refuge behind exalted Biblical expressions: to be one spirit with the Lord (1 Cor. 6:17), to be partakers of the divine nature (2 Peter 1:4). Oh, would they but consider that these high and holy phrases are boundary-stones which we are not to cross and that we must accordingly forbear venturing and climbing up into what we have not seen! These high mysteries are unspeakably far beyond our conception. Hence we should accept them with the simple obedience of faith but not extend them, as is done by going beyond the mark and teaching that a pious person is essentially one with God, has the divine being, divine attributes, is made well in the being of God without Word or means, etc. Although such things may seem to follow from the lofty Biblical words, yet our reason is not free to conclude thus from these high mysteries without the Word, especially when such arbitrary extension of the Biblical words leads to the danger of falling into error. May God grant that this be taken to heart everywhere! Then the church will soon have rest in this matter as in others."

[21] Albrecht Ritschl, *Geschichte des Pietismus in der lutherischen Kirche des 17. und 18. Jahrhunderts* (1884), II, 32.

[22] Cf. Ch. 5, no. 41.

181

the services, and only there. God dwells in His congregation, when "two or three are gathered together in His name." But the presence of Christ is not a mere encounter, for then He would remain only outside of man and beside man. In a most profound and final sense this presence becomes communion and union. Hence classic Lutheran theology presents the thought of God's presence not only *with* men but also *in* men.

One could contrast these two teachings, looking upon the presence of God that dwells *with* us *(praesentia Dei cohabitationis)* and shows itself in help and assistance *(assistentia et auxilium)* [23] as an expression of "prophetic" piety; and regarding the presence of God that dwells *in* us *(praesentia Dei inhabitationis)* and culminates in the spiritual union *(unio pneumatica)* [24] as an expression of a "mystic" piety. It is characteristic of Orthodox theology, however, to draw formal distinctions here but to posit no material differences. This is revealed when on the one hand God's indwelling in the believers as described by St. John is merely identified with God's presence *(adessentia)* in His church, while on the other hand the promised presence of Jesus with those gathered in His name (Matt. 18:20) is also referred to the *unio mystica* of God with the believers. The gracious presence of God with the believers *(gratiosa Dei apud fideles praesentia* — Matt. 18:20) [25] is but *one* name among many others, oftentimes symbolic, for one and the same matter.[26] Dilherr, for example, also completely unifies the two series of thought.[27] A seeming excep-

[23] Philipp Nicolai, *Sacrosanctum omnipraesentiae Christi mysterium* (1602), p. 307.

[24] Ibid., p. 312.

[25] Brochmand, *Systema,* II, 304.

[26] König, for instance is acquainted with the following designations: (1) the dwelling of the Holy Trinity with the believer (John 14:23); (2) the dwelling of Christ in our hearts (Eph. 3:17; 2:22); (3) the espousal of believers with Christ (Rev. 21:9); (4) the mystery of the marriage of Christ and the church (Eph. 5:24, 25); (5) the ingrafting of the spiritual branches in the spiritual vine, Christ (John 15:4-7); (6) the union of the members with the Head (Eph. 1:22, 23). (*Theologia positiva,* pp. 209 f.)

[27] Dillherr, *Augen- und Hertzenslust,* p. 12: "Although the Lord Jesus is no longer with us visibly as He was 1600 and more years ago, He is still always among us invisibly. For He Himself said: Where two or three . . .

tion occurs in Gerhard, who states that the external communion of God with men, which must be conceived of as imperfect on earth, will pass over into an inner and perfect union in eternity. *Cohabitatio* and *inhabitatio* seem to be contrasted like inception and consummation.[28] Gerhard actually contrasts the union of grace *(unio gratiosa)* and the union of glory *(unio gloriosa)*. The former is accorded to man as a believer and must be daily granted anew; the latter reveals the indwelling of God in all its glory. Gerhard, too, holds the union of the believing soul with God to be reality already in this life.[29] The oneness of the believers with Christ, however, becomes possible only by virtue of their membership in the body of Christ.[30] Union with God is rendered possible only by the presence of Christ in Word and Sacrament, the presence realized in the service.

It appears, then, that Asmussen wrongfully accused Orthodoxy of not having dared to assert or even to think that the Christian service is the point of paramount importance in the Christian church.[31] This reproach may be justified over against certain tendencies of that period but not over against Orthodoxy as such. Further proof should

and I am with you always, even unto the end of the world. If we hear His holy Word devoutly and use His blessed Sacraments zealously, our Lord Jesus is undoubtedly with us; not only according to His general presence but also with His special gracious presence, in which no godless person can rejoice. Well for those who have this God with them! Alas for those from whom He has departed!"

[28] Gerhard, *Loci,* IX, 378: "From this it is clear that that communion will be not merely inceptive, as in this life, but complete and perfect; not merely external, but also and chiefly internal, because God will be all in all (1 Cor. 15:28). He will dwell not only *with* them but *in* them, and by the beatific vision of Himself He will most amply satisfy and gladden all powers and faculties."

[29] Ibid., I, 530: "As from the personal union of the two natures in Christ there arises the personal communication of attributes, so there arises from the spiritual union of Christ and the church of God and the believing soul a certain spiritual communication, both in the kingdom of grace in this life and in the kingdom of glory in the future life."

[30] Ibid., I, 561: "As the ointment flowed down from the head of Aaron upon his members, which were not detached or disjointed but joined most closely and effectively to the head, so the oil of the Holy Spirit descends from Christ as the Head upon the faithful, as members of His mystic body, not separated from the Head, but united with it most closely and effectually."

[31] Asmussen, *Die Lehre vom Gottesdienst,* p. 47.

not be necessary to show that "what should take place between God and the soul" can occur only in indissoluble connection with the service, if not always in the service itself. To regard the service of the congregation, in principle, as something that takes place *alongside of* the true spiritual experience is precisely the new feature introduced by Pietism. There were important forerunners of this movement in the 17th century. But the Lutheran Christian could be sure of the *unio mystica,* of the presence of Christ, in no other way than by receiving from God the gift of justification anew daily through Word and Sacrament. And where else does this occur but in the service?

This thought, moreover, emerges strikingly from the manner in which classic Lutheran theology employs the term *meditatio.* The modern connotation of the term does not come into question here. If Asmussen were right, meditation in Orthodoxy would be capable, as a special kind of activity, of bringing about "the spiritual occurrence" apart from the relation of preaching and faith. But meditation always appears only as a special form of readiness to receive aright the Word of God when read or spoken. It is a function of the intellect and has for its object exclusively the *proclaimed* Word of God;[32] that is, it relates to the only possible "spiritual occurrence" that takes place in the sequence of preaching, hearing, faith. That this relation has its place in the public service of the congregation is the unspoken but self-evident presupposition.

There is, however, another sort of *meditatio* which, ignoring the relation just indicated, believes that it can bring about the spiritual occurrence in a sphere of its own. Hollaz, again following the linguistic usage of the mystics, calls it *contemplatio.*[33] Its distinguishing mark is that it works without an object, as it were, attempting to be creative of and by itself. It disregards the medium of the plain, unmistakable Word and seeks to attain to insight by direct seeing. What results, however, are but indefinite, vague specula-

[32] See the definition which Hollaz adduces from Molinos: "Meditation is properly so called when the intellect considers attentively the holy mysteries of our faith, to understand their truth, by examining their separate heads and pondering the circumstances, in order to stir up the emotions in the will." (*Examen,* p. 221)

[33] Ibid.: "Contemplation is the sincere intuition (=viewing), sweet and quiet, of eternal truth without discussion and reflection. It is otherwise called the prayer of faith, the prayer of silence, internal recollection."

tions.[34] Hence there is no room for it within Christianity as a means of knowing God. It is true that Hollaz, when repudiating the *contemplatio,* is in this context not yet leading up to the gathering in the name of Jesus, which alone transforms God's presence into dynamic action, but only to the occupation with the Word of God in general. But if the Word of God has been given to us as the only source of cognition, it follows that, in line with what has already been said on the externity of the Word and the gathering for worship, we are led on to the visible, external divine service.

Thus we need not, in order to preserve the right Lutheran conception of worship, turn against the Orthodox teaching of the *unio mystica.* But we must reckon with the possibility of wrong inferences. As piety must not stray off into attempts to grasp and experience the union with God psychologically, so the service must not try, by means of a "sacrament of union," to force this inscrutable union of God with men, which must simply be believed "against all sense-perception." In the older liturgical movement, for instance, Rudolf Otto sought to achieve this as the "culmination" of the service. Finally the service must not become a "double-track" affair; that is, there may be a danger that, while the divine grace of justification is indeed dispensed, the individual may be drawn too little into the general liturgical action and may seek compensation in a mystical feeling of devotion that has no connection with the gathering of the congregation. Granted that the Roman Catholic ritual is exposed to and has succumbed to this danger in far greater measure, yet the Evangelical service will also do well to be aware of the relation between liturgy and inward "mystic" piety.

At a time when the juxtaposition of productive and visualizing action in the service was still relevant, endeavors were made to apply the views on worship current in the earlier epochs and to designate one of these two principles as the authoritative and decisive one. For Orthodoxy, charged with always having placed much stress on doctrinal matters, only a pedagogically effective view of the divine ser-

[34] Ibid., p. 229: "From the assiduous and attentive meditation on the divine Word there is born a distinct knowledge of God, of the divine Persons, of the attributes and works of God, of His commandments and the means of salvation. But from contemplation there proceeds knowledge that is confused, obscure, and general."

185

vice could come into consideration. Yet Graff makes the statement that in the Orthodox writings on worship "the genuine Reformation principles of the service as being an offering of praise and thanks by the congregation are enunciated much more strongly than one would expect." [35] He proceeds from the hypothesis that in Reformation worship "the independent value of the service" and not a "pedagogy of salvation" must be the principle.[36] Our investigation has not pursued the aim of demonstrating which view actually predominated in the period of Orthodoxy. The confrontation of these two factors is outdated today.[37] The attempt to prove a conscious or unconscious emphasis on either of these sides at a time when the contrast was not known at all would be a mistake. The very fact that Orthodoxy (like the Reformation age) allowed both principles to stand side by side unconcernedly, is proof that it did not sense a contradiction. To express the matter in familiar concepts: the purpose of the service is at the same time the salvation of men and the glorification of God. When we minister to men with Word and Sacrament in order to win them for eternal salvation, this is nothing else than solemn praise of God's mercy; when we offer our thanks and adoration to God with heart and mouth, we make known the grace of God that achieves the salvation of mankind. If, then, we find in the classic Lutheran teachings on the service productive and visualizing actions side by side without apology, that does not involve a contradiction; it rather proves that the alternative mentioned, which emanated from Schleiermacher, does not do justice to the essence of the Evangelical service. Following Luther, Orthodoxy knew that there can be right worship of God only where there is the right faith. There can be true faith only where there is a continued "invitation to faith." Not only such as are to be newly won for Christ need such an "invitation to faith," but also those who are believers already. For faith is "the constant receiving of the works of God." [38] God's saving purpose is presented to us in the proclamation of the Word and the administration of the sacraments. The divine service consists not in the mere fact that

[35] Graff, *Geschichte der Auflösung,* I, 66.

[36] Cf. Graff, p. 6.

[37] Althaus, Jr., *Das Wesen des evangelischen Gottesdienstes,* pp. 46 ff.

[38] Vajta, *Theologie,* p. 230; *Worship,* p. 128.

these actions are carried on by the church, but also in the grateful reception of these actions on the part of the worshiper.

This dogmatic discovery leads to a historical one: On the whole the period of Orthodoxy faithfully preserved the heritage of the Reformation. Our presentation has shown the curtailments of Luther's teaching which doubtless occurred in the 17th-century dogmaticians. But these departures from Luther's views are in no case a special characteristic of the teaching on worship. Although the unevangelical thoughts (on verbal inspiration, on the Law, etc.) did exert a marked influence on the conception of the service, yet this doctrine itself in broad outline reveals the true evangelical spirit. The departures from the views of Luther could change neither the doctrine of worship nor the practice of the service. It remains true, then, that Lutheran Orthodoxy displayed great faithfulness in understanding, retaining, and celebrating the divine service as "the real spiritual occurrence." The decay of liturgical forms that began already in the 17th century was not due to Orthodox theology; it was caused by those spiritualizing and individualizing tendencies which Orthodoxy was always at pains to resist.

Orthodoxy can indeed not be absolved of having fairly provoked the reaction of Pietism by an increasing hardening and stagnation in its own theological development. The sad feature of the clash is that Orthodoxy and Pietism became mutually exclusive and that Lutheranism lacked the energy to produce a real reform whereby the conservative and the reforming elements could have been reconciled in the right manner.

We have every reason to acknowledge gratefully the zeal of the Orthodox fathers for "the beautiful services of the Lord." From them we can relearn the truth that the appropriate form of the service must always grow forth from the right understanding of what is the faith corresponding to the Gospel. It is true that liturgical research at all times must build upon what it has discovered in earlier epochs. It is equally true that this research must always busy itself anew with the questions of true faith and right worship and supply the answers to both.

SOURCES

Arndt, Johann. *Vier Bücher vom wahren Christentum,* 1722. "Paradiesgärtlein."

Arnold, Gottfried. *Unparteyische Kirchen — und Ketzerhistorie.* 2 vols. 1699 f. Cited according to the 1729 ed.

Baier, Johann Wilhelm. *Compendium Theologiae Moralis,* 1698.

Balduin, Friedrich. *Tractatus luculentus . . . de . . . casibus . . . conscientiae.* Wittenberg, 1628.

Brochmand, Jesper Rasmussen. *Universae Theologiae Systema,* 1664.

Calixt, Georg. *De veritate unicae religionis Christianae . . . dissertationes,* 1658.

Calov, Abraham. *Systema locorum theologicorum.* 12 vols. Wittenberg, 1655—57.

Chemnitz, Martin. *Examen concilii Tridentini,* 1565—73, ed. Edward Preuss. Berlin: Gustav Schlawitz, 1861.

Dannhauer, Johann Konrad. *Collegium decalogicum,* 1669.

————. *Hodosophia Christiana seu theologia positiva,* 1666.

————. *Theologia casualis,* 1706.

Dilherr, Johann Michael. *Augen- und Hertzenslust, d. i. emblematische Fürstellung der sonn- und festtäglichen Evangelien,* 1661.

————. *Heilige Sonntagsfeier,* 1649.

Dunte, Ludwig. *Decisiones mille et sex casuum conscientiae,* 1628.

Gerhard, Johann. *Homiliae XXXVI seu meditationes breves,* ed. Berbig, 1898.

————. *L Meditationes sacrae ad veram pietatem excitandam . . .,* 1606.

————. *Loci theologici.* 9 vols. Edward Preuss, 1863.

Grossgebauer, Theophil. *Wächterstimme aus dem verwüsteten Zion (Drei Geistreiche Schriften),* 1667.

Hafenreffer, Matthäus. *Loci theologici.* Rev. ed., Tübingen, 1603.

Hollaz, David. *Examen theologicum acroamaticum.* Rostock and Leipzig, 1741.

Hutter, Leonhard. *Compendium locorum theologicorum,* 1610, ed. August Twesten, 1855.

Kesler, Andreas. *Theologia casuum conscientiae . . . d. i. schriftmässige und ausführliche Erörterung unterschiedener . . . Gewissensfragen,* 1683.

König, Johann Friedrich. *Theologia positiva acroamatica,* 1665.

Löscher, Valentin Ernst. *Vollständiger Timotheus Verinus.* 2 vols., 1718—21.

Lütkemann, Joachim. *Harfe von zehn Saiten,* ed. Heinrich Lütkemann, 1909.

Luther, Martin. *D. Martin Luthers Werke.* Weimar ed., 1883—. Weimar: Hermann Boehlaus Nachfolger.

Meisner, Balthasar. *Collegium adiaphoristicum,* 1663.

Melanchthon, Philipp. *Loci communes.* eds. Gustav Leopold Plitt and Theodor Kolde. Leipzig, 1900. *Corpus Reformatorum,* vol. XXI.

Mentzer, Balthasar, Jr. *Evangelisches Handbüchlein,* 1698.

————. *Kurtzes Bedenken von den eintzelnen Zusammenkunfften* (1st. ed., 1691).

Müller, Heinrich. *Ausgewählte Predigten,* ed. Leonhardi, 1891.

————. *Geistliche Erquickstunden, oder 300 Haus- und Tischandachten,* 1888.

Nicolai, Philipp. *Sacrosanctum omnipraesentiae Christi mysterium,* 1602.

Quenstedt, Johann Andreas. *Ethica pastoralis,* 1678.

————. *Theologia didacticopolemica sive systema theologicum.* Wittenberg, 1685.

von Reinkingk, Dietrich. *Biblische Polizey,* 1701.

Saubert, Johann. *Die neue Kreatur,* 1625.

————. *Predigten,* 1642. Appendix to *Die neue Kreatur.*

————. *Psychopharmacum pro Evangelicis et Pontificiis,* 1636.

————. *Seelen Music,* n. d.

Scherzer, Johann Adam. *Kurtzer Weg und Handgriff durch einen einigen Hauptsatz, den Kern Heiliger Schrifft, die ganze christliche Lehr und reine Theologiam leicht zu fassen,* 1686.

Schroder, Joachim. *Hellklingende Zuchtposaune,* 1671.

Spener, Philipp Jacob. *Theologische Bedenken,* 3 vols. 1712 ff.

Stryk, Johann Samuel. *De iure Sabbathi* (Opuscula tergemini argumenti), 1733.

Tarnow, Paul. *De novo evangelio,* 1697.

LITERATURE

Allwohn, Adolf. *Gottesdienst und Rechtfertigungsglaube,* 1926.

Althaus, Paul, Jr. *Das Wesen des evangelischen Gottesdienstes,* 1932.

————. "Der Sinn der Liturgie," *Luthertum,* 1936, pp. 235 ff.

Althaus, Paul, Sr. *Forschungen zur evangelischen Gebetsliteratur,* 1927.

Asmussen, Hans. *Die Lehre vom Gottesdienst,* 1937.

Bauer, Walter. *Griechisch-deutsches Wörterbuch zu den Schriften des Neuen Testaments und der übrigen urchristlichen Literatur.* 4th ed. Berlin: Alfred Töpelmann, 1952.

Bertholet, Alfred. "Kultus," *Die Religion in Geschichte und Gegenwart.* Vol. III, 2 ed., Tübingen, 1927—32.

Bornkamm, Heinrich. *Mystik, Spiritualismus und die Anfänge des Pietismus im Luthertum,* 1926.

————. *Protestantismus und Mystik,* 1934.

Brunner, Peter. "Zur Lehre vom Gottesdienst der im Namen Jesu versammelten Gemeinde," *Leiturgia, Handbuch des evangelischen Gottesdienstes*, I, 99—361. Kassel: Johannes Stauda Verlag, 1952.

Eisenhofer, Ludwig. *Handbuch der katholischen Liturgik.* 2 vols. 1932. 5th ed., 1950, ed. Joseph Lechner: *Grundriss der Liturgik des römischen Ritus* (Freiburg: Herder); trans.: *The Liturgy of the Roman Rite.* New York: Herder & Herder, 1961.

Elert, Werner. *Das christliche Ethos: Grundlinien der lutherischen Ethik.* Hamburg: Furche-Verlag, 1949; trans. Carl J. Schindler: *The Christian Ethos.* Philadelphia: Muhlenberg Press, 1957.

————. *Der christliche Glaube: Grundlinien der christlichen Dogmatik.* Hamburg: Furche-Verlag, 1940.

————. *Morphologie des Luthertums.* 2 vols. Munich: C. H. Beck'sche Verlagsbuchhandlung, 1931; trans., Vol. I, Walter A. Hansen, *The Structure of Lutheranism.* St. Louis: Concordia Publishing House, 1962.

Engelhardt, Johann Georg. "Speners Pia Desideria," *Zeitschrift für historische Theologie*, XV (1845), 157 ff.

Fendt, Leonhard. *Der lutherische Gottesdienst des 16. Jahrhunderts*, 1923.

————. "Der reformatorische Gottesdienstgedanke," in Curt Horn, ed., *Grundfragen des evangelischen Kultus*, 1927, pp. 20—47.

Flemming, Friedrich. *Die treibenden Kräfte in der lutherischen Gottesdienstreform*, 1926.

Frick, Heinrich. "Protestantismus und Liturgie," *Theologische Blätter*, 1924.

Gass, Wilhelm. *Geschichte der christlichen Ethik.* 2 vols. Berlin, 1881—87.

Graff, Paul. *Geschichte der Auflösung der alten gottesdienstlichen Formen in der evangelischen Kirche Deutschlands.* 2 vols. Göttingen: Vandenhoeck & Ruprecht, 1937—39.

Hamel, Fred. *Johann Sebastian Bach, Geistige Welt.* Göttingen: Vandenhoeck & Ruprecht, 1951.

Harnack, Theodosius. *Praktische Theologie.* Erlangen, 1877.

Heiler, Friedrich. *Das Gebet*, 1918.

Höfling, Johann Wilhelm Friedrich. *Das Sakrament der Taufe.* 2 vols., 1846 ff.

Holl, Karl. *Die Bedeutung der grossen Kriege für das religiöse und kirchliche Leben innerhalb des deutschen Protestantismus*, 1917.

————. "Was können wir für die Neugestaltung unseres evangelischen Gottesdienstes von Luther lernen?" *Lutherjahrbuch* 1924.

Kappner, Gerhard. *Sakrament und Musik: zur liturgischen und musikalischen Gestaltung des Spendeaktes.* Gütersloh: C. Bertelsmann, 1952.

Kempff, Georg. *Der Kirchengesang im lutherischen Gottesdienst und seine Erneuerung.* Leipzig: Heinsius, 1937.

Kliefoth, Theodor. *Theorie des Kultus der evangelischen Kirche*, 1844.

Knolle, Theodor. *Bindung und Freiheit in der liturgischen Gestaltung*, 1932.

————. "Luthers Deutsche Messe und die Rechtfertigungslehre," *Luther-Jahrbuch* 1928.

Koepp, Wilhelm. *Johann Arndt. Eine Untersuchung über die Mystik im Luthertum*, 1912.

191

————. "Wurzel und Ursprung der orthodoxen Lehre von der unio mystica," *Zeitschrift für Theologie und Kirche,* New Series, Vol. 2 (1921).

Kressel, Hans. *Erneuerung des lutherischen Gottesdienstes im Spiegelbild der Bayrischen Liturgiegeschichte.* Erlangen: Martin Luther-Verlag, 1937.

Leube, Hans. *Die Reformideen in der deutschen lutherischen Kirche zur Zeit der Orthodoxie.* Leipzig: Dörffling & Franke, 1924.

————. "Die Theologen und das Kirchenvolk im Zeitalter der lutherischen Orthodoxie," *Allgemeine evangelisch-lutherische Kirchenzeitung,* vol. 57 (1924), nos. 16—20.

Löhe, Wilhelm. *Der evangelische Geistliche.* 2 vols. Stuttgart: Samuel Gottlieb Liesching, I (1935), II (1876).

Maurer, Wilhelm. *Gemeindezucht, Gemeindeamt, Konfirmation,* 1940.

Mensching, Gustav. *Die liturgische Bewegung in der evangelischen Kirche,* 1925.

Preuss, Hans. *Die Geschichte der Abendmahlsfrömmigkeit in Zeugnissen und Berichten,* 1949.

————. *Martin Luther, der Künstler,* 1931.

Realenzyklopädie für protestantische Theologie und Kirche. 24 vols. Leipzig: Heinrichs, 1896—1913.

Rietschel, Georg. *Lehrbuch der Liturgik,* ed. Paul Graff. 2 vols. in one, 1951 to 1952.

Ritschl, Albrecht. *Geschichte des Pietismus in der lutherischen Kirche des 17. und 18. Jahrhunderts.* 2 vols., 1884.

Schlink, Edmund. *Zum theologischen Problem der Musik,* 1945.

Schrems, Theobald. *Die Geschichte des gregorianischen Gesanges in den protestantischen Gottesdiensten,* 1930.

Scholz, Heinrich. "Fruitio Dei: ein Beitrag zur Geschichte der Theologie und der Mystik." An excursus to *Glaube und Unglaube in der Weltgeschichte,* 1911.

Söhngen, Oskar. "Zur Theologie der Musik," *Theologische Literaturzeitung,* 1950, no. 1, cols. 15—24.

Stählin, Wilhelm. *Vom Sinn des Leibes,* 1930.

Strasser, Ernst. "Der lutherische Abendmahlsgottesdienst im 16. and 17. Jahrhundert," in Hermann Sasse, *Vom Sakrament des Altars* (1941), pp. 194 ff.

Tholuck, August. *Lebenszeugen der lutherischen Kirchen aus allen Ständen vor und während des Dreissigjährigen Krieges,* 1859.

Thomas, Wilhelm. "Die liturgische Bewegung," in Carl Schweitzer, *Das religiöse Deutschland der Gegenwart,* II, 259—277. Berlin, 1929.

Vajta, Vilmos. *Die Theologie des Gottesdienstes bei Luther,* 1952. 2d ed., Göttingen: Vandenhoeck & Ruprecht, 1954. Abridged English trans., *Luther on Worship,* Ulrich S. Leupold. Philadelphia: Muhlenberg Press, 1958.

Wallau, René H. *Die Musik in ihrer Gottesbeziehung,* 1948.

Wolf, Erik. *Musikalischer Gottesdienst?*